A Sudden War in the Bering Strait

A story written in the finest tradition of some of the good ole classic Tom Clancy and Dale Brown cold war novels.

Other books written by Thom Mindala

Nonfiction
Lambert Tales
Ride Across Colorado
The Lazy Gourmet: A Fast and Easy Guide to Cooking
The Lazy Gourmet: Cooking With Love in Mind
Little Green Travel Book
Picket Fence
Return to Thurleigh
Flying the B-17 Flying Fortress

Fiction
Mission to Mars

TRAIN2WIN Corporate Training Series
TRAIN2WIN Manifesto
TRAIN2WIN Performance Guide
TRAIN2WIN No Harassment Zone
TRAIN2WIN Winning Presentations
TRAIN2WIN Why Training Fails
TRAIN2WIN Coach to Win
TRAIN2WIN A Team Built to Win
TRAIN2WIN Working for Tips

"Like always, I write this book in the loving memory
of my father, who never lost his curiosity about things,
and continued to love to read about the stuff
he didn't know right up to the end of his life."

"I think that dad might have actually liked this book
with its reference to history and current events,
and with just a tad of spicy human interest."

Forward

Ever since those exciting days of my youth all the way back in the late 1960s and 1970s when I discovered my love for history and international affairs, I've continued to be a huge fan of reading the classic cold war novels that so eloquently depicted the deadly competition between our country and the Soviet Union in all corners of the world, probably just as much because I am in fact what often gets referred to as a "Post World War II Cold War Baby." And as such I've often wondered about what it would be like to write my own "what if" novel about some of those events. It all intrigued me because I simply couldn't help but wonder why we couldn't seem to get along with the Russians. All around me as a young boy I heard the adults talking about the evil Communists or those in the Russian Soviet empire who intended to invade or take us over if we failed to remain vigilant. Conversely, we in the United States were always described everywhere I looked as the "defenders of freedom and democracy" throughout the world. During college, where I majored in History and Political Science with an emphasis on the Soviet Marxists and Russian, and I soon became a huge fan of the work of author - novelists such as Tom Clancy, Dale Brown, Allen Drury, Robert Ludlum, and Larry Bond who all seemed to base their intriguing stories mostly on some of the more than likely events during the Cold War with a close eye on international relationships and techniques. I also liked the fact that these authors based their stories for the most part on some very realistic possibilities that could actually take place, our most basic fears, and where the most likely confrontations might happen.

A Sudden War in the Bering Strait is the first of what I like to describe as my "Post Cold War" novel series, and as such is a story where a real true to life potentially dangerous confrontation, in this case the current situation (2014 and 2015) in the Ukraine which is continuing to cause so much friction between the West and an increasingly aggressive post Soviet Russian Federation, which leads to a future unexpected conflict between the United States and Russia. It's a hypothetical story about what could eventually happen if there were to continue to be a tit for tat back and forth upping the ante of political discourse and mostly flawed negotiations that end up ultimately breaking down with huge numbers of military assets arrayed in direct confrontation against each other. And, like so many stories about people and things, my story attempts to take a look at some specific aspects of our past histories as well as how people react and relate to each other when thrown together in unexpected circumstances. My hope, of course, is that I've done so in some manner of understanding in a way that is hopefully interesting to the reader.

And, let me say before I go further that any mistakes or missteps that I've made about historical details during the telling of my story are completely unintended and I apologize where I have been in error and done so. I admit too that in some historical cases I've played a bit with the realities of what really did happen. Some aspects or details of the story, including the St. Lawrence island lighthouse and the individuals involved in particular, are entirely fictional and not at all intended to represent any known personality or actual events. Of course, where the story requires, I have used the names and positions of international political leaders where they're both useful and relevant. I do this to add an essence of credibility to the story from my point of view. Cases in point are Jeb Bush (I do decide that Jeb does in fact win the 2016 Presidential election you might note) and Vladimir Putin (the current all powerful President of the Russian Federation), among others. And, where they apply I do make every attempt to properly describe the known personalities involved as well as the relevant capabilities of military vehicles and equipment used to tell the story.

5

Hopefully, those of you who do read the book won't find some of my descriptions of historical or intimate events too graphic or uncomfortable. As such I use some pretty graphic and even profane language here and there in conversations that we are remiss if we think they don't get intense and more than a little vulgar at times. Frankly so, I also think that too often there's a tendency to "wash over" to a degree the humiliating violence and many times evil brutality of the regretful slave era in our own country. Personally, I think it needs to be told as it was just as despicable and horrifying as historical records show in a manner that does nothing to romanticize it in any possible way. In addition, I think we tend to gloss over the raw emotions of human interaction and sexuality in the world of historical events, especially when it takes place in stressful circumstances such as during war. I have tried to be tasteful if descriptive when doing so.

Much like my first novel, Mission to Mars, I have taken license in A Sudden War in the Bering Strait to write about the intimacy and love between human beings in a manner that hopefully is in the tradition of the romance novels my mother loved to read so much throughout her life. Frankly and admittedly so, I'm a hopeless romantic and it's my honest and selfish opinion that love between people is grand and it becomes even grander when it's described in all its splendor and it ends with a "happy ever after." To be honest, it mirrors in a sort of way my own experience where I out of the blue met a girl, fell hopelessly in love, then loved forever after in the bliss of our happiness (so far at least).

As always, I must thank my lovely wife, Jenny, for all of the loving support she has in the past and continues to offer an aspiring author, which includes her willingness to put up with weeks and weeks of me sitting at the computer typing away literally for hours at a time, and how she somehow manages to actually act interested when I talk about some of the crazy things I'm writing about. Not surprisingly to any who know her, Jenny always comes up with many useful suggestions for how to make the story better and more readable. Often, she saves me the embarrassment of a poorly written text when I actually allow her to do so. She's simply the best. And also as always, I owe both "Mr. Google" and "Mr. Wikipedia" huge debts of gratitude, since without "them" and "their" vast reservoirs of resources what little research I actually choose to do for my stories would literally take months or even years to complete. I also owe a debt that will never be fully repaid to my high school senior English teacher, Jane Bales Starner, for the inspiration she gave a young teenager all those years ago to read, and to also make him realize that he could write so that he could eventually discover how much he loved doing so. And, I do owe an enormous debt of gratitude to authors like Tom Clancy, Dale Brown, Allen Drury, Robert Ludlum, and Larry Bond who not only have provided many, many hours of reading enjoyment through the years, but have all proved to be an enormous inspiration.

Thom Mindala

Event Calendar

8001 BC - Igor's family group gets stranded on the newly formed island just south of what is now a never seen before ocean strait between newly separated continents

December 25, 0000 - The birth of Christ and a day when a first whale is killed on the other side of the planet

September 14, 1792 - The first Russians arrive on St. Lawrence island

April 12, 1861 - The start of the Civil War in the United States

April 9, 1865 - The conclusion of the Civil War in the United States

February 9, 1989 - Jonathan Anderson Jr. is born in Kalamazoo, Michigan

December 23, 1994 - Ihsapie (Elizabeth) Quviariatukuluk is born in Gambell, St. Lawrence island, Alaska

January 20, 2017 - John Ellis (Jeb) Bush is inaugurated as the 45th elected President of the United States

February 19, 2017 - The newly elected President proclaims support of the Ukraine in their dispute with the Russian Federation and announces new sanctions and trade restrictions

December 9, 2017 Russian Federation President Putin makes his first threat against St. Lawrence island

April 2, 2018 - The Russians invade St. Lawrence island and occupy the villages of Gambell and Savoonga

October 1, 2018 - The officially stated deadline for the removal of all of the Russian Federation forces on St. Lawrence island and its return to American control

October 22, 2018 - The United States Marines retake St. Lawrence island

November 23, 2018 - Captain Jonathan Anderson leaves St. Lawrence island to return home to Michigan to finish his tour of duty in the Marine Corps

December 1, 2019 - The Russians quietly pull out of the Eastern Ukrainian region and sign an agreement with the Ukraine formalizing once again that the region is Ukrainian with Russian rights to the Black Sea port in Odessa

July 19, 2019 - Joshua Kendall Anderson is born

August 14, 2020 - Jonathan Anderson returns to St. Lawrence island

September 12, 2020 - Jonathan Anderson and Elizabeth Quviariatukuluk are married in a traditional outdoor Inuit wedding ceremony

Main Characters

Evelyn Anderson - Captain Jonathan Anderson's youngest sister

Jonathan Anderson Jr. - Captain in the United States Marine Corps, and leader of E5 Charlie company

Jonathan Anderson Sr. - Captain Jonathan Anderson's father

Mary Anderson - Captain Jonathan Anderson's mother

John Ellis "Jeb" Bush - Current Republican President of the United States

David Cameron - British Prime Minister

Admiral Viktor Chirkov - Russian Federation Naval Chief of Staff

Paula Dobriansky - President Bush's National Security Advisor

General Valery Gerasimov - Russian Federation Chief of the General Staff

Igor - Name of ancient Siberian tribal family group leader and hunter

Jillian Henderson - Member of the Stonehouse Hedge Fund wet operations team

Gregory Jones - Leader of the Stonehouse Hedge Fund wet operations team

General Arkady Islonovich Kamanisky - Commander of the Russian Speznet occupation forces on St. Lawrence island

Arkady Kamorensky - Russian SVR computer expert

Sergey Lavrov - Russian Federation Foreign Minister

Mia Love - Vice President of the United States

Dmitri Medvedev - Russian Federation Prime Minister

Angela Merkel - German Chancellor

Robert Natter - President Bush's Secretary of Defense

John Negroponte - President Bush's CIA Director

Roger Noriega - President Bush's Secretary of State

Vladimir Putin - President of the Russian Federation

Ihsapie (Elizabeth) Quviariatukuluk - Inuit native American resident of the village of Gambell on the western shores of St. Lawrence island

George Rafferty - Head of the Stonehouse Hedge Fund

Prince Robert - Former Nigerian prince who's captured, enslaved, and then transported to the slave markets in Savannah, Georgia

Randy Robertson - Member of the Stonehouse Hedge Fund wet operations team

Sergey Kuzhugetovich Shoygu - Russian Federation Defense Minister

Sinuwin - First wife to Igor, leader of the ancient Siberian Native Indian family group

Princess Yoruba - Former Nigerian princess who's captured, enslaved, and then transported to the slave markets in Savannah, Georgia

Emma Vonderlinden - St. Lawrence island mistress to Russian Speznet general Arkady Kamanisky

Key Terminology

A-10E - American Air Force ground attack fighter

AH-64 Apache - Frontline attack helicopter for the United States military

AK-74 - Russian special forces assault rifle

B-1 Lancer - Heavy bomb load low flying swing wing fast attack bomber operated by the United States Air Force

B-2 Spirit - Heavy bomb load stealth bomber operated by the United States Air Force

C-130 - Venerable 4 engine turboprop short field cargo aircraft operated by the United States Air Force

Delta Star - Name of an Alaskan crab boat

E3 Sentry - American Airforce AWACS radar control aircraft

Elmendorf - United States Air Force Base located just outside of Anchorage, Alaska

F/A-18 Hornet - Main line carrier based fighter bomber for the United States Navy

F-22 Raptor - United States Air Force air superiority stealth fighter built by the Lockheed Martin Aerospace company

F-35A Lightning II - Newly developed U.S. Air Force stealth fighter built by the Lockheed Martin Aerospace company

F-35B Lightning II - Newly developed U.S. Marines stealth fighter with vertical take-off capability built by the Lockheed Martin Aerospace company

Gettysburg - Aegis Ticonderoga class United States Navy anti-aircraft missile cruiser

HK MP5N - Short barreled assault rifle carried by United States Marine Elite Special Forces troops

Hellfire - Name of the air to ground missile used by American AH-64 Apache helicopters

Humvee - United States military ground transport support vehicle

Ice Breaker - Type of ship designed to travel through and break up ice fields

Leningrad - Moskva Class Amphibious Assault and Helicopter carrier operated by the Russian Navy

MARSOC - Marine Corps Forces Special Operations Command

Maverick - Common name of the American shoot and forget air to ground missile

May - Name designation given to the Russian AWACS radar plane

MH53E Sea Dragon - United States Navy heavy lift transport helicopters

Mig-35 - Russian frontline fighter, designated the Fulcrum F by NATO

MQ-1 Predator - Remote drone operated by the United States Air Force

MQ-9 Reaper - Remote drone operated by the United States Air Force

Pearl Harbor - Name of the United States Naval Base in the Hawaiian Islands

Port Royal - Aegis Ticonderoga class United States Navy anti-aircraft missile cruiser

RQ-70 Sentinel - Low observable drone used by United States Air Force

Ronald Reagan - Name of the United States Navy nuclear aircraft carrier

SA-21 Growler - Russian anti-aircraft missile battery

Su-27 - Aging Russian frontline fighter, designated the Flanker by NATO

Tomahawk - American cruise missile launched from U.S. Navy ships

Tu-95 Bear - Aging Russian turbo-prop long range surveillance aircraft

Tu-160 Blackjack - Russian supersonic intercontinental bomber

Typhoon - Russian long range ballistic missile submarine

U2 - The venerable U.S. high altitude spy plane

V-22J Osprey - Specially designed black ops twin engine vertical take-off aircraft used by United States Marines Special Forces for transport on the battlefield

Virginia - American Navy Seawolf class fast attack submarine

ZSU-57-2 - Russian mobile anti-aircraft cannon with 4 50mm rapid firing cannons

1

8,001 B.C.

The ancestors of the small Siberian band of hunters and their families have been traveling on this same ancient foot path for literally thousands upon thousands of years, as they follow the annual migration trail of the Wooly Mammoth herd while they go from their Asian arctic summer to their north American winter range to the east. The native Indian band is an extended family group that includes 9 adult men, 16 adult women, and 20 children that range from 3 to 11 years. Leading the family group of hunters as he has for eleven seasons now, is Igor with his life mate and first wife, Sinuwin, at his side. They've already walked hundreds of miles as they do each and every year in search of the meat and fat they will need to survive the coming winter season. Hunched over with his collection and storage bag strapped tightly over his shoulders and carrying the treasured carved walking stick that indicates his status, Igor is the very picture of the northeast Asian hunter gatherer with his stocky 5 foot 4 inch body, sun burnt rugged and brownish leather like skin, jet black coarse and straight hair with its touch of gray around the edges, and deep set dark oval eyes that seem to take in and notice everything that goes on around him, which of course is his most important job as the family group's trusted leader. In his other hand Igor also carries the sling spear he will need if and when they do find the mammoth herd, as he knows they will soon, because all of the signs point towards them doing so. Warmth on this year's trek has been more plentiful than in past seasons of the sun due to the unusually large amount of wooly dung they've been able to collect to burn in their cooking and heating fires while they've traveled. This pleases Igor

16

immensely, both for the comfort it has brought to his small tribe as well as the indicated prospect the fact represents of a successful annual hunt that will need to sustain his tribe for another year. All of the signs they see point to a herd of wooly mammoth that includes several adults and many young that if they are blessed with the heavenly fortune the Gods will provide his people the food and warmth they need to survive. Strung also across his back is the pack made for him by his first wife that carries the carefully made perfectly straight and smooth 4 foot long feathered ash arrows with their razor sharp obsidian blades that Igor, like all of the adult men in his tribe, will use with his sling spear to kill the Mammoth when the time comes, which will be soon it appears.

Igor is an excellent and respected hunter who has led their annual hunt for the wooly beast successfully for over 10 seasons now and all in the small tribe who have chosen to follow him are filled with confidence that soon they will locate the migrating Mammoth herd, and to be ready when they do the men and boys who have reached hunting age in the family group have all been busy these past few moons sharpening the razor edges of their slated obsidian stone spearheads and making sure that the rawhide straps of their sling spears are unfrayed, supple, well tied, and ready to use. The oldest of the hunters are spending time each day teaching the youngest to throw their arrowed spears straight and true. There's only one chance with the beastly mammoth, so having properly cared for slings, straight shafts, sharp edged blades on their spears, and well practiced throws will all be essential to every member of the tiny hunting party if they are to hope to have the success they require to survive another year.

Not a big man, even by the standards set by the ancient tribes of 8,000 years before the birth of Christ, Igor is still well muscled and literally doesn't have the sign of a single ounce of fat anywhere on his weathered body as he moves carefully with a deceptively slow and efficient stride over the windswept tundra with his people in tow. Covering his body is Igor's treasured supple reindeer skin garment and leggings, having been both harvested and crafted himself with skills taught him by his grandfather during his own man making ceremony, that has on it now the picture stories that proudly document his many successful hunts and the birth of his children in the ancient traditions of his people. It's the tradition of his people, in fact, that the male children who have reached 12 seasons of the sun are sent out from the village, armed only with a sling spear, one single spear, one stone knife, and a single fire making stone without a stitch of clothing anywhere on their body to protect them from the harsh elements to hunt the wily reindeer so that he can cut out and eat its heart, then make his personal man garment out of its valuable skin before returning proudly to the extended family camp with the meat he's harvested. Like all of the other male and female children of the tribe Igor has only been allowed to wear a simple loincloth until the age of adulthood arrives. All of the men of the people are expected to do their ritual hunt for the reindeer not only to make their passage to adulthood and provide themselves with clothing, but to also provide the people with more stories to tell their young about their ancient traditions, which remind them all that if the Gods above will it a son will be strong enough to find and kill the reindeer, but if the Gods fail to do so a son will necessarily parish in the attempt. And some do, because there will be no help or rescue for those who do fail in the endeavor, but there will be a great celebration for those who do succeed, which of course will include all of the much appreciated meat from the fresh kill proudly supplied by the tribe's newly minted adult member.

The men of the people are born to hunt for the sake of their people's survival, and every single bit of their upbringing and training is designed to prepare them to do so successfully when their time comes. They learn to recognize all of the many signs that indicate the presence of reindeer and mammoth in season, they learn all about the relevant habits of these animals who are so essential to their very survival, and they learn all they need to do to hunt and kill them efficiently with the sling spear that they

18

are taught to make themselves out of straight branches of ash wood, woven strands of reindeer rawhide, and sharpened obsidian stones found near the water. Of necessity they also learn the habits of and methods to be used to protect themselves and their tribe from the Siberian saber toothed tiger, a dangerous predator to be feared and respected. Igor is by all estimation a fine example of this ancient tradition and training, and is now passing on all he knows to his own male children.

Also part of the ancient native tradition is that once a male child has succeeded in his man making ceremony it will be his right to select a life mate from the group of "eligible maidens" in the small tribe who have also reached the appropriate age for their own adulthood. For the maiden girls, it will be the bleeding that will announce their arrival as a child bearing member of the tribal group. In Igor's case he's had his eye on Sinuwin, a comely young maiden only one season of the sun younger than he with strong legs for trekking and already large and healthy breasts for baby feeding who comes from her own honored tribal family background. He knows these things of course since like he, Sinuwin until quite recently has only worn a simple loincloth and nothing else, allowing he and others to see the not to be mistaken development of her strong well muscled legs and milk providing breasts. The young couple's marriage ceremony will include Igor having to once again kill the buck reindeer for its supple hide that will provide the skin for his new wife and life partner's own adult garment, which she of course will make herself.

The womenfolk and not yet adult girls of the small family tribal group are themselves all busy with the work of sharpening the surprising variety of obsidian stone knives they will use to skin and butcher the enormous mammoth beasts after the men have killed them, and are also making preparations for the large fires they will also use to render every valuable ounce of meat, fat, and marrow harvested from each of the dead animal's body and bones. Nothing, not even the tiniest of bone or tissue will go unused. Buried under the rendering fires will be the huge amount of meat the women have carved from the bones of the animals that will be heat smoked and dried so it can be preserved and distributed among the tribal family throughout the coming seasons of the sun after a successful hunt. The family group will need to kill at least 2 and hopefully 3 of the enormous and dangerous animals to sustain them with what they will need over the coming year, and this essential fact always keeps the women on edge, nervous, and anxious until it does in fact successfully take place. They know their group's very survival depends on it, and while it's the traditional role of the men to be confident and sure of their success, it's the just as important role of the women to worry and fret until it happens.

Survival is in fact so difficult in this harsh north Asian and American climate that no tribal family group can afford the luxury of feeling sorry for or taking in the neighboring group who fails to supply themselves with the essential meat, bones, and fat of the mammoth they need. Even those groups who experience the annual hunting success so desired and is in fact so absolutely necessary to their very survival are living so close the edge of disaster that they can little afford to share their meager means with another in need. Every season of the sun sees such a group who has failed in their annual effort become no more than desperate beggars over the crushing winter cold and snow who eventually wither and die of starvation or simply disappear to never be seen again. The sad reality is that there is so much dire competition for the food and sustenance needed to survive from season to season in their harsh environment that there's little interaction except for the occasional seldom seen incidents of open competitive violence between the tribal groups that populate the region.

We should note here that even though there is severe competition between tribes to sustain themselves from season to season, there is in fact very little if any actual violence between them. Organized war between tribal units is in fact a social interaction that won't appear for another 5000 or so years. Violence against another is so "taboo" in the ancient

Siberian culture that there are but a few examples of it in any adult member of the tribal group's memory. And, as such, their ancient culture dictates that when such infrequent violence does in fact occur, the perpetrator will necessarily be ostracized by the family group, and sometimes even exiled to a life of starvation and death unless of course some other family group takes him in, which rarely happens except in those cases where another group is desperate for an additional hunter. This would only be the case if disease or injury has caused a premature death. It's a harsh and competitive world, truthfully, that the Siberian tribal groups live in. What the tribal units must be prepared for more than anything else are the real life dangers presented on a daily basis by the harsh elements they live in and the occasional saber toothed tiger who gets a rare taste for human flesh.

Like Igor, Sinuwin is the classic example of 80 centuries before Christ adult womanhood in northern Asia, with her also somewhat stocky sun baked bronze tone body that's even more hunched over by an even bigger gathering and storage pouch strapped to her overworked back. It's the job of the tribal group's women by ancient tradition to carry the vast majority of the family unit's few possessions so that the men in the group can be free to track the game they seek and hunt when the opportunity presents itself, as well as defend them from danger when necessary. This, of course, is nothing more than a matter of pure expediency and survival for the people, and the women know it without thinking, worrying, or complaining about it. From birth, tribal girls are taught that this will be their role in addition to providing the family with future members. They don't know of and can't even imagine any additional role than these. Their entire being revolves around taking care of the domestic needs of the group, which gives them little or no time to even begin to consider that there could be more to their lives. As the life partner and first wife of the tribal family's leader, it's Sinuwin's unique role to organize and lead the rest of the women and girls of their small tribal group. And, Sinuwin has been well taught by her own mother and her mother's mother

21

all of the many things she needs to know to properly do so and make it happen. At first glance she looks little different than her husband with her greasy straight black coarse hair with more than a little gray streaked through it that hangs well over her muscular shoulders with a stocky build that's covered by her own reindeer skin garment. In her case, like all of the women of the people, the reindeer skin for Sinuwin's supple rawhide garment has been provided by her husband and life partner when she turned 11 seasons of the sun, became betrothed, and was deemed ready to take her own place as an adult woman in the tribe following her first bleeding. Like the men in the tribe, Sinuwin is wearing thick rawhide sandals and leggings made also by her to protect her feet and lower legs from the rocky ground as they travel. The Siberian women of the time are by thousands of years of ancient necessity and the resulting selective breeding thick legged and large breasted so they can walk the distances needed to follow the annual migrations and supply their young with the nutrient rich milk they need to survive their first seasons of the sun. Honestly, as the tribal family group travels, it's only the size of their hefty bosoms and lack of picture stories on their reindeer skin garments which allow any to see the difference between the adult men and the adult women, since they are otherwise so very much alike in stature and appearance.

In addition to their jobs as raisers and nurturers of the young, keepers of the domestic chores, and butchers of the meat they harvest, the women of the people are also responsible to gather the wide variety of available non-meat food stuffs the group will need to provide the essential vitamins and minerals not provided by the fat and protein rich red meat they eat. Every young girl in the tribe learns by the age of 5 seasons of the sun how to quickly determine which leaves, roots, and stalks are edible and which ones are to be left alone as they travel from place to place. They also learn to harvest the nutrient rich kelp just under the surface of the deep blue sea close to shore for their stews and soups. Kelp is especially important to the group when the meat supply gets low, as it always and must do at the very end of the seasons of the sun before more is harvested on their annual trek for the wooly mammoth.

And, as is expected and is in fact an essential requirement to the human tribal groups long term survival, Sinuwin as well as all of her adult female sisters and cousins must provide the young for the tribe to survive into the future. Sinuwin has been taught by ancient tradition that her husband will provide the seed of life to make a child during their making of love if the Gods from above so will it, but knows from learning that it is the woman who will provide the nest of incubation that will bring their young to life at the proper time, and it will be the woman who will then provide the new helpless child the milk of life to allow them to grow from infant to toddler. Sinuwin, like all of the people, has heard the ancient stories and shudders at the very thought about a time when women were nothing more than the sole vessels to be used by any man who wished to spread his seed at any opportunity when he felt the need or desire and were forced to do so on demand without question. Sinuwin is nearly frozen at the dreaded idea or thought that by tradition in ancient times a young women could expect to be violently brought to adult womanhood at the first sign of bleeding by the strongest males in the group, and repeatedly treated so at his or any male in the group's pleasure. She's heard the abhorrent stories about fathers violating daughters or even older brothers raping younger sisters and is glad she has never had to live such a life. There are even rumors that there are some tribes of people in distant lands who still practice such a despicable and horrific tradition. Sinuwin can't even begin to imagine a life without the gentle making of love she shares with her life partner and first husband, Igor. She in fact looks forward to those frequent times when Igor is of a mind to share his seed with her in that most pleasurable of manners, especially since she knows she is no longer young and supple and that there are many other much younger women in the tribal group who must be more appealing to share a bed with at night, which of course would be her husband's absolute right as the leader of the tribal family. Unlike many of the women of the tribal family who

23

sometimes complain about the physical needs of their men while in their marriage bed, Sinuwin does not since she in fact takes much joy in giving her mate the pleasure he seeks and deserves. Sinuwin has counseled her own daughter who will soon reach her 10th season of the sun and will experience her own bleeding soon after, that she must be sure to pick a life mate and husband who is gentle and loving if she is to experience her own joy of life that her mother has been blessed with.

Tonight Enu, the elderly and grizzled sage of this Siberian family group (he's seen an astonishing 54 full seasons of the sun and moon and is now old, wrinkled, and completely gray), is quietly talking to his eldest and favorite nephew, Igor, and muses in a worried tone about how the simmering blue water of the sea beyond seems to grow more and more with each passing season of the sun. It's an admitted mystery that he in fact can't at all comprehend he says, but he now is quite sure with little doubt that if the blue water continues to grow as it has in recent times what has now become a narrow passage on their annual treks will soon most likely disappear altogether as early as next year's season of the sun. Igor wonders to his respected uncle in a purposefully low voice so not to worry the rest of the tribal family group what could cause such a horrible and devastating thing as he suggests, but the sage like Emu says that he can't know the strange mysteries that must encompass the minds of the heavenly Gods in the mountains, the sky, and the blue sea; and that they must be very angry with the people for some inexplicable and unexplainable reason that he can't begin to fathom or understand. He offers to his worried nephew that he's observed this worrisome change for some seasons now and has been offering the "smoke of life and peace" to the angered Gods above to ask for their forgiveness for what transgressions the people must have committed with no apparent success. Emu continues to tell his nephew in an even softer and more worried voice than before that in his estimation if the water from the blue sea beyond continues to grow as it has over the past 2 seasons of the sun it could even become possible that they will very soon no longer be able to travel to hunt the migrating wooly mammoth herds in their winter range like their ancestors have done for all the time that we know, which will mean they will not have the meat and fat they will need to survive another Siberian winter.

The weathered but still almost smooth brown skin of Igor's forehead and brows crinkle in worried thought as he tries with all of his effort to process the shocking and distressing information he's just heard from his respected elderly uncle, who he trusts more than any human being he's ever known. Nobody in the family tribe, nor maybe among the entire tribal peoples, know more about the strange and unexplainable goings on in the world around them or what the heavenly Gods might be thinking than does Igor's honored uncle Enu. Finally, not knowing what else to say, Igor simply whispers almost too low to be heard, "uncle what is it that we should do?"

"Nephew, there is nothing we can do I'm afraid. The Gods for whatever reason that we cannot know appear to have cast their decision on our world and I fear that our people will soon be gone from it," muses the sage uncle in a worried and troubled voice.

"There must be something I can do to save us," whispers Igor with the drip of a tear appearing in his dark colored eye.

"There is not my son. Go now. Go to the woman who waits for you in your bed. Enjoy love making with her so you can ease your worries. There's nothing more that you can do my son," murmurs the sagely elder of this small Siberian tribe with what amounts to a sigh of resignation.

Igor's ancient Siberian native Indian band of 45 souls is traveling on the wide but shrinking land bridge that has existed for as long as humans have populated the region in their annual search of the wooly mammoth whose meat, bones, fat, and skin provide over 80% of what they need to survive the seasons of the sun. The Siberian land bridge for tens of thousands of years has been a hundreds of mile wide pathway between the Eurasian and

North American continental land masses that are ever so slowly moving further apart as the millennia go by. In a strange and over simplistication of what has been happening over the last thousands of centuries, the bridge is quite literally stretching itself apart which is causing the tenuous link between the continents to weaken in an ever narrower strip. At the very same time a massive global warming trend caused by the highly increased volcanic activity all around the world is causing ice to melt on both the Arctic and Antarctic shelves which is now supplying the Earth's gigantic oceans with an enormous volume of water that will eventually raise sea levels by as much as 200 feet or more, which will cause a massive change in topography all across the planet. North and South America will stretch from being one massive continent into two separate ones with only a narrow strip of land in between separating the two. An enormous island continent will break away from the Asian land mass to form what will one day far in the future be called Australia. A massive atlantic land mass will disappear completely, leaving behind only the island of Greenland to announce that it ever existed. And, the now seemingly narrow Siberian landmass bridge that has for more than a millennia formed the connection between the upper Asian continent to the west and its north American counterpart to the east will eventually completely disappear as well.

The Siberian land bridge, along with the vast low lying coastal areas it connects in both Siberia and what will one day be called Alaska, is no more than 50 to 275 feet high in elevation, with the exception of the one high mountain like peak in its virtual middle. That single sentinel like peak rises majestically from a 50 foot high plain to almost 2300 feet at its summit in the far distance on that night when Igor is quietly speaking with so much worry and concern to his uncle about their disappearing ancient path. By the time the worldwide volcanic activity finally diminishes over time (which it in fact has been well underway for more than a century as Igor and his uncle speak), the atmospheric and surface heat of the planet will ultimately begin to cool down, the ocean's waters will no longer continue to rise

26

around the world, and the Siberian land bridge will have completely disappeared and in its place will be a narrow strait with a small island left behind as the only sign that it had ever been there. That island will one day be called St. Lawrence island with its 2200 feet high mountain summit that close by native residents will name Mount Atuk.

And as so accurately predicted by Igor's uncle Enu, it's the very next year when the same Siberian Indian tribal family who is once again making its long annual trek in search of the precious wooly mammoth meat, bones, and oil when disaster does in fact happen as he had predicted that it would. Tonight the large extended family tribal group are camped at the base of the highest point on the ancient land bridge they are crossing that is even far narrower than the year before. Igor is now alone in his thoughts since his treasured uncle whose knowledge of the world he has relied on so dearly for all of the seasons of the sun that he has been honored to be the leader of his people has passed on to the heavenly world of the Gods who surround them this past summer, having quietly warned his nephew before doing so that this will most likely be the last season of the sun that their small tribe will be able to follow the mammoth on their annual migration to their winter feeding grounds to the east. Still not wanting to believe it Igor sadly wonders if what his uncle has told him could possibly be true and if so why would the Gods above want to destroy the people, but when he looks around to see that again the blue sea has grown even more and the road to the mammoth hunting grounds has shrunk further from the last season of the sun to a mere pathway he must believe that what his uncle has told him will one day soon have to be true. Sinuwin comes to where he's sitting in contemplation of a bleak future with the bright full moon shining above in the night sky to urge Igor to come to their bed, but he tells his amorous wife that he's not ready to do so because he needs to think some more. Sinuwin puts her arms around her husband's broad shoulders in a manner making evident what she has in mind as she murmurs that he shouldn't worry so much about the things that he can do nothing about,

27

and that he should instead come to their bed. The hug and kiss she gives him while saying so tells him with absolute certainty that it's not immediate sleep his first wife and long time love mate has in mind. Igor takes pleasure in that he and his first wife's relationship is one of mutual and intimate respect and feelings of love, and in fact is a relationship that gives him little opportunity or even much desire to visit his younger second wife's bed at night. Igor takes a moment to kiss Sinuwin on the lips and fondle one of her sagging breasts through the thin fabric of her well worn reindeer hide garment. Sinuwin has seen 31 of her own seasons of the sun and moon, and has the graying hair and wrinkling heavily weathered skin that her advancing age demands and in fact deserves, but still Igor knows without doubt that he loves her more than any other. "Go to sleep my dear, he tells her, I don't think this worried man who no longer has Emu to counsel him about the strange goings on in this world will be in the mood for lovemaking before sleep tonight."

It would be not a full hour later after Igor's wife, who is deeply worried about her longtime husband, sadly retires alone to their blankets that it begins. For all the time Igor's been an adult he's known the teachings about the mysterious phases of the moon above, but nothing could have prepared him for what he sees tonight as the big and bright full moon is suddenly and inexplicably being devoured by some strange being, causing it to literally slowly disappear right before his eyes. Of course, what Igor is seeing is a lunar eclipse (the first in 47 years so none alive among Igor's people has ever experienced one) where the unseen sun is passing behind the earth in a manner that's slowly covering the light of the moon on the other side. He, however, has no understanding of celestial mechanics as don't any among his people, not even the now gone Emu. Frozen in sudden fear and dread since he's heard the whispered stories told in the night about the dreadful disappearance of light in the sky above, Igor watches completely mesmerized while slowly but surely some absolutely relentless force continues to eat the light of the moon. He can see the left behind hulk of lightlessness on the other side that seems to almost glow in the increasing dark with

28

an orange red hue, which in itself looks forbidding. And then, as he knew it would in his increasing dread, the light of the moon completely disappeared, and all that is left behind is a dish of a sickly reddish shadow of what had once been a shining beacon in the night sky, and all he can think about are those whispered stories that claim that the disappearance of the light in the sky portends something of great disaster is soon to come. Igor, like all of his people has experienced the complete darkness caused by thick clouds or the phase of the moon where all of the light almost disappears except for a thin sliver, but never has he felt as he feels now in the eerie night with the reddish cast of dim light from the now dead moon above. "What sort of being could do such a thing?" wonders an astonished and rightfully scared tribal leader. "What's going to happen to the world?" he's forced to wonder as he stares into the sky. "If only Emu were here to explain it all to him," he thinks. And then, just as he thinks he's seen or experienced the most horrific of things, Igor quickly realizes in moments that there can be even more fearful and dreadful things take place than the eating of the shining moon, something that seems to confirm all of the late night murmured stories of predicted disaster. He knows this because suddenly with the moon dead as it is there's a strange silence that is now blanketing the world. Not a single bird, not a ground squirrel or an insect, nor is there a puff of wind to indicate a single element of life is present, as if a vale of evil has fallen upon the world.

And then, in the silent black darkness of the now strangely moonless night there's a sudden rumble of mysterious noise that seems to be Mother Earth herself rising in growing anger from the hidden depths below and beyond. In the far and near distance Igor can easily see in the dark of the moonless night that there appears to be even more belching of smoke and bright embers of fire rising from the angry "fire mountains" (volcanoes) that surround them than usual. A quick thought crosses the tribal leader's conscious mind that the heavenly Gods must indeed be especially angry tonight. The biggest "fire mountain" located on the horizon far to the east rumbles even

29

louder, and as Igor continues to watch there's an explosion of fire that rises from its massive summit high, high, and even higher in the dark night sky as if a fiery rocket is in fact launching to the twinkling stars high above. The rumbling fireworks all around in the distance are so bright and so fearful that the man watching them fails to notice that the moon who only so recently appeared to be eaten is now reemerging a small bit at a time in the dark sky. And then, Igor literally feels the ground begin to move underneath him and shift where he stands, something that he has in fact felt before, and his uncle had informed him is actually a sign that Mother Earth is awaking from a sleep. Never though, has he felt the shifting be so strong or lasted so long as it has on this night. The movement he feels, of course, would be an earthquake that proceeds a major volcanic event, but Igor and his small group of native people are unaware of the fact, as all in the tribal family are now fully awake and watching the skies and seas around them in worried fear as the volcanic eruptions continue and even appear to be increasing both close and far in their frightening violence, and the increasingly rumbling at their feet gets noticeably louder and louder as the minutes go by. Both small and giant rocks are beginning to move in a manner all around them which strikes even more fear in the hearts and minds of all who see it happening.

"Is the world coming to an end father?" cries out Gregor, Igor and Sinuwin's oldest son.

"I don't know my son, if Emu were still here with us he could tell us," Igor tells his scared 9 year old son as he puts an arm around him while he continues to look around in the fiery dark with his own increasing apprehension.

But, before anything else can be said by any of the 44 members of Igor's extended Siberian tribal family, there's an even louder rumble coming from the bowels of Mother Earth, and far out in the night black water of the night time sea beyond they can all see rising a massive fountain of water, fire, smoke, and rock that comes cascading in their direction with a whooshing boom that sends the entire group diving for cover to protect themselves. It's an underwater volcano that they could not know exists which has just exploded in a sudden eruption to add its own destructive violence to the warring cascade now going on amongst the 40 some volcanoes on the northern Pacific rim that will add the last and final chapter to the changed geography of the entire area for the millennia to come as uncle Enu has so aptly predicted and warned his nephew about the year before. And, as Igor and the rest of the native family watch fearfully from the scant protection of the high ground they've desperately sought, a gigantic cresting wave of ocean water makes its destructive and relentless way towards them in the night.

The 44 frightened native Indian men, women, and children will huddle in abject fear throughout the rest of the stormy night in what little fortunate elevated protection that are provided by the still stationary large rocks that managed somehow to save most of them from the violence of the close by undersea eruption, mostly due to their 50 foot elevation from the shore of the raging sea. Sadly, 9 members of the tribal group (1 man, 3 women, and 6 children) would not survive the devastating Earth shattering event and were all crushed under the smashing weight of a single giant falling molten rock from the volcanic explosion. Somehow, by the very graciousness of the heavenly Gods above they would later decide, 35 members of the tribal family group were all spared with surprisingly few injuries from the rocks, fire, and rampaging lava of the explosion that in a few short moments turned the world around them completely upside down.

It would be the very next morning that the tribal group survivors would wake up from a fretful night of worried restless sleep, and would look around to see how their world has changed after sadly burying the crushed remains of their dead brother, sisters, and children in the still growling tundra while a strangely red sun peeks through a sky full of haze and falling ash. The raining ash is so deep in fact where the entire family group continues to

31

huddle themselves that it's more like one of the blizzarding snows they know so well, except for its gray color. Igor takes stock and is relieved to find that at least none of the survivors has suffered any serious injury outside of some cuts and bruises and one leg and one arm who refuse to work as they are supposed to, then notes also that what was just last night once a relatively distant shoreline is now only several feet beyond where they now stand not 20 feet up the mountainside from where they so recently camped. The rising deep blue sea seems to have settled some and even the distant fire mountains appear to have gone to sleep from their anger which created the awfulness and destructive death causing sadness of the night before. And, it would be some days before the shrunken tribal group discovers to their great relief that the wooly mammoth herd appears to have also survived the catechism and they do have a successful hunt where two healthy adults are killed by the surviving men and butchered by the women, meaning that for yet another season of the sun they won't be forced to wither and die as desperate and starving beggars from the lack of food and warmth.

But then, and only then, is it that the tribal group first discovers the full truth of what the recently departed elderly sage uncle (Emu) has so accurately predicted when they shockingly come to an impassable shoreline during their western trek on their return back to their summer village following their successful hunt. All Igor and the rest of his family group can do is stand and peer with confused consternation at the featureless sea beyond the new shore that must have been created by the frightening anger shown by the heavenly Gods only a few moons before. It would take Igor's group over a year of the sun to determine that they were in fact trapped on an enormous island formed by the devastating night of smoke and fire. They would discover two other things during their exploration of their new and very changed world, one that a herd of wooly mammoth has in fact survived with them on the new island world, and two there is another tribal family trapped on this strange new island world with them. And, given that the other tribal group has selected a flat plain on the eastern shore of the newly formed island for their village location, Igor and Sinuwin would lead their tribal group back to the island's western shore to seek out and find a location for their own permanent village. And, over the eons to come, the Gambell and Savoonga communities are born out of a need to find the protection of the village against the harsh conditions of their new land. It would be, of course, some many dozens of centuries before either village would become named so by their residents. One of the immediate and most serious consequences of the new world formed by their angry Gods were the decline and ultimate disappearance of the wooly mammoth herd so essential to their past survival. The newly formed topography simply lacks the year round vegetation required to sustain the massive mammal at the levels needed to sustain the two village communities, and with that change also came higher average temperatures that spelled the ultimate doom for the massive thick skin and haired animals. So, over time it became obvious to both native Indian communities on the island that a new source of foodstuffs must be found if they are to survive into the future, and for that source they were forced to look to the nearby sea for the very first time. Their new land is barren with no reindeer, who have themselves been trapped on the vast landmasses to the west and east by the new geography, so out of a desperate urge to survive in their newly isolated land Igor's decedents would ultimately turn almost completely to the deep blue sea for what they need to survive and flourish. They would learn to hunt the crustaceans who live in abundance in the shallow water, and they would learn over time to become fishermen of the fishes swimming off the shores and coves of the island, as well as up the streams during an annual migration. And then, as must have happened with the wooly mammoth many millennia before, they discovered the bounty of the seaborne mammal they eventually called a walrus, who became a near perfect replacement for the shaggy mammoth for plentiful hearty meat and blubber that would sustain the tribe over the cold winter months in a way the fishes and crustaceans never could.

And as such, over the eons and millennia to come, an entirely new kind of society was being born out of the destructive formation of St. Lawrence island. Gone forever were the hundreds of mile ancient migrations that followed the greatest portions of food and sustenance they needed to eat and survive. Gone also was an ancient culture that placed a high value on being able to move long distances as the seasons passed and a conversely low value on permanent communities. Yes, the decedents of Igor were still hunters by nature, and the descendents of Sinuwin would continue to be gatherers and domesticators, but the hunting and the gathering would change radically from what it had been before as the men were forced to learn all they could about the sea and the women increasingly plowed and tended their gardens instead of foraging for foodstuffs. As there have been for hundreds of generations, there would continue to be rendering, smoking, and cooking fires when the harvested meat and fat arrived, as there would also continue to be long cold winter nights of lovemaking under thick covers that would inevitably result in an annual seasonal appearance of new life in the community. Likewise, the continued harsh weather conditions in their near arctic world also meant that young and old alike could succumb to its unrelenting severity, either from disease or injury. And also, for literally many hundreds of generations, the 2 communities spread apart by not 100 miles of topography and a single high mountain would continue to live in near isolated unawareness of the other as both struggled to survive the unforgiving harsh conditions of the southern mouth of the Bering Strait.

2

A Whale is Killed

Blue whales rarely come this far north, and only do so at all during their annual summer migration to the krill rich waters of the north Pacific and Arctic oceans beyond. And, of course, it took many, many hundreds and even thousands of years before the residents of the new island in the middle of the newly created sea born out of Mother Earth's fire and anger would actually discover what the strange and unexplainable spouts of water rising out of the surface of the sea in the distant beyond really were. In the minds of the native St. Lawrence islanders whose entire outlook has been limited to what they can readily see around them nobody who has ever lived on this isolated world could in fact even remotely begin to fathom a being so large as a blue whale, an animal that is larger by several factors than the most massive animal the people have ever known, the long gone wooly mammoth. The gargantuan blue whale is larger than the mammoth in fact by an astounding factor of 80 or 100. For centuries now, there have been whispered stories told in the dark of the night around warm fires about unspeakably massive animals suddenly appearing from under the sea to overturn the dugouts of fishermen and walrus hunters. But having never seen nor experienced it for themselves, none of these strange tales are truly believed by any who hear them until one day when closer to shore than ever before is witnessed the appearance of an up to now unexplainable spout of water which they now can without further doubt clearly see is being caused by a behemoth of some sort of animal struggling on the surface of the water. Many in the village proclaim it to be a monster of the deep come to swallow them all as so eloquently described by the centuries old wise tales, while others predict that it represents an apparition of condemnation created by the same mysterious heavenly Gods who are once again clearly angry with them for some inexplicable and unknown reason.

The enormous and strange animal is a darker version of the blue sea itself rather than the known dark brown black of the walrus the native people are accustomed to seeing congregate on the rocks just off the shore of their island village during summertime. More to the point it's a full 30 rods long, more than 15 times that of even the largest bull walrus, and possesses a massive rudder like tail the size of a huge sail that literally slaps the surface of the water with an enormous and frightening splash. On closer inspection the men of the village discover to their immediate horror that the monster has huge blinking reddish eyes almost the size of a person's head that seem to look straight into theirs, and a spectacular mouth that's more than 25 feet long as it stretches along each side of its gargantuan head and looks like it could swallow an entire house in their village when opened wide. Upon closer inspection and to their great relief the monstrous beast doesn't appear to have the bone crushing teeth they might have expected to see when it opens its mouth, but instead has rows and rows of what can't be easily explained. Instead of the expected razor sharp teeth, they look like rows of some sort of woven filter, almost like the fine nets the women weave for the men to use as they dredge the shoreline of the deep blue sea for shell fish and crustaceans. The villagers had no way of knowing the irony that this biggest of mammals on the planet actually survives by feeding on and eating some of the smallest, the trillions upon trillions of plankton and krill that inhabit the deepest parts of the near freezing ocean waters located just off the shores of their island. Just the same, as they stare in wonder and admitted fear into the mouth of the monstrous animal, it does in fact look as if they are staring down the corridor of some enormous cave that goes to who knows not where.

The mysterious animal in question is in fact a full size 11 year old adult female blue whale who is in some serious trouble and is totally disoriented due to its inability to give proper birth to the almost full term calf still trapped inside its lower abdomen. She weighs a massive almost 190 tons in her 85 foot long body, and has instinctively swam nearly 8000 miles from her summer grounds in the southern Pacific ocean off the coast of Australia far to the north to where will be her and her unborn calf's ultimate grave in the cold of the Arctic sea. Growing steadily weaker from her illness and long distance travel, the doomed whale is now locked in a desperate struggle against the fierce ocean waves that are relentlessly driving it closer and closer to land as the hours and days go by, and away from its normal open deep sea. Sadly, her calf has long died in her womb. And, it's this tragic circumstance why the men of Gambell village have suddenly come upon and discovered the impossibly large and strangely mysterious beast wallowing in the shallow coastal waters just west of St. Lawrence island.

It's a revered village elder who first suggests that the strange animal off their shores is an unexpected opportunity to be taken advantage of rather than a feared monstrosity of an abomination to be feared as some others in the village loudly proclaim. And so after much sometimes loud and contentious discussion and argument among those same elders (the women and children in the village have no input or say in the matter), boats are immediately launched so they can hopefully harpoon it with their rope attached sling spears and haul its enormous carcass to the shore of the island so it can be harvested for what must be its unimaginable supply of meat, fat, and bones. It would take no less than every single adult male in the village (52 at the time) with every sharpened spear in their possession and 14 long dugout boats to finally finish off the massive blue whale, and it would then take literally hundreds of feet of rope made by the women of the village out of weaved seaweed to haul it out of the water to finally beach it safely on the shore.

Long skilled at their job of butchering the animals their men kill, the women of the village immediately attack the massive but strange animal now lying on their beach with their razor sharp stone knives, and it doesn't take long for them to realize the true bounty of their great fortune which has unexpectedly delivered to them literally hundreds upon hundreds of pounds of savory whale meat, and thousands of pounds of blubber that they will quickly discover they can melt into oil for future cooking, fires, and candles. And, it's with an eager delight that they discover the body of the unborn calf inside with its especially succulent meat and fat. And, the massive pile of strong and heavy bones left behind after the women of the village finish their work will provide any number of uses to build homes, furniture, and the wide variety of implements needed to make their lives better. The beached whale and her calf all by themselves will provide most of the supplemental food and blubber the native Indian citizens of the small village will need for almost a full year. So, the once thought mysterious monster of the sea turns out to be nothing less than a great boon and bounty to the local subsistence economy, and a great boon to all who live in the village which must have surely been delivered to the people by no less than the divine heavenly Gods above.

After the successful beaching and butchering of the massive creature, there follows an enormous village wide 3 day feast of meat, blubber, and bones, as the villagers continue to joyfully celebrate the great and unexpected fortune delivered to them by the revered Gods of the great blue sea and sky above, and it's quickly decided by the village elders that they must do all they can in the future to hunt and harvest any additional "whales" as they begin to refer to the enormous monster of the sea in the future. The word whale in their ancient Indian dialect literally means "enormous animal of the sea." So it's thus at that very moment in time, that the new and great tradition of the seasonal whale lookouts posted off and along the coast of St. Lawrence island is born, and soon the discovery is made by the villagers that there is, much like there were with the once upon a time ancient wooly mammoth herds of an earlier age, an annual migration of the enormous beasts of the sea that they can rely upon for their future community hunting plans and living requirements. This discovery all by itself will have an enormous impact on the village culture, not only because it drives a new and abundant source of food and wealth, but because the very hunting of the enormous whales cause the islanders to move out into the ocean with their boats.

And on those sunny days of wild and excited celebration of their newfound and unexpected bounty, the village of Gambell (a name by which it won't be called yet for centuries) has grown from the 35 ancient souls who first founded it on the coastal shore of the island over 7 thousands of years before, to what is now a thriving community of well over 100 persons. There too is a newfound comfort in their community that is now supported by a new religious faith born of the sea that has replaced the mystical ancient religion of the mountains and sky. For another almost 1800 years the people will give all of the credit to the Gods of the deep blue sea beyond the sky for so gratefully enriching their lives with the fishes, the crustaceans, the walruses, and the annual migrating whales that make their modern comfortable lives possible.

Entirely unbeknownst that day to the dozens of celebrating men, women, and children of the remote and isolated seaside Gambell village community on St. Lawrence island, their glorious celebration day is no other than December 25th on the zero year of what would one day soon become known as the Christian calendar, and is in fact the very day when a baby who would be named Jesus of Nazareth is born in a strange and unknownland far, far away on the other side of Mother Earth. It will be another 1792 years before the people of Gambell are told of this great event.

3

St. Lawrence Island

Life is almost always quiet and peaceful for the most part for the residents of tiny St. Lawrence island, except for during the frightful fierceness of the winter storms that annually come bursting out of the Arctic reaches of Siberia just to the north and northwest in winter time, which in fact does make life more than a little difficult for months at a time for the local mostly native Indian population. Even well into the 20th century the local economy on the remote island will have no more than three major industries with the exception of the village priest, unofficial local mayor, and the operation of the 3 story lighthouse that stands on the northern coast several miles outside of Gambell. They being fishing, which include the annual whale hunts, walrus hunting, and reindeer herding as the native American population have done now on the remote island for just over 200 years since their entrapment and introduction of the animals from the Eurasian continent a mere 50 miles away to the west. Most jobs of course, as would be expected from such a remote and isolated location, provide little more than a subsistence economy for the people who live on the island and in the 2 small villages that have emerged over the millennia on its east and west coasts.

Almost completely windswept and treeless for the most part St. Lawrence island, which lies less than 60 nautical miles from the eastern Siberian coast of Russia to the west and nearly the same distance from the southwestern Alaskan coast to the east, is all that remains of what was once a 100 to 600 mile wide land bridge that connected the north Asian Siberian continent to the

Alaska and Canadian north American land mass tens of thousands of years ago. The tiny island today is little more than a near featureless and rocky 90 miles long and no more than 22 miles wide at its widest point, with not even 1800 square miles of landmass to call its own. The highest point on the small island is Mt. Atuk, which is a mere 2200 feet high (670 meters), while the rest of St. Lawrence island averages nothing more than 25 to 150 feet in elevation.

St. Lawrence island is frankly one of the remotest and most isolated places on the entire Earth, not because it's so far away from anything else because it's not. But it's in fact so surprisingly remote for no other reason than it's in such an incredibly difficult place to go to or survive in. The island is in fact a mere 60 air miles "as the crow flies" from the Russian shoreline and just a bit further from the Alaskan, but in terms of geographic or weather conditions it might as well have been on the far side of the moon for all it would do for anybody caught unawares in its violent grip. The shallow and barren island itself is a relatively safe haven for the most part so long as you have both clothing and shelter, but the impossibly difficult and shivering cold even at their warmest wilderness seas around it are full of danger due to constant high wind, enormous ocean waves, and mind numbing almost freezing cold even in the highest of heights of summertime. In winter you would last exactly about 12 minutes if you fell into the icy waters without the protection of a thermal wet suit, and even if you are lucky enough to have one somebody had better rescue you sooner than later if you wanted to come out of the experience unharmed or even alive at all.

And, because if its relatively remote location, barren geographical nature, and surprisingly small population, so many aspects of modern life over the past hundred years or so seem to have just serenely passed by without taking any notice at all of St. Lawrence island or its native American residents. There's shockingly no local modern signal tower that can provide them either over the air television or internet service on a consistent basis. Radio service that has become so readily expected and assumed for the rest of us is even sporadic at best for those who live there. The only station in fact is one based in Savoonga that only beams its signal a couple of hours a day and is managed by a few volunteers dedicated to providing some information about world events to the island. Cell phones, what very few there are, are intermittent if even usable with signals that constantly break up and telephone land lines just don't exist on the island at all. Truthfully, above ground lines would suffer frequent breakdowns from the constant blowing gale like winds and digging underground lines in the rock hard tundra would require diamond tipped drilling equipment, both of which would involve levels of investment that less than 1500 souls don't justify to those with the capability to make them happen. Even the local newspaper is more an occasional newsletter or leaflet handout than a real professional news reporting piece, which is written and distributed by a staff of two when they have the time to do so with not a single reporter to bring the news in. Most of the sharing of information on the island comes from a pretty dedicated network of HAM radio operators who maintain a constant contact with their brethren both to the east and the west on the Eurasian and north American continents. But, contrary to what we in the modern twenty or twenty first century world might want or choose to believe or would more than likely assume, there's little concern about any of this lack of the ability to communicate or what they on the island might miss, even though by the latter part of the 20th century most if not all on the island are well aware of world events and possibilities. And those few who are in fact so bothered by it, simply leave the island to find another life somewhere else to the east or west, but even those who do are surprisingly few and far between in actual fact. Most of the residents on the island just shrug their shoulders and say for the most part that they really don't need the world's problems anyway when asked if they feel left out.

Life goes on in 2015 almost as it always has for literally hundreds if not thousands of years on St. Lawrence island, with the exception that there are now mostly well built wood framed and block built houses to replace their thrown together thatched predecessors from yesteryear, a stone Russian Orthodox Church now stands in Gambell as does a small wood framed Congregational Christian Church, and there's a small restaurant that serves greasy seafood and little more to go along with the local bar hangout. The village grocery is more farmers market where towns people barter services for a small variety of food stuffs than an actual or real professional business. You might find milk and locally made cheese on hand one day, only to find the shelf empty for days, and likewise that same is true with fish, reindeer meat, eggs (provided by the family owned chickens in town), and what few vegetables are available for sale while in season. The one fresh fruit available in abundance at the right time of year are the blueberries that grow wild for the picking all across the island, which every citizen of the island looks forward to with great anticipation. August blueberry picking season is a time of great celebration and shared culinary delights without question that the entire island population takes great joy in. Gambell village also has that one bar that serves as the town "watering hole" for mostly the men around the small village where they sit, drink, and discuss the most pressing issues of the day (women are in fact invited and even welcomed to imbibe though they rarely show and only the very toughest and most resilient such as Emma Vonderlinden dare to do so). Checkers, darts, and dominoes are the favored sports in the dim light of the bar where games are typically played and watched on a daily basis. And, while Gambell may be a remote place, Gambell Saloon as it's called by its loyal patrons does have a ready supply of 86 proof whiskey, 100 proof vodka, and even a selection of Alaska brewed craft beer that gets shipped to the island on a fairly frequent basis.

More amazingly in the second decade of the twenty first century, there are not more than 200 cars or trucks on the entire island with only two gas stations (one in Gambell and one in Savoonga) to serve them, and only a single bus that travels back and forth between the two coastal villages. And part of the reason is the simple fact that gas on the island is two bucks higher per gallon than it is even in remote Alaska since every drop of it has to be shipped in from the mainland. Even the richest of oil companies shudder at the cost of building a sea floor pipeline to serve the needs of only 1300 or so people and no more than 200 cars. And, even though gas is so expensive and many of the modern lighter and smaller vehicles with more gas saving engines might seem to be a favorite choice on the island, nothing could be further from the truth since those same lightweight automobiles simply couldn't handle the rugged terrain or lifestyle on St. Lawrence island. So, given those facts, the vehicle of choice on the island tends to be a 70s or 80s vintage iron solid body pick-up truck or jeep without a whole bunch of anti-pollution devices since the meddling EPA has a near nonexistent presence, all kept in pristine running condition by their owners.

There is one runway on the island that's more scrub than grass (even asphalt let alone concrete would be difficult and impractical in this harsh environment) in the very center of the island at the base of Mt. Atuk that services the single bush plane that regularly flies back and forth from the Alaskan coast and Nome to the east, as well as the few occasional tourist flights that come their way. Most of the residents of the island use the bus when traveling any distance, as they seldom do in any case, but for their personal transportation most who live on the island use their beloved 4 wheelers in summer and their snowmobiles in winter. And, of course as one would expect in an ocean side community, nearly every St. Lawrence household has a small boat or kayak. The statistics bear the point as the single bus, the one airplane, and the 200 or so cars and trucks are vastly outnumbered by the 752 4 wheelers, 643 snowmobiles, and 581 boats or kayaks. There are even almost half as many dog sleds (82) than cars or trucks on the island.

About the dogs of St. Lawrence island. There are no less than 1568 dogs on St. Lawrence island and not a single cat, goldfish, pet pig, or parakeet. That's more dogs than people on the island, and when you subtract the 656 dedicated sled dogs for the 82 dog sleds on the island, it still leaves more dogs (912) than households (519) by a factor of almost 2. Dogs as loyal work and household companions are simply a way of life on the island as it's been for its mostly native American Indian population for at least a couple of centuries now. For the most part all of the dogs on the island are actually the direct decedents of dogs brought to the island by the Russians when they arrived in 1792 since the original entrapped natives had no dogs with them on their annual mammoth hunt. And not surprisingly, they are tough dogs, no Pekinese or Poodles here, since like their human masters the dogs of St. Lawrence island have to be hearty to survive and flourish in their harsh environment, especially during wintertime when there is so little extra left over for them to eat. In fact, a common sight at the end of summer and early fall (August and September) is to see the dogs along the salmon stream fishing for much needed flesh born nutrients to fatten themselves up for the coming winter much like the brown bears on the Alaskan and Siberian mainland not far away. Unlike the continental locations just to the east and west of the island the hungry dogs looking for the spawning salmon don't have to worry or fear the appearance of the beastly brown bears since there are none on St. Lawrence island.

The just under 1300 inhabitants on the Bering Strait island (there are actually 1237 according to the last official census count in 2010) have over the past couple of hundred years settled into a sedate and pleasant existence far away from the goings on and hubbub of the hectic modern world that surrounds them. And frankly, it's still a mostly male dominated world, but gently so, as the men go about their business of finding food and providing, while the women go about taking care of the home and the children. They may lack many of the modern conveniences that are taken for granted in most other places but the men and women of Gambell and Savoonga do have a plentiful supply of electricity generated by the island's only water turbine generated power plant. Flowing water is something they do have plenty of. Their radios or computer connections might be a little hit or miss, but almost every household has a washer and drier, and many have the latest style dishwashers to make life more convenient for the daily work around the house. And the men have gas powered generators they can rely on for the work they do as well as the most modern hunting and fishing equipment that make possible a vibrant hunting and fishing economy. And, those who choose or can afford to, can hook up their satellites to receive the very latest of television, but the surprise is just how few on the island choose actually to do so. The Gambell Saloon does have a large screen satellite TV where the men can watch pro baseball, basketball, and football (football of course is the crowd favorite), where the favorite teams tend to be the Seattle Mariners, Portland Trailblazers, and Seattle Seahawks. But, when asked about TV at home, most of the men simply laugh and say they would rather spend time making love to their wives than watching the nonsense being televised these days.

The occasional visitor to the island amounts to what few fishermen venture into these dangerous waters and what few geological or marine scientists who might pass or stop by from time to time. All of course are without exception heartily welcomed by all who meet them when they arrive and treated to a wild celebration as if they were long lost friends to be treasured, which of course they in fact were and are in fact. There's no hotel, motel, or official bread and breakfast establishments in Gambell (there is a B&B with 2 bedrooms in Savoonga that stays open for guests during the June, July, and August summer months of the year), but not a single visitor to the island has to ever worry about a place to sleep or eat, because when they do arrive occasionally the entire community simply rallies up to determine where they will bed themselves down. And, the competition to earn the right to play host to their infrequent guests is quite surprisingly stiff as a matter of fact. More to the point, any who visit the island will discover very quickly that they will be treated as truly honored guests who can expect to not only be wined and dined by the entire community, but can also expect far less sleep at night than expected since they will be kept up in constant celebration by their excited hosts.

4

Strangers Arrive and Build a Lighthouse

It's another typical windswept morning on September 14, 1792 when a group of village fishermen see a strange never seen before apparition appear on the distant horizon just off the western coast of the island as the sun is rising in the sky above the deep blue sea, which is actually nothing more than an enormous 3 mast Russian sailing vessel. Before this day none alive on the island have ever seen such a vessel with its huge hull, enormous sails, and indecipherable rigging, without a single oar to be seen to propel it. Having never seen sails before this day the men on shore are left to wonder what these enormous square structures are and what they do. As the mysterious thing they would all soon learn is a "first line ship of the empire" comes closer they see a banner at the top of its tallest mast with bold white, blue, and red horizontal stripes, and on the huge platform of the ship they can already see in the distance what can be none other than dozens of oddly dressed men who must be traveling on the huge but strange vessel. And as the mystified fishermen continue to watch, the enormous ship approaches just a ways down the shore from where they stand and drops with a huge splash the largest anchor with its long iron chain any of them have ever seen, which of course is a sight that none of them have ever in fact seen before. There is as should be expected some bit of anxiety for what it all must mean as the native men watch an amazing number of the strange looking men appear and scramble over the side of the biggest sea going vessel any of them have ever witnessed into 2 smaller boats (which themselves are bigger than any boat currently on the island with their six pairs of oars) that will apparently bring them to the shore where they stand. These enormous paddled boats, much like their own except far larger, are powered by the common paddle like oars they know from their own world, except that they seem to be working in pairs in comparison to the single oars used by the individual sailors on their small boats. All on the shore continue to watch in worried but curiously highly focused silence as if they intend to mark this historical day for some future time, as the smaller but still large boats with their many sailors finally reach the wavy shoreline to be pulled onto the rocky sand of the desolate beach so the strange men can disembark and come ashore.

There are 5 distinct things the native men who are dressed in simple hand crafted animal skins immediately notice about the strange men which are; that they have strangely and almost sickly pale light colored skin, have oddly thick bushy hair all over their faces, are dressed in never seen before brightly striped blue, white, red, and gold clothing with bright metal "hats" on their heads, speak in a never heard before strange language that is completely incomprehensible, and are carrying what must be without a doubt a variety of weapons of a sort that look more than a little frightening. The islanders can only stare in wonder at the oddly strange men since none in their lives have ever seen such pale skin or full facial beards, and are amazed that they can only barely see the mouths and noses of the men standing before them. The men standing on the island have to marvel at and even fear a little men who look more like ghosts than real people with a proper brown skin. One of the newly arrived men who seems to be in the lead so must be the group's "elder" is carrying an enormous dangerous looking broad sword made of shiny steel with a golden hasp in his hand. Never having seen a sword before, those on the island would only learn of its dangerous power much later. His strange looking uniform, while the same dark blue color with red and golden appointments as the others in the group, is clearly fancier with more decorations, another indication for those watching that he must be a man of some importance to the others. Another of the strange men is carrying a long wooden pole with a large cloth banner waving on

49

the top that exactly matches the wide white, blue, and red stripes on the one located on the top of the huge vessel they've just come from. The islanders would later, of course, learn that this tricolored banner is what these odd men proudly call the flag of their nation empire, a great and powerful country they call Russia. As the native fishermen from the village continue to watch carefully, the men from the ship stand around their leader as he appears to say something to all who can hear in a loud voice in their strange and undecipherable language, then in response to what the apparent leader says the man holding the banner on the tall pole jams it into the sandy ground of the beach so that it stands blowing in the seaside breeze.

Only then do the dozen or so strange men who have just arrived on their shore turn and look in their direction, almost as if seeing the native fishermen standing down the beach for the very first time. By now a second group of strange men have arrived in another oar driven boat from the enormous sailing ship now anchored off their shore and are now unloading a very odd looking bright metal tube with large wooden wheels that must be very heavy, along with some other what must also be heavy round balls and small drums of something none of them watching can determine what is inside. By now another dozen or so village men and women have arrived on the scene wondering and curious about what is going on and who the odd looking men are. All watch as a half dozen of the oddly dressed men fan out and aim long tube like what appear to be weapons of some sort in their general direction. While they do so, the other men are moving the huge tube on wheels which is also being aimed in their direction, and as they continue to watch in increasingly anxious silence one of the men takes a strange and never seen before black powdery like substance out of one of the small containers and pours it down the opening of the tube on wheels, then another uses a big pushrod of some sort to shove one of the round balls down inside. None in the village crowd has ever seen or heard about a gun or cannon, but what they see before them is still nerve rendering while they watch one of the strangely dressed men put what looks like a short length of rope into a hole on the far end of the wheeled tube. And as the growing group of Indian natives continue to watch in silent fascination, the new arrival on their beach who they've already identified as the leader of the strange men points to a spot just to their right not far from the village itself where their community garbage dump is located, after which 2 other of the strange leader's colleagues move the undecipherable device they have been working on to point in the indicated direction. Once this is done, yet another man strikes what must be a flint device because a fire starts on its end, and then touches the rope at the end of the metal tube.

In absolute stunned and frightened beyond belief shocking horror, the entire Indian group dives for the ground while screaming and grabbing at their ears at the astonishing explosion that comes from the tube on wheels device. And, when they do finally find the nerve to look up from where they lay, they see thick gray smoke rise from the end of the tube, and when they look to where it was pointed their pile of garbage is in exploded smoldering ruins. The same gray smoke is rising from their now destroyed dump as a fire that has appeared out of nowhere burns around it. As frightening as the event is, it still doesn't make any sense to the villagers how the strange men used their never seen before device to create smoke, fire, and destruction on their waste dump across the way. And then, as if a further demonstration of their magical power needed to be made, one of the men carrying one of the much smaller wheeless tubes in his hands repeats the process of loading powder and ball, turns in the other direction and kneels on one leg, puts one end of the long tube to his shoulder, takes careful aim at a buck walrus lazing on the beach a full one hundred yards distant, and appears to somehow make it fall dead from where he kneels with the same explosive smoke and fire as all watch in stunned and frightened amazement. While not nearly as fearful as the blast from the cannon before, the shot from the musket also includes the same loud bang and inexplicable rise of smoke just as the animal slumps. And, as the almost 3 dozen village Indians continue to stare and quiver in fear at what they have just witnessed, all wait in silence as one of their group runs to inspect the animal to see that it's not only dead, but bleeding profusely from a huge wound which was clearly caused by the strange weapon in the man's hands. A few of the native women folk would later furtively sneak out to harvest the valuable walrus after the strangers finally leave their shore and before it could spoil in the daytime sun. The man who must be the leader of the strange men quickly strides up to where they continue to stand, along with the other men with their own long tubes which the natives now must assume can do the same thing they've all just watched the others do to their garbage dump and the walrus, and starts speaking loudly to them all in a commanding and authoritative voice.

"I hereby claim this island for Mother Russia, and all who live on it are now subjects of Tsarina Catherine, Empress of all of the Russias."

Of course, none of the watching Indian natives can understand a single word of what the man is saying or means. But, they continue to listen in more than a little fear and curiosity as the strange man continues to speak to them.

"Do you have gold?"

During the uneasy quiet interlude after the undecipherable question is asked one of the youngest girls in the native crowd timidly approaches one of the odd men standing before them and tentatively with a look of wonder in her eyes reaches up and touches the thick brown hair on his face. She giggles at the touch, causing the man to relax into a smile in response.

Again, the men and women from the village don't understand a single word of what's said to them, but when the strange man reaches out to show them the shiny yellow metal on what he calls "a watch" they nod with understanding. So, after a combination of indecipherable words and barely understood hand signals the village crowd comes to understand that the men want to see anything made out of gold especially that they might have. And, of course, unknown to them before they did so, all of the treasured iconic and valued community relics shown are immediately confiscated by the new arrivals as they make additional comments that are completely un-understandable. What is clearly understood, however, is that if they don't comply with these strange men, they will use their destructive weapons only recently demonstrated to get them to do so.

Over a short period of time a language of understanding is found between the what they now know are Russians and the Inuit Indian villagers, and they learn that they must now be servants to a "woman-god" they call the Empress who lives in a distant far off place called St. Petersburg. They learn also that all gold, silver, and gemstones of value belong to this so called Empress who the Russians refer to as Tsarina Catherine the Second. They will also learn that their new queen is often called Catherine the Great because she is so loved and revered by her subjects.

To all their great fortune no man, woman, or child dies at the hands of their newly arrived conquerors and their astonishingly powerful weapons, and things settle quickly into a routine that soon differs little from before. Another enormous sailing ship soon arrived with its own tri-colored white, blue, and red flag on top of its high center mast to take the place of those who first arrived. And with them they brought not only never seen before goods to trade with the natives for fish, whale, and walrus meat, but building supplies for what they called a "church" and a "lighthouse." One of the new advantages of the recent arrivals was that their long barreled guns (the natives now knew they were called guns or muskets and quickly learned to appreciate their power) were very effective at bringing down the walrus that sun bathed on their island shores but also the reindeer that would be soon grazing on the island. The reindeer would come from yet another Russian sea vessel as a "gift" to the island's people from the Tsarina Catherine. Where it had once taken weeks previously to hunt enough meat for their village winter larder, it now took only days to their amazement.

In the weeks after the arrival of the second Russian ship, the villagers learned that they would be required to stop praying and make offering to their "pagan sky and sea gods" and would be taught the "right way to believe," a religion the Russians called "Orthodox" which had its own true God who looked after all of the people on the Earth with great love and benevolence they were told. The Russians promised to build what they called a place of worship, or church, where all members of the faith would go to honor their new God. And they did. In weeks a new "church" rose from the path through the village, built from stones collected from the island and never seen before smooth wooden boards, nails, and caulking brought in the ship from Mother Russia. A third ship would soon arrive on their shores with an Orthodox priest and his fat wife who would live in their village to teach the villagers their new religion and faith.

Once the new church was completed in the spring of 1793, St. Lawrence island's new masters announced plans to build something they call a lighthouse with materials brought to them from Mother Russia on the second and third supply ships that arrived as soon as the winter weather abated. Of course, none on the island had any idea what the Russians meant by a lighthouse or what it would do when built, so they listened to the promise with polite and friendly interest. Life under these new masters was frankly not so bad the native villagers have by now decided. Yes, they did have to turn over all of their precious metal and gemstones (the truth is they don't have many to matter much about losing), and they did have to submit to a strange new inexplicable religion, but aside from those oddities things were for the most part better for the villagers since their arrival. Meat and oil supplied by the highly efficient Russian guns was more plentiful than it has ever been, and they even learned that they could travel out into the ocean deep and use the same guns to easily kill a whale while in season to their great excited joy. In addition to their guns the Russians also demonstrated an oddly effective hunting weapon they called a harpoon, which was an amazingly efficient sling spear like device that was launched out of a tube with the same magic black

54

powder just like in their cannons and muskets. All in the village were greatly astonished and a little intimidated at how easy hunting and killing the behemoth blue whale was with the powerful harpoon device. The Russians also brought on their ships more and more trade goods that included warm and colorful clothing to wear and improved building materials for their homes. All they asked in return was their loyal allegiance to a far away Empress and a commitment to the faith they called Russian Orthodox.

And, as could only be expected with the continued arrival of more additional Russian sailors and such, relations began to spring up between the newly arriving men of the ships and a few of the women of the island. Most of the time these relationships were mutually consensual and desirable, but sometimes they weren't unfortunately. What did happen as a result of the intimate intermingling of Russians and Inuit women were what would be a new breed of St. Lawrence islander, girls and boys with lighter skin and never seen before lighter hair color. Some even had light colored eyes, something never seen except for the occasional albino who was mercifully put to death immediately in the thousands of year history of the people until these strange "Russians" arrived so recently. Some of the children born of the new blend of peoples were taller and slighter boned than their full blooded native Indian cousins. This "blending" of peoples, as it always is among small and isolated tribal populations, turns out to be a great fortune genetically over time as it introduces some much needed variety and diversification into the island gene pool. One day, Ihsapie Quviariatukuluk would be an outstanding modern example of this interbreeding of Russian and Native American cultures. But, in a real sense, the joining of the two peoples after 1792 is almost like a return home for the islanders of St. Lawrence island who almost 10,000 years ago were separated and stranded from their Siberian heritage by the sudden disappearance for the land bridge between the two continents.

In 1796 the famous St. Lawrence island lighthouse was completed by the Russian sailors on the northern tip of the island to serve ever after as a shining beacon and much appreciated guide to ships and sailors entering and leaving the always dangerous Bering Strait to the north. It became the sought out guard post to the southern entrance of the narrow Strait that sailors for over 200 years have kept an eye out for, and still do, especially in windy, blizzarding, and high ocean wave weather conditions during wintertime. One of the oddities that took place during the lighthouse's completion celebration was the solemn announcement that Tsarina Catherine had died and that now the islanders would be required to swear their allegiance to a new man Tsar named Paul. The islanders had certainly experienced the death of revered leaders before, so the announcement was received with a frank shrug of the shoulders along with nods of acceptance of the new Tsar. And, it would be only a short five more years before they were told that there was to be yet another new Tsar named Alexander.

Still living in thatched dugout like shacks built out of rocks, mud, and what few sticks would wash up on the shore of the island in the late 18th century, the local native population watch in utter amazement as the mostly pasty white skinned and brown bearded sailors built the strange building out of never seen before square blocks and a glue like mud mortar they mixed on the shore out of sea water, sand from the beach, and some odd stuff they added in that they brought from their sailing ship anchored off shore. The Indian villagers first thought it must be some sort of community center or fortress when they saw how big the footprint of the new building was going to be. But as the Russians continued to build row after row of the strange glued together blocks stacked on top of each other, the growing tower rose from the rocky beach one story, then two stories, and then finally to an amazing three and one half stories high before they announced that they were done. By a full two and one half stories, this new but very odd building would be the tallest and most impressive structure on the entire island in 1796. And, by the choice of future generations to come, it would always remain so.

And, the St. Lawrence lighthouse was a strange sort of thing to the Indians who watched it rise into the north Pacific ocean sky over the months that followed. It was agreeably huge by any standard at the bottom, over 12 long steps across, but what became odd about the structure as layer upon layer of block and mortar were applied, was that it appeared to be getting narrower and narrower the higher it got into the blue sky above, and at the very top it couldn't have been much more than 4 or 5 long steps across its narrowed width. The Indian elders couldn't but wonder why? Why would these strange pale skinned men who spoke an indecipherable language, prayed to a so called benevolent God that none can see, and paid homage to an emperor who lives in a distant place build such a strangely shaped building that has no distinguishable purpose? None on the island, of course, had ever seen glass or stairs before, so when the stairway that circled the inside walls of the strange abomination of a building began to rise step by step, all who looked at them were left to wonder at the impressive abilities of the curious men who had appeared on their shores not that many moons ago. They also looked with wonder at the amazing see through wall that the Russians put over the square openings in the building that they could look and see through while the rain and wind from the other side couldn't come in. They decided right then that these men who called themselves Russians were wondrous men indeed when told that they too could put the strange walls on their huts so that they could see outside when indoors even when it rained, snowed, or blew.

And, when the circling stairs were finally finished all the way up to the top opening of the what is now an enormous building by 1796 St. Lawrence island standards, those who dared climb to its highest point were now sure without any doubt that they finally understood the real meaning and reason for the strange building. Surely it must be a lookout point since when at the top you can literally see for miles and miles in every direction, and to a point they were right that it was and would be a lookout of sorts. And, for the very first time in all of the many centuries that the people have known about them the migrating blue whales could now be seen in the waters off the coast of their island without launching boats into the dangerous waters to go in search of them.

But, it was when an enormous amount of what the Russian men called steel and some more of that wondrous transparent glass were carried up the circular stairway that the people watching began to wonder and in total curious mystery about what they might represent and foretell. Some in the village actually feared that the strange machine being built on top of the new building was some new and powerful weapon in the hands of the Russians sent by this unknown new Tsar in St. Petersburg to kill them all. And, when completed the strange apparition the men had constructed looked almost like a gemstone in the sky when the sun shown as it literally sparkled a beaming light to the ground below from the prism of its glass enclosure. However, it was during a balmy summer evening that the true shock came to the native Indians when suddenly for no reason that they knew the gemstone like structure at the top of the strange building began to shine in a blinding beam of light that turned night into day wherever it pointed. Some wanted to run for their lives in abject fear, while others watched in near horror at the amazing development. And as they all continued to watch with some amount of dread, the blinding beam of light began to rotate around the building, around, and around, and around, shining its impossibly bright light out across the ocean and across the land behind as it turned. Again, some proclaimed it to be a dangerous new weapon. Only when the Russians told them that the new building was intended to help the great ships of the great blue sea find their way did many of the villagers even begin to lose their sense of fear and dread.

Once the building was finally completed, the Russians took the tri-colored flag of their nation that had up to this time been flying from its pole on the shoreline where they had first placed it when they arrived, and installed it on a new far sturdier pole on the summit of the lighthouse with great celebration and ceremony. After a time, the strange foreigners whom they in the village have come to accept as neighbors came to the village elders and announced that they will be leaving soon, but they are in need of somebody willing to occupy and watch over what they now call their lighthouse. They once again explain carefully what the lighthouse does to guide and protect sailors as they ply the ocean beyond, and promise to provide all of the necessary provisions for life to any who accept the responsibility to live in and manage the lighthouse. They also point out once again how any who reside in the lighthouse can see the arrival of the blue whale that has become such an important part of St. Lawrence island life. They show the men the living quarters with its front room, kitchen, bath, storage, and bedrooms. They are also shown the massive light at the top of the stone structure that is the lighthouse's lantern, and are shown how easy it is to operate. There is one slight problem with the proposal made by the Russians, which is that in spite of the required new religion the sailors have introduced onto the island, in private the natives still practice their own long held traditional non-Christian faith which is based on the essential approval of all that they do by their heavenly sea Gods, and one of the key elements of their belief is that any new living residence must be properly ordained to the service of the non-Christian pagan Gods and the people.

Following the demonstration and announced soon to be departure there's much discussion and argument over the coming days as the elder men of the village carefully consider the proposal made by the Russians. The women of the village, of course, have no part in the contentious discussion or say in the ultimate decision. Some of the men want to turn the Russians down flat since the building is in fact seen by many still as an abomination not approved by the true Gods that must be torn down as soon as possible to avert the anger of said Gods. Others are intrigued but don't want to leave their fishing boats. Still others want to accept the offer to only burn down the abomination as soon as the foreigners leave. A few converts insist that the building has the approval of the Russian Orthodox God. Finally after much discussion and worry, it's decided that the village elder himself and his wife will take up residence in the lighthouse since no other in the entire village is willing to do so, and will take the great risk to live inside its walls until the building can be properly blessed by the rightful Gods after the Russian sailors do finally leave the island. And as thus, the St. Lawrence Lighthouse Manager is born, and in many ways it represents the very first paid position and job in the thousands of year history of the island and its Native American people.

5

How the Island Becomes Part of the United States

There are a couple of other significant developments that result from the Russian arrival at the shores of St. Lawrence island in 1792 to go along with a strange new religion and the new lighthouse. The first result was the introduction of dogs into the village life of Gambell. While dogs held captive and tamed as pets had in fact been a part of their ancient Siberian past, never during the thousands and thousands of years in the tribal history of the villagers who had become trapped on the island had the Native Americans experienced dogs or pets of any nature, so the reintroduction of them by the Russians brought a new and joyous phase into their lives. In fact, by the beginning of the 21st century little more than 200 years later dogs would be so much a part of St. Lawrence island life that it would be hard to believe that there had not been a single one present on the island only two short centuries before.

Even more important to their subsistence economy was the reintroduction of the reindeer back into the food chain of the people of St. Lawrence island. Reindeer haven't been a source of food and clothing to the tribal people of the island ever since that fateful night almost 10,000 years ago when they were separated from their Asian tribal grounds by the sudden change in topography brought about by the violent volcanic activity that formed their island. The violence had left the abundant grazing animals as before on both the American and Asian continents, but not a single one existed on the newly formed island. The reintroduction of the reindeer by the Russians soon after their arrival would prove to be a valuable additional source of meat and protein for the island, and over time raising and herding the growing reindeer population would become one of the key pillars of the St. Lawrence island economy.

However in many ways, the most important and likely the most significant change of all brought about by the Russians was when the first Russian woman appeared on the island on the fourth ship to arrive in 1794. Her name was Elaina Rosovishka, and her arrival on the island along with 5 others was almost just as sensational as had that been of the first Russian men to arrive two years earlier. Her appearance and image were in fact possibly even more shocking to all who saw her get off the ship, since no man or woman on the island has ever seen such a coifed and elegantly attired being in their lives. Elaina Rosovishka is a classic example of St. Petersburg womanhood with perfectly pale skin unencumbered by facial hair, sparkling blue eyes, dazzling red hair piled onto her head in well coiffed curls, and a much taller and decidedly shapely body physique with unquestionably "un-Indian" facial features. But, it was the woman's dress attire that had the entire native community abuzz, especially the native Indian women. Her sweeping hoop bottomed dress left nothing to the imagination as all of her pale shoulders and shelf like sloping chest were exposed for all to see with its low scooping neckline that showed a massive bosom that could compete with any of the native women on the island. While the native women are as a group just as well endowed as the new arrival in general, native tradition dictates that a woman's breast is to be hidden except when breast feeding an infant child or behind closed doors with a husband or lover, so the undisguised and unapologetic showing of the pale and fleshy tops of her massive bosom makes Elaina Rosovishka a matter of huge conversation and wonder to all who see her. And of course, none of the women have ever seen anything remotely like a corset before, and when they do, more than a few wonder a bit derisively among themselves why Russian women appear to be so eager to painfully squeeze their bellies so in order to highlight their "boobies" and their "bottoms." In their experience no such effort is necessary to get and keep the attention of the men in their lives. And, just as much so, the native village women also marvel and wonder at the huge and uncomfortable pantaloons, slips, and undergarments worn by the Russian woman new to their midst.

In any case the long accepted history of the island thereafter would mostly for some reason claim that Elaina Rosovishka and her 5 associates were in fact St. Petersburg prostitutes brought to St. Lawrence island for the specific purpose of further Russifying the gene pool on their newly proclaimed territorial possession. And, whether or not the often told story or legend is true that the women were in fact prostitutes brought to the island for the purpose of procreation, what is without question true is that they did indeed introduce new European elements to the gene pool of the island as all 5 quickly formed intimate alliances with native men that eventually over a short few years resulted in a tribe of no less than 3 dozen lighter skinned offspring, since while there might have been some issues with accepting a new residential building to accept and live in, there were no such hesitations about enjoying the mutually desirable activities made possible by the women. Just as well, there were no hesitations also in accepting the wonderment of new life on the island as represented by the children born of the new native American Euro Asian alliances.

All of these many and significant changes brought about by the Russian arrival were immensely beneficial to the St. Lawrence island culture and economy, so much so that by the beginning of the third millennia of the post Christian era, the vast majority of islanders are a combination of Indian and Russian blood, both dogs and reindeer are seen as critical parts of the St. Lawrence island culture and food chain, and with their lighthouse, 2 churches, and increasing numbers of consumer goods brought about by trade the Russians have changed the island way of life forever.

The Russians would in fact serve as the overlords of not only St. Lawrence island in the middle of the Bering Strait, but around the same time they arrived there they also arrive in the Alaska and north American territories to the east and southeast where they established thriving colonies in Anchorage, Juneau, and Sitka, as well as all the way down to what one day be the states of Washington, Oregon, and northern California in the United States. Like on St. Lawrence island they would incorporate Russian imperial Tsarist ideas and policies, and build Russian Orthodox churches to establish their rule over the rich and vast territory. The problem was that the Russian imperial government never quite figured out just how to be an effective colonial overlord, so for over 70 years they struggled to turn their established investment in the western hemisphere into a source of revenue instead of a drain on the Tsar's bank account. Riches in minerals, furs, and fisheries were discovered all the way down the Alaskan territories to the northwest of the north American continent to the south. Never though in 70 years could the Russian traders or naval commanders figure out just how to manage the massive territory and its sparse native population. In the meantime Mother Russia herself, and the world of Tsar Alexander in particular, were paying an enormous financial price for standing as the eastern bull work of independence against Napoleon's Continental System in Europe, and the 3 wars they had fought during that time against the French nation and her allies. By 1850, Imperial Russia could little afford to be the owner of a vast territory that served only to drain precious gold from the Tsarist coffers, so very quietly the foreign negotiators and diplomats were instructed to seek bids for parts or even all of the vast lands under their possession. At the time both England and France were entirely engaged in their own colonial issues (England mostly in India and France in Indo China and North Africa) as were the already declining Spanish in South America, so none of the 3 powerful powers offered much of a role as suitors in the competition, and soon the bidding came down to Canada and the United States. Canada was interested since an expansion the rest of the way across the forested tundra of the northern western hemisphere continent was desirable, while at the same time further expansion of the ever problematic United States north to the

64

Alaska territories was something to be avoided if at all possible. Frankly, by the 1850s American attempts to intrude into Canadian territories earlier in the century are still fresh memories in Ottawa, and there's real fear in the Canadian government that if the United States is allowed to expand into the northwestern Alaska territories they will be soon faced with a renewed threat to their very existence from not only the south but from the west as well. On the other hand, in Washington, during an era when the entire country is immersed in the idea of manifest destiny following the successful annexation of the former French Louisiana Purchase and the near theft of the southeastern Floridian territories from the declining Spanish empire, eyes are feasting on the possibility of adding the great northwest and even all of the greater Alaskan territories to the Union. And, there are some radicals who still dream of a great north American nation they would create by the subjugation of all of English and French Canada. Men like Andrew Jackson, William Harrison, Zachery Taylor, and Abraham Lincoln argued that the United States has a responsibility to spread its unique form of freedom and democracy all the way across the north American continent, and even further if at all possible. Even the intervening Civil War between the northern Federalist states and the southern Confederate states does little to stop the march towards further expansion of the country. In fact, both sides in the Civil War would agree hardily that annexing the northwest and Alaska was highly desirable, and the only question involved was that of future slave ownership and states' rights in any future territories.

Conversely, by 1865 Russia is absolutely desperate to generate some much needed revenue by getting rid of its troublesome Alaskan territories, so once again opens the bidding at a time when Ottawa is being governed by a the conservative party who wants nothing to do with further expansion of their country. On the other hand, the new bidding meets much approval in the halls of Washington City to the south, and within months Secretary of State John Seward is able to come to an agreement to buy from Russia all of their north American territories, from the arctic circle to the far north, all the way down to north of California to the south for the grand sum of 7.2 million dollars to be paid in gold bullion. So, in one fell swoop, all of Alaska, all of the islands that range to the south, west, and east of the land, and all of the territories that represent north California, Oregon, and Washington fall under the control of the United States with the exception of that vast area called the Yukon and Northwest Territories that Russia convinces a once ambivalent but now very concerned Canadian government to buy as a brake against the potential American hegemony in the west.

And, as they so often say in the world of the classroom, the rest of course is history as the United States quickly divides the newly acquired possessions into the Alaskan, Oregon, and Washington territories and places them all under the shield of territorial government in 1870. That sliver of territory just south of Oregon will be added to California who only became a state in the union in 1850. Oregon territory, with its already well established white trader population quickly met the standards for statehood and was added to the American Union in 1871, while those same standards weren't met in Washington until almost two decades later in 1889, and wouldn't be accomplished in Alaska until well into the 20th century in 1959, almost a full 100 years later in fact.

And, when finally Alaska territory did formally became the 49th state in the American Union in 1959, included in its vast and massive territory was that of the never heard before St. Lawrence island located all by itself in the middle of the southern entrance to the Bering Strait from the north Pacific Ocean.

6

On the Plantation

It's impossibly pitch dark, incredibly hot and stiflingly humid, and the putrid smell after 17 long days at sea while imprisoned in the bottom hold of the slave ship with 63 others is both sickening and obnoxious to say the very least. There are no "facilities" and the 70 foot boat is rocking in the heavy violent seas, making the scum and sweaty odiferous smelly stench even worse by the vomit of the combined retched seasickness of the manacled prisoners. With not a bath offered since departure the 30 men and 34 women are not only dirty, but are dressed in nothing but grime soiled rags with crawling lice living in their oiled up hair. Worse yet, the beady red and hungry eyes of the scampering rats could be seen in the dark as they skittered around and competed for the impossibly small amount of rancid food and slimy water given to the retched now and future slaves. They, too, were hungry which meant that the destitute prisoners had to be ever vigilant as the desperate rodents would nip at fingers and toes whenever the opportunity would come about. What little food they were provided consisted of bug infested moldy black bread that's more sawdust than nourishing grain, a gruel that smelled like urine and tasted like much worse, and some rotten long overdue fruit and vegetables that sickened their noses and stomachs more than anything else. The pathetic amount of so called fresh water they were given in dirty buckets seemed to have been left over from what was used to mop the decks of the grimy slave ship, which of course it was in fact, but they were forced to drink it anyway to avoid dying of thirst, making them all even sicker. Even worse than all of the above, a brutal treatment would have been better of a sorts than the silent and abject disrespectful ignorance they received from the ship's entire crew who did little more than throw the meager garbage scraps down from above at the appointed times. They didn't even bother to remove the dead bodies of those poor folks who finally succumbed to the dire and impossible heat or diabolical food they were fed, let alone bother to remove any secreted offal that resulted from their despicable captivity.

Sir Robert (the "T" is silent) is a 20 year old former prince in his village back home who had once not so long ago held not unreasonable personal aspirations to be a future king of his people, right until the darkness and horror came with the recent arrival of the hoards of mean spirited pale skinned bearded Europeans with their many guns, vicious swords, and snapping whips. Robert's a proud man of great blackish bronze physical stature and represents a perfect example of the powerful virility of his tribe who would have in any rightfully normal and fair world provided a dozen healthy heirs with as many as three or four wives before he died of old age according to the long held traditions of his people.

The decidedly lovely and sanguine 17 year old Yoruba, is like Robert a former princess in her own tribal village, has been highly educated in the traditions of her tribe and position by both her mother and grandmother in preparation for her future regal role, is highly prized for her acknowledged startling deep bronze beauty, and in fact still rightfully considers herself so even in the face of the brutal and abusive treatment delivered by the white men. There's a regal and royal haughtiness about her demeanor still even now in the despicable hell hole of this slave ship that won't finally be extinguished or entirely disappear until it's literally beaten out of her in the physical and emotional humiliation of a future white master's bed.

While the slave auction in Savannah comes as no real surprise to any of the 51 captives who have somehow managed to survive the 17 day cross ocean voyage, 9 even less fortunate ones were simply thrown overboard to have their rotting dead flesh eaten by sharks and crabs, and 4 dead souls who didn't make it were simply taken off the ship when it docked and tossed into a gristly pile to be cast aside under the dirt surface of some forgotten unmarked burial ground. It takes less than an hour for the 51 African negroes who have been cleaned of their two and a half weeks of dirt and lice to be auctioned off to the instantly feared and hated gun carrying white men who are in great need of cotton field pickers and household staff. Even with their retched condition following their long voyage, seeing the immediate undeniable value in the healthy and strong looking Sir Robert and the regally beautiful Yoruba as a potential "breeding couple" the Georgia plantation owner bids top dollar and soon has the man and woman slaves securely tied in the back his wagon for the long 60 mile trip home. The irony of the situation is that if left back home in their African tribal villages it wouldn't have been so odd to suggest that these two royal specimens of their world might have also one day ended as a couple who would be rightfully expected to procreate to the genetic future benefit of their respective people. The trip in the wagon itself will take over 3 days of body chilling bouncing and pounding over the never ending rutted dirt roads of Georgia, during which the two Africans will be freed only long enough to relieve themselves in the most humiliating of circumstances and will be fed only hard bread, greasy lard, and almost putrid water. They are never spoken to by the man who's bought them except to give shouted orders neither can understand with a short leather whip in his hand. When Yoruba only once makes a brief whimpering attempt to resist when the man puts a hand on one of her barely covered breasts she receives an immediate full blown back handed strike across the face that leaves an enormous dark red bruise on her cheek and a swollen bleeding lip. Sir Robert received the leather whip across his back for doing nothing more than taking too long to take a bowel movement, leaving his thin cotton shirt ripped open and bloody open wounds to fester painfully in the summer heat.

Once at the Georgia plantation with all of its enormous cotton and tobacco planted fields, the now miserable couple's new master makes no attempt to hide his intentions and what he expects from them. He houses them in a broken down one room wooden shack with no heat and no plumbing and a pathetic example of a roof over their head that lets more weather in than it holds out. There's no hint of a floor outside of the hard packed red colored dirt under their feet. The only warmth would come from 2 tattered and thread worn blankets that both had seen far better days and their only toilet was a steel bucket in the corner that they would both be required to use when needed whose contents they were required deposit as fertilizer and work into the fields close by afterwards. The only cooking they are allowed will take place at a communal wood fireplace and iron plated stove located outside their pathetic living quarters. And the white plantation owner makes it clear through sign language and an interpreter to Robert and Yoruba that he expects and requires them to breed like cattle for the delivery of a suitable "offspring" every nine months or so. At least one per year he announces along with a promise that there will be actions taken that insure that this will be the case. It wouldn't be long before both Robert and Yoruba understand what these promised actions will be.

And, after finishing the introduction of the couple to their pathetic new home and his brutally frank speech about his expectations, the leering white master grabs Yoruba by the arm and hair and literally drags her out of the shack to the back of his mansion where he keeps a room for "special occasions" such as now when he will test the favors of his newest possession. Never in all her short life has Yoruba been taken so brutally or humiliatingly, as the man forces her to strip naked, then physically abuses her breasts and her loins before literally raping her in a most repugnant manner before sending her back to her "new home" with instructions to procreate with her new "mate" so that he can get the return he expects on his investment. He also announces to the humbled and shocked woman who now has both blood and semen oozing down her legs that he will be expecting more of the same that he's just enjoyed a couple of times per week, and that he would send his overseer to get her when the proper times to do so come about, and that if her "new breeding partner" can't make her pregnant he sure as God in heaven will.

While still not quite able to make himself quite totally believe, accept, or comprehend his newfound circumstance even after weeks at sea in the slave ship and another week of continued torture at the hands of their captors, Robert goes so far as to beseech his new white master for better and less brutal more respectful treatment due to the royal tribal stature of both him and Yoruba. Unfortunately, Robert has little understanding of the mentality of the American slave holder, so in doing so fails to realize the horrible mistake he's making by announcing his and his female partner's former royal status while making his plea. He can't know that the discovery of the onetime status of his human property now demands that the plantation master demean the man and woman under his control all the more to establish his own brutal authority, so in response to Robert's beseeching cry for improved treatment his master actually moves to humiliate and humble him even more each and every chance he gets. Every single perceived failure, shortcoming, or regarded resistance are all met with the severest punishment with the whip and cane to the point that Robert's entire body is soon covered with the bruises, welts, and scabs from his constant abuse. Sadly, Yoruba's punishment for her former royal status will be more emotional than physical, as her master takes every opportunity to let her know that it's he who now has full control over her once exulted status. And of course, he does so in a most physically humiliating manner every chance he gets in that back room bed.

Unfortunately for Yoruba especially, their master's wife, who was at first more than a little compassionate in her treatment, soon became nearly as humiliating in her actions once she came to realize that the young negro woman had become her husband's favorite. She at first had intended the young girl to be trained to become part of her own household staff, a prized position amongst the slaves, but when she realized how her own husband was using the girl, rejected her immediately to work in the fields with the other women. Worse yet, in her own frustration at the young woman's obvious beauty and desirability, the mistress of the house took every opportunity to see any possible failure in Yoruba so she could either herself whip her or have her whipped for some transgression or shortcoming.

If anything, the club carrying overseer of the plantation's slaves was even more brutal than his employer. He liked nothing more than to whip and beat the men under his supervision severely with his leather whip or club at any perceived provocation or misstep, and would literally laugh with glee as he brazenly pinched the nipples and fondled the butt cheeks of the slave women with impunity every chance he got almost on a daily basis. There were those times that he would make a woman undress in front of the others down to her waist as he pretended to measure and weigh the exposed mammary glands while he openly leered at and fondled them. And, of course, any one of them could expect to be pulled into the overseers cabin to be raped and abused at the whim of his desire, something their master didn't seem to mind. Only Yoruba was immune from the overseers attentions, simply because she was being saved for the master's own special form of attention. Ironically, the long work days would be crushingly hard but did in fact provide some respite of relief from the misery and brutality of their captured existence in this strange and violent new world they call the United States of America. They are told that it's called the New World and is the "land of the free and home of the brave" but to all in the slave quarters free is the furthest idea that could ever describe their retched and brutal existence and brave is the last thing they would describe their masters, since it's made clear from the very beginning that the barest of complaint or uncooperativeness will be met with the most severe punishment by the whip or worse, and any attempts to run off or escape will be met with immediate death.

As if the whip or the owners special room were not bad enough, there was the "punishment hole" where particularly uncooperative slaves were sent for a period of "repentance." It was literally a deep five foot square hole cut in the ground with a wood slat ceiling, no heat, no toilet, no lights, no bed or furniture, with only a single small cup of "liquid nourishment provided every couple of days that would barely keep the smallest of them alive for long. The sentenced prisoner would be stripped naked, and then thrown into the "punishment hole" for periods of 3 days, a week, or even 2 weeks, depending on the so called crime committed. Those thrown into the hole learned from others to keep a lookout for the black widow spiders who liked to hide in the dark corners of the prison cell. More than one such prisoner failed to survive his or her confinement, and would simply be taken out and buried in a shallow unmarked grave in the back corner of the plantation without further comment. Even Robert was sentenced for 3 days in the hole now and then for reasons that had no meaning other than to further humiliate and control him so as to entirely break his will.

Ironically, as stark and bleak as their circumstances were in general, the food the plantation slaves have to eat (except when being punished) is relatively good for the most part if not quite enough since the white landowning master was quite aware that keeping his slave property decently fed meant more work could be done and productivity would increase. They were allowed to raise a few chickens for their meat and eggs, and even were given one pig a year to harvest and eat. Savory grits that they made from corn and pig lard provided some much needed sustenance to the small portions of meat, potatoes, and eggs they ate. They also had a scraggly cow that provided them milk to drink and butter for their bread.

Love does in fact grow from the mutual emotional need of their imprisoned and desperate circumstance to go with the sex that Robert and Yoruba knew they dared not try to avoid, and within weeks the couple were not just copulating as required by their white master, they were willingly and joyfully making love day in and day out, and 101/2 months later Yoruba would give birth to

73

a healthy 81/2 lb baby boy who was so ebony black that both were sure the child was from the loins of Sir Robert and surely not their brutal master. The parents are joyful if not officially married, because their white masters didn't think there was any reason they needed to be since low minded black folks intended only for breeding obviously lacked the human capacity to love and understand marriage like proper white folks, and besides they were never to be allowed to keep the child in any case. Not surprisingly, both Robert and Yoruba are deeply heartbroken when the child is quickly taken from them. And, when the baby is in fact taken away from his parents, he's Christened James Daniel Anderson (the paternal family name of the plantation owner - a common occurance with babies born into slavery at the time and yet another example of the humiliating arrogance of the master and slave relationship) and sold for a handsome price to another plantation owner not far down the road.

And, just as promised, Yoruba is "summoned" to her master's private bed usually more than once a week since it soon becomes clear to him how humiliated the woman feels when he abuses and takes her so brutally. She's, in fact, a most exquisite example of womanhood to be appreciated, but all the landowner knows is to do all he can to destroy her haughty self image by forcing himself on her repeatedly in the most humiliating and painful manner he can. Even the children he causes from their frequent times together only interest him by the amount they bring at the slave auction. In the end what finally breaks a determined Yoruba's will is when her white master casually offers her one day as a reward to his even more brutal overseer for the service he's done, then stands and watches with open glee while drinking his whiskey and smoking his cigar as the man literally tortures her for hours in every lustful manner possible.

Robert and Yoruba will provide 11 more healthy children to their white master after James Daniel (three times she had twins), along with 3 brown skinned babies who are obviously his, all to be sold into their own world of imprisoned slavery before

Yoruba finally dies at the shockingly young age of 30 more of a completely broken heart than any real physical health problem from her almost constant pregnant condition. Her slave master would always claim afterwards that she and Sir Robert were the best damned "breeding stock" investment he ever made by bringing in over 16,000 pounds with their and his 15 offspring, and that Yoruba was also without question the best piece of ass in his entire slave inventory. He suggested even that he was actually sorry to lose her, almost as if she were a prized milk cow. Robert would outlive his slave companion who he grew to love as the wife he wasn't allowed to have by almost 20 years, a time in which he would in fact sire another 14 sellable children for his master to put on the bidding block, before he died a broken man from decades of backbreaking hard work and the emotional abuse of captivity by another.

In the spring of 1860, civil war breaks out between the Federalist northern states and the Confederate southern states over the issue of slavery and state's rights. Some will claim that the war was always more about who would run the country (the industrial north or the rural agrarian south) than it was about true freedom or democratic rights for the black slaves, and to a great degree they would be correct. The simple fact has always been that the southern states, Virginia, North Carolina, and Maryland were the true leaders of the rebellion against the British and have never forgiven New York, New Jersey, or Massachusetts for their increasingly dominant political and economic role in the American Union that came after. Not surprisingly, the outbreak of the Civil War between north and south fills slaves all over the rebelling southern states with both apprehension and hope. Apprehension because they know that their cause is dim and any real hope for freedom is limited at best given the strength and determination of the Confederacy. Hope is never entirely lost however because, if the northern Federalists find a way to somehow defeat the southern rebellion, the northern leaders, President Lincoln in particular, have promised to give them their long wished for freedom in this new land. And, to their amazed and happy astonishment, the war does end on April 9, 1865 with a not anticipated Federalist victory and the announcement of the immediate emancipated freedom from slavery for every negro American (that announcement of intentions had actually come in 1863). There's great and wild celebration at first.

Then comes the dark reality of reconstruction as the bent upon revenge northern radicals sweep into the southern states to exact what they insist is owed to them for the death and devastation that the south has reaped on the rest of the country. What price freedom the former slaves would soon ask themselves? And, the answer was abject poverty with no real fundamental rights that will enable the former slaves to truly or even have a chance to realize their long held dream of a better future. Restrictive Jim Crow laws soon appeared throughout the south that made impossible for any real participation in the main stream of society or its economy by any person of color regardless of background (ironically men of color in both the north and the south who had never been slaves and had in fact had some status in the former free and slave worlds now found themselves with no status at all under the new defacto framework of anti-slave laws), and it very soon became apparent as well that their former northern supporters were no longer interested in their fate nor did they want for the most part their presence in their northern communities now that the war is over. The brutal horrors and humiliation of slavery had now been replaced by the almost worse humiliation of abject poverty and total rejection of every part of what white American society offered. The vast majority of former slaves became poverty stricken sharecroppers who worked their pathetically small pieces of land so they could provide for their families at the barest of subsistence levels. And, worst yet, any who stepped up to argue the point ended with either a bullet in the back of the head or a thick hanging rope around their neck. Not long after the end of the war so called Christian based white power groups sprouted up everywhere to police the new social hierarchy with the Ku Klux Klan as its leading force, and just like on the old plantations of the past black women continued to face the humiliation of white men who raped them at will in their beds while black men faced the humiliation of mistreatment or even death if they dared step out of line.

Then World War II happened in late 1941, and overnight an America that had rejected and shunned its former black slaves for almost 8 decades was now desperate for additional sources of labor and suddenly needed their help to fill the tens of thousands of new factory jobs on the enormous assembly lines being set up all across the country in support of the massive war effort needed to fight the Germans in Europe and the Japanese in Asia. Waves of recruiters from places like Boeing Aircraft, General Motors, Douglas Aircraft, Consolidated, General Electric, and the Ford Motor Company were suddenly on the hunt all over the country for able bodied men and women of any color willing to come to northern cities to build the weapons of war needed to defeat the Axis Powers. And, just as suddenly, concerns about perceived mental capability or color seemed to not be important at all in comparison to the need to keep the assembly lines of war going day and night. The result of these recruiting efforts to the war making factories that were mostly located in the industrial north would later be called the largest single migration in the two century history of the United States as literally hundreds of thousands and millions of former unemployed or unwanted white and black poor folks looking for a better life flooded into the factories in the north, mostly from the rural southern states.

One such American who moved from the deep south to the new opportunities offered by the north was Robert Jonathan Anderson, his young wife Viola, and their 3 year old boy Jonathan. They had been poor sharecroppers in Mississippi who had been barely able to scrape along on their 2 1/2 acres of dirt, until they had been offered an amazing $50 cash on the spot to come north on the train to work in the newly built mile long Ford Motor Company Willow Run assembly plant located not 40 miles outside of Detroit and be paid an astonishing fifty cents an hour with food and housing thrown in to build the B-24 bomber.

Little did the Anderson family know the highly dangerous working conditions they would find at Willow Run and the abject squalor they would find in the worker's camp that was set up in a muddy field with nothing more than square canvas walled tents to live in and trenches to pee and poop in. But, to the Anderson family the squalid living conditions in the beginning were worth it and soon things did improve with better housing, better sanitary facilities, and better and safer working conditions in the plant. There was even education for the kids provided free by the Ford Motor Company, something that had been absent on the farm in Mississippi, so that their son Jonathan would soon receive an education that closely rivaled that of his white counterparts, also something new to the American experience.

Once the 4 1/2 year long war against the Axis powers was finally over and won, and the relatively high paying assembly line jobs were quickly and sadly gone as the jobs that still existed were now being taken by young white boys coming back home from the war fronts, and the once again struggling Anderson family moved from the Detroit area to Kalamazoo, Michigan where Robert set up a small shop as a machinist repair man, using the skills he learned while on the assembly line at Willow Run in fact, while his wife, Viola, became a day care worker in the local Catholic private school. Many who had worked the wartime assembly lines that shut down after the war was over had also been forced to leave to find new opportunities, which meant that in a short year's time Kalamazoo had a large new and vibrant negro black community who needed Robert and Viola's skills and services. Life would not be particularly easy for the Andersons in the newly established negro neighborhoods of Kalamazoo, but over the years they would be able to eke out a decent living and live in a suitable 2 bedroom clapboard home with their 3 children.

Robert and Viola's eldest son, Jonathan Joseph Anderson would grow up in the black neighborhoods adjacent to downtown Kalamazoo, where he would meet his future wife Mary while

78

attending the all black high school where he played sports and she was a cheerleader. After graduating from school Jon and Mary would have a son that they would proudly name Jonathan Junior in 1989.

7

Captain Jonathan Anderson

Jonathan Anderson Jr. hails from the classic Midwestern middle sized industrial city of Kalamazoo, Michigan, where he grew up on the city streets delivering newspapers, mowing yards, and playing baseball in the summer and basketball in the winter with the rest of the boys his age. By the time Jonathan arrives on the scene in the late 1980s Kalamazoo is the very picture of a midsized American multi-racial city with white folks, black folks, Hispanics, central Africans, and Muslims all living together in fairly well defined even if distinctly separated city and suburban neighborhoods who experienced more than a little interaction while attending many of the same public and private schools. For the lower middle class Andersons it would be public school for their children with some insistent tutoring by their mother on occasion. Jon is the third and youngest boy in a family of five children, who has two adoring and doting younger sisters to go along with a couple of older brothers and two fine hard working parents who are highly respected throughout their community, both at work and in their church.

And, the Anderson clan is in fact the modern product of one time slaves who can proudly trace their heritage "as it exists" all the way back to when their ancestors were kidnapped on the Gold Coast of Africa and brought to this country in slave ships by the English slave traders in the earliest decades of the 19th century. Jonathan Anderson's great, great, great, great grandparents were in fact identified as one time members of African tribal royalty who had been kidnapped by the slavers, brought to American on a slave sailing ship in the most horrific of conditions, who actually worked the cotton fields of Georgia in the years before the civil war, and he's heard throughout his childhood the hard to believe stories about how the overseer would scream at and literally whip the backs of his regal ancestors in a most brutal way with a tasseled leather bull whip when angry. There were also horrific stories that were told in hushed whispers about how the women slaves (including his great, great, great, great grandmother) were forced to procreate with the male slaves held in captivity and even often "used" for the pleasure of their white masters at night between work shifts in the field with their offspring taken away and sold back into slavery for profit. Other hushed stories were told about torture and death at the hands of brutal slave masters and overseers in the cotton fields before the war came that ended it all in 1865. Anderson family lore claims that they can trace their own history to such a forced union between slaves.

Jon and his brothers and sisters have also heard many of the stories about the abject poverty that came with the "so-called" emancipation and freedom brought about by the northern victory in the Civil War, and the struggles to survive as sharecroppers in a world where those of their kind were unaccepted and hated in a manner that left them on the outside looking into an unapproachable white dominated world of opportunity and happiness. They heard too about the raw fear created by brutal beatings and murders perpetrated by "nigger haters" that included more than a few of their own family. They, like all black folks, know stories of people hung or shot by the Klan. But, it wasn't all about struggle and poverty in a world of prejudice, so Jon and his 4 siblings also learned much from their parents and grandparents about the rich heritage of their African and early American ancestors who all somehow through all of the brutal captivity and struggles to survive in an alien and racist world managed to not be forgotten from generation to generation. They learned how their grandfather had dared leave Mississippi to come north with his young family to work in the Ford assembly lines at a pittance wage for no other reason that a hope for a possible better life. They learned too about

81

how a strong commitment to hard work and common decency would ultimately lead to the ultimate promise of their share of the American dream even though so many of their ancestors had been cheated out of it.

Roger, Dennis, Jon Jr., Kate, and Evelyn Anderson would all learn from parents and grandparents that they were themselves the products of those ancestors of former slaves who had been recruited by and hired to be assembly line workers in the enormous Ford Motor Company built factory located not very far from Detroit city that assembled thousands of B-24 Liberator bombers for the American war effort against the Germans and Japanese during World War II. They were told with pride how black men and women who had previously been rejected and left out by society as far too dumb for such skilled work, answered the call when their country discovered that it needed their unsuspected talents and abilities. They were also told how their grandparents had literally lived in little more than mud soaked canvas tents with no clean running water or sewage for a time while building the bombers before suitable housing could be built for the tens of thousands of migrating factory workers.

While still a youngster, Jon Anderson was taught to both hunt and fish by his father and his grandfather along with his two older brothers, who always insisted that the young boy do things the right way. His grand dad bought him his first spin casting rod and reel when he was only six years old, and spent hours teaching him the fine art of casting for bass and bluegill in the lakes and ponds around Kalamazoo. His brothers introduced him to drift fishing for Carp down at the river and the secret of the eating delicacy that was so rejected by white folks offered by the bottom feeding fish. Jon didn't get his first real gun or be allowed to hunt with his father and grandfather until he was twelve, and then only after passing a hunter's safety course followed by some severe instruction from his elder mentors. But when he did go hunting for the first time it was to hunt squirrels with a trusty Remington 22 caliber single shot rifle with no scope that had also been used at first by his brothers. His elders informed the almost teenager that a gun with only one bullet and open sights would teach him to value each shot he took, and it did. That same year, Jon received a used but serviceable Mossberg 20ga shotgun with a 3 shot clip with an adjustable choke that he used with is elders to hunt doves, rabbits, pheasant, and even a few ducks down on the river. He used his own skills to re-stain and varnish the scratched up stock and carefully re-blued the barrel of that prized shotgun so it looked like new. Jon wouldn't be allowed to hunt alone with his friends until he was 16 years old, but by the time he did he was both an accomplished woodsman who knew not only how to use his rifle and shotgun (he still in fact used the Remington single shot rifle and Mossberg shotgun) but also knew just where the game they were hunting could mostly be found because of what he'd been taught by his father and grandfather. Jon's friends (even his white friends) always preferred hunting with him over others, saying that when they did they usually had a much better chance of coming home with something for the table. The same was true in fact at the lake or by the river, since it would almost always be Jon Jr. who caught the first or any fish for that matter. He loved everything about the outdoors, and loved especially pitting himself against a wily largemouth bass or cleaver rabbit by the lake in summer or in the brush during the coldest wintertime.

Jon would eventually grow up to be a healthy, attractive, and universally recognized smart young man who would at 18 years old earn an academic scholarship to Michigan State University in East Lansing after finishing in the top 10% of his high school class. He did participate in athletics while in high school (baseball, basketball, and football) but never really excelled in any to any real degree. He was a decent outfielder on the baseball field who struggled to hit breaking pitches, while on the basketball court he only managed to be second string on the varsity as a senior. He tried football as a quarterback but soon discovered that the brutality of the physical contact in the game really wasn't for him in a program that only wanted to run the football unless so desperate to do otherwise, so he quit after his sophomore year to run cross country instead where he lettered but only managed to earn a ribbon in a couple of meets. By the time he was 18 years old, Jonathan Anderson was 6'2" tall and a svelte 175 pounds to go with his dark complexion and good looks. Even the white girls in high school showed more than a passing or curious interest in him, but to their disappointment Jon Anderson mostly refused to reciprocate. Not because he didn't like white girls, but more because he was simply too shy to approach let alone speak to any pretty girl period, regardless of race or color. Because this was so even though he did have a few dates from time to time (mostly at the behest of some girl or friend), Jon would never have a serious girlfriend during high school or even in college, something that did in fact bother him some and certainly concerned his very traditional thinking parents who looked forward to their own grandchildren and even wondered at times if their son might actually be gay.

After 4 years at Michigan State University in East Lansing, Jon Anderson was awarded an undergraduate bachelor's of liberal arts degree in marketing, and after giving some serious consideration about going to law school he eventually decided to join the Marine Corps to the strongly voiced chagrin of both of his parents, older brothers, and at least one of his younger sisters. Frankly, in 2011 the idea of serving in the military and becoming a United States Marine appealed to Jon's independent and patriotic outlook in a world where the United States and what it stood for were under constant attack throughout the radical world, as well as in many corners of his own country. Jon Anderson was by then at not quite 22 years old absolutely determined to map out his own life's path in a very confusing world and discover his own personality in a quest to find understanding about who he really was and wanted to be. Jon's parents or siblings, with the exception of his youngest sister Evelyn, didn't like his decision to join the military much, but once the decision was made by him to do so they all stood up and supported him in every way possible, even if outwardly reluctantly in more than one case.

As a newly minted E-3 Lance Corporal fresh out of 6 arduous and sometimes brutal weeks in a physically demanding United States Marine boot camp the just under 23 year old Jonathan Anderson Jr., whose above average intelligence and relentless determination have already been recognized by his training command superiors, is sent immediately to officer's training school in Quantico, Virginia, after boot camp where he will spend an additional 4 full weeks in the most rigorously physical and mentally demanding training he can imagine where 38 of the 45 men and women candidates washed out before they could qualify as Marine officers. Jonathan himself came so close to quitting during the exhaustive training regimen that he doesn't really want to think about it, but he does in fact manage to meet the harsh standards and qualify to be a United States Marine Corps junior officer, and following yet another mentally taxing 3 months of just as demanding class work is finally commissioned as a proud 2nd Lieutenant in the United States Marine Corps. in the late fall of 2011 and given his own infantry unit platoon to lead. His family couldn't have been more proud of their son and brother in his impressive blue, red, and white Marine dress uniform with gold piping and his shiny saber on his hip.

And then, following two 9 month long tours of duty in the remote provinces of Afghanistan fighting the Taliban (an experience that Jon will never in fact speak very much about), during which time he received a field promotion, a newly minted 1st Lieutenant Jonathan Anderson makes application to be considered for the Marine elite special forces called Force Reconnaissance and when finally accepted returns yet again to Quantico, Virginia for some even more vigorous and even more intensely demanding physical skills training and tactical study over the next six months. Graduation from the rigorous course came with yet another promotion to the rank of Captain in the Marine Corps and allowed him to wear proudly the red and black Force Recon unit patch. So, by the late summer and fall of 2015 the now battle hardened and well trained Captain Jonathan Anderson is a fine example of the best that the United

States Marine Corps Special Forces can offer to the American taxpayer.

Jon is still the same 6'2" tall, but now weighs a full 10 pounds more (180) than he did at his high school graduation. But, that 10 additional pounds on his well chiseled body is made up of nothing more than battle tough muscle, making him the very picture of the impressive perfectly straight back rigid statue of a Marine in his deep blue, white, red, and gold pin striped uniform with his shiny Captain's bars on his shoulders and silver saber hanging from his left hip while standing at attention. And, with his already impressive string of regimental service and duty medals displayed on his chest, Jon Anderson is literally the picture of a handsome Afro-American male. He by now makes both of his parents very proud, even though they worry incessantly about his whereabouts and safety much of the time. And, even more than in high school or college, all of the young women, black, white, and of any color or culture, literally swoon over him wherever he goes, something that his maturity level and confidence is far better able for him to handle now as a 26 year old minted Captain in the United States Marine Corps Special Forces.

Compared to Jon, his two older brothers follow a much more normal, traditional, and far less dangerous path to adult success as a very successful corporate tax lawyer (Roger) and an equally successful corporate accountant (Dennis). Like all of the rest of the Anderson family (brothers included), Jon Jr's two younger sisters grow to be handsome and attractive young women by the second decade of the twenty first century. Kate, the spitting image of her mother, will eventually marry a high school classmate and become a respected wife, mother, and clinical psychologist of some standing in her own right. It would be the irrepressible but doubtlessly beautiful Evelyn who would, like her older brother Jon, choose a much different and quite unordinary path to her own future life, to the often times worry and sometimes disappointment of her parents and older brothers (including her closest brother Jon at times). The lovely

86

Evelyn is without question the most outspoken and willful of the 5 Anderson children at the same time she has what's described as the most creative and compassionate mind in comparison to any of her 3 older brothers and sister.

Of special note before we continue forward with our story is that, while never having a steady long term relationship with a person of the opposite sex before his final mission as a Marine Special Forces Captain to the island of St. Lawrence, Jonathan Anderson Jr. does in fact experience a number of short term romantic and intimate liaisons in and out of the bed room as a young adult once he finally gains the self confidence to do so. Jon's not at all gay as his parents sometimes feared in his late teen and early adult years, but he does by his mid twenties seem bane to make any lengthy commitments to the women he comes into contact with to the ongoing chagrin of his two younger sisters and parents who all feel that he needs to settle down so he can begin to build a life and family for the future. Jon simply tells his worried siblings that he's yet to find the right person to settle down with, but once he does he promises that he will be quite ready to make the commitment they all seem to find so necessary. The truth is that he's just too unwilling to let himself fall into or commit to a relationship at a time when he's not only not at all sure where he will be, but is definitely sure that he doesn't want a loved one to have to sit at home and worry about his safety when he can't even tell them truthfully where he is or what he's doing. He also doesn't want to make a life commitment to another before he can provide a stable home, and while in the military he knows doing so would be difficult, especially as a member of the Marine Corps Force Recon Special Forces unit.

8

Ihsapie (Elizabeth) Quviariatukuluk

While she doesn't feel entirely of either world nor is she forced to most of the time, Ihsapie Quviariatukuluk, or Elizabeth as she's commonly known among her people and closest friends, is part Inuit native American and part Russian by genetic heritage. She's the product of a union between a half Russian and half native American mother and a full blooded Inuit father, making her in fact three quarters native American. At not quite 5'6" tall and just over 135 pounds, Elizabeth has a strong but not really all that stocky of a build that comes with a strangely atypical deep brown (the most common hair color on the island is jet black) hair color with a highly visible near blond or light brown strand down the side that seems to be completely out of place on her classic Eurasian face that's heavy on native American Indian features in a very pleasant sort of way. To go with her almost olive colored brownish skin pigmentation, Ihsapie has the classic wide set oval dark brown eyes, flat shaped but tiny nose, and deep rosy colored full lips that mostly define her ancient native American Indian culture. One would never describe her figure as exactly hour glass, but there is no question that Elizabeth has full and lush feminine curves in all the right places. And, even though she doesn't realize all of the truth of it, with her enormous bustline, wide hips, and strong looking legs she's the epitome of a modern living example of her long forgotten Siberian ancestors from thousands of years ago. Ihsapie, or Elizabeth, always has a ready smile and gay twinkle in her eyes when she so chooses to show them, which unfortunately hasn't entirely been all that often for the most part in recent years, and even so is by any estimation a strikingly beautiful young woman.

Like virtually all of the rest of the girls on St. Lawrence island, Elizabeth Quviariatukuluk is raised by her male dominated family (her dad) and community (elders) according to a set of out dated archaic ideas and traditions that demand that she eventually take her proper place as the wife and mother of a future family unit. And, as such, she's prepared early for what will be a most likely arranged marriage of a most suitable husband from a respectable Inuit family in the village, something that frankly young Elizabeth starts to dread from the time she's not even 11 years old and just starting to bloom and flower as a young pre-teenage girl. Ihsapie is taught the traditional wifely skills in fishing net repairing, blubber rendering, reindeer harvesting, weaving, quilting, and crocheting along with all of the other traditional homebound chores by her mother and aunts at a time when she would rather be reading about the world and things outside of the prison of her existence on St. Lawrence island and the remote village of Gambell. There, of course, aren't many of these types of books available to read, but those few that are on hand fill the young woman with ideas of a vast and exciting world out there beyond her own that she can only dream about taking part in.

By her own mother's admission, Elizabeth would have undoubtedly been a scholar had she been born anywhere else besides her remote village on St. Lawrence island. Her same mother, though, would always be careful to caution her young and sometimes unhappy daughter that she must find a way to accept her fate and live her life as determined by her culture and long held established traditions in a manner that finds the happiness and fulfillment she's looking for. The stated caution about her ultimate fate by her mother only served to frustrate and make the young native girl even unhappier as the next few years of her life pass by. Ihsapie is, however, a devout Russian Orthodox Christian example of St. Lawrence island womanhood who possesses great faith, to whom her mother gives a shiny

89

gold necklace with the "double cross" as the symbol of her faith for her 12th birthday. Her 12th year would also be the time that Elizabeth truly becomes a woman, and takes part in a long held tradition of the Inuit women where her blood soaked underwear are burnt with great but private ceremony amongst her female elder mentors as an offer to the Gods for fertility and good health to the children she bears.

At the instance of her very traditional thinking native Indian father, Ihsapie "Elizabeth" Quviariatukuluk is betrothed and married to her husband to be in a traditional Inuit wedding ceremony mostly against her will at the still young age of 15 in the early summer of 2009, after which she is immediately carried to she and her husband's wedding night hut to consummate the marriage partnership to the pleasure of the family and village elders who celebrate outside after the couple disappears into the shack made out of traditional walrus skin and whale bones. It's of course the greatest hope of all who participate in the ceremony that a child will be the result of this night of wedding bliss. Let's just say that it can go without saying that young Elizabeth was ill prepared for marriage either physically or emotionally at 15, and was especially ill prepared to submit to the amorous demands of her new husband during their wedding night. Her young 18 year old not quite an adult yet husband was just as ill prepared as she, even if eager to enjoy the pleasures of his supple and beautiful new wife. Sadly, Elizabeth would find the almost nightly intimate but mostly unskilled demands of her husband as nothing more than painful reminders of her fate and represented little more than emotionally difficult interludes of misery filled with his grunting and groping on top of her body, something she both came to dread and couldn't wait to get over with. That fact that her well meaning husband was much larger than normal in his "manly tools" didn't help matters much. She, as any good Inuit wife is supposed and expected to do, Elizabeth did try to hide her feelings from her husband while submitting silently to his frequent but painful desires.

But, by any form of measure, the marriage between Elizabeth and her young husband represented a failed relationship at best, and as a result the young wife took every method she could to prevent a pregnancy, to the ongoing frustration of her husband, her father, and the Gambell community as a whole. In fact, had any known what she was secretly doing, Elizabeth would have surely not only been chastised by them all for purposely preventing a pregnancy, she would have been openly shunned by the entire community as a near despised outcast. And, the fact is that she secretly uses the contraceptive herb Queen Ann's Lace in a tea she drinks to kill her husband's sperm after they have sex. Often following her marriage, the once former gay and vibrant young woman could be seen treading around the village with her head down in a abject sadness of her imprisoned circumstance with no real hope of release or pardon, a burden that is far too often the case in a traditionalist St. Lawrence island society where young women are forced to marry men they little respect or care for. By no means was her young and faithful husband cruel or did he hurt Elizabeth in any way, either physically or emotionally. In fact he was solicitous in every manner as he made every attempt to love her and get her to love him in return. Like his father, and his father before him, and all of the fathers before them, Ihsapie's husband was a walrus hunter and a fisherman, who plied his trade on a daily basis to provide for him and his wife, who lived in the very same small cottage at the end of the street on the edge of the village where they had all lived. Sadly, the two of them simply don't have much of anything in common as Elizabeth continues to pine for a world she can't participate in and her young husband is left to wonder why he can't make his wife love him as he loves her. More sadly even, her distraught husband over time became a quiet drunk who tried to drown his growing despair in cheap Vodka, mostly down at the tavern after returning home from fishing or hunting each day. The saddest truth of all for the couple is that Elizabeth doesn't really mind that her husband doesn't come home, since she prefers her own unhappy solitude to sending time with his, and especially appreciates it when he comes home too drunk to grope at her in their marriage bed. The good fortune for Elizabeth is that her husband is in fact a quiet and miserable drunk who somehow due to his kind and gentle nature never becomes loud or physically abusive out of his frustration. Over time, even her husband's ardent demands in their marriage bed no longer continue except on infrequent occasions even when sober, something that too the young wife isn't at all disappointed about. And because all of this is the stark reality of their lives, for 4 years Elizabeth is forced to live her dreary life as an involuntary wife to a kind and generous man she doesn't even begin to love (the honest truth is that she could love him as a doting brother just not as a husband) and has in fact lost all respect for while she spends her increasingly dreary days rendering walrus blubber, fixing fishing nets, and preparing the reindeer meat in a manner that's so boring to her that she wonders from time to time if she should do something to end her life in some manner, yet another thought that would have been considered an abomination by her community had they known.

And then, as miserable as her life has been for almost 5 years, even more misery and sadness is added when her husband shockingly dies in a walrus hunting accident when a sudden unexpected storm comes out of nowhere that causes his dugout boat to capsize where he drowns in what is more than likely a drunken stupor in the swirling surf before he can be rescued. Now Elizabeth, by long held Inuit tradition, will be forced to mourn her departed husband by wearing nothing but black clothing from head to toe in public for a period of a full year, during which time she's to remain celibate, which neither of course are in fact really a problem at all. It's the sadness of being forced to mourn the loss of an admittedly decent man she knows she didn't love as required and maybe she should have but is in fact sad that he's now dead and gone from his family and their village. Even though she hadn't loved or much respected her husband, Elizabeth does feel a great deal of guilt about her life with him and how she had in fact emotionally rejected him and never gave him the love he so much wanted from her. And of even more concern to her, Elizabeth is quite well aware that she will be expected at the end of a year to either select another available unattached potential husband in the village or become by tradition the "cohabitational" wife of another already married male in the village who's willing to take the recently widowed woman in. In so many of these cases the ancient tradition is more about a middle aged husband who is bored with his middle aged wife than a willingness to step up and help. In this particular case it's a wealthy fisherman who immediately indicates he and his wife are both willing to accept her into the "safety" of their home. She knows of a few women who have fallen into such a circumstance, living lives and having the offspring of men much older than themselves, something she finds even more repugnant than her previous marriage situation. So, contrary to the long held tradition and her native community's expectations, Elizabeth resolves to her mother in private that she will more than likely never accept another, especially the kind wealthy but clearly lecherous older man, but will instead live in solitude for the remainder of her life, and afterwards informs the man himself of the determination of her decision and tells all of the various other eligible suitors who also appear as much.

To her misfortune, Elizabeth is "not meant for this world" her mother sadly expresses to her in the privacy of their conversations with great empathy to her daughter's plight. To the unfortunate contrary, her traditionalist father is already not six weeks after the death of her husband insisting that his daughter seek out and eventually marry another eligible man in the village, especially the rich fisherman who's made the most generous offer to add her to his family. His interest is merely in the future security of his daughter as the ancient traditions of his people dictate, and there are, in fact, besides the already married fisherman many other unattached and already attached men in Gambell who would be more than interested in such an arrangement with the still quite beautiful young woman. So, at not yet 21 years old, Elizabeth has already experienced more sadness and frustration in her life than any could want, but worse is the fact that she knows what's expected of her and knows that life for her will continue to be a constant and continuous reminder of her plight and circumstance.

It was right at this very time that the elderly couple who have lived in and managed the lighthouse on the furthest northern point of the island for the last almost 40 years are suddenly found dead together in their bed from old age. While the passing of the couple is not entirely unexpected, the difficulty in replacing them is due to the fact that none as a whole in the village can be expected to want to take their place of residence or their jobs in the remote lighthouse located a full 10 miles from the nearest neighbor. Theirs is a hunting and fishing culture, so the idea of spending a life living in and maintaining the strange building located in the middle of nowhere and watching the sea instead is abhorrent to most, but not to the recently widowed Ihsapie Quviariatukuluk when the unexpected opportunity offered by the vacancy is quietly pointed out to her by her understanding and compassionate mother who suggests that taking on the responsibility might be at least some of the escape from her unhappy circumstance that her up to now miserable daughter is looking for. Her dad, of course, is immediately against any such suggestion, but while being an admitted traditionalist who is desperate to find security for his wanton daughter, he eventually relents in great frustration and worry to her desire to lead a very different existence than he can perceive.

So, without further ado and without looking back for a single moment, but to the very real consternation of her father who wants a safely married daughter and future grandchildren at his hearth, Elizabeth applies for and is quickly accepted by the United States Coast Guard to run and manage the St. Lawrence island lighthouse and live full time in its small residence. And, over the next few years, Elizabeth would grow more and more comfortable with the near hermit solitude of her new life far from the demands and constant pressures to conform to the ancient traditions of her people, that was only interrupted

94

during her infrequent visits to Gambell village almost 11 miles to the south for the supplies she needs. She loves her quiet life where she can do pretty much as she pleases while making sure the lighthouse is operating as needed, without the mind numbingly boring demands of being an "Inuit Indian" wife and mother, and is even allowed to experience a newfound world of books and ideas made possible by her Coast Guard supplied computer and satellite based internet connection to the outside world. Life is suddenly good for the most part for Elizabeth, right up until that strange and unexpected night in early 2016.

Like all of the other Inuit children on St. Lawrence island Elizabeth Quviariatukuluk had been regaled by bedtime stories that included some of her peoples greatest memories from long ago, such as even before this island was their home and when the island was discovered to be a newfound prison detached forever from their traditional lands to the east and west. There were the stories of great eruptions of volcanoes and devastating earthquakes that created upheaval and changed the entire landscape. And, there were also stories about great mammoth, whale, and walrus hunts, and stories of survival during difficult winters. One of the favorite stories told often to the young children by their parents and grandparents, however, was the story about when the Russians first arrived on the island in their great sailing ship almost 225 years ago. The kids loved it because it started out scary with the talk of never seen before guns and cannons, and the shocking destruction of the garbage dump and killing of the walrus, then ended in happiness as the people and the new arrivals settled into a combined community at the behest of both the sky Gods above, the sea Gods below, and the great Russian God all around. Never in her imagination would Elizabeth had thought that she would actually witness a modern recurrence of the two centuries old event told in her bedtime stories as a child.

9

Eastern Ukraine 2013

Seemingly or not so seemingly, it all began with the Russian incursion into the Eastern Ukrainian region commonly called the Crimea in 2013 at the behest of the rebellious ethnic Russian majority who lived in the region, and who identified themselves more with Moscow to the east rather than Kiev to the west. And, slowly but surely over the next two or so years, the Russian Federation under the near dictatorial leadership of Vladimir Putin and his pro-business antidemocratic cliché made every effort to consolidate their hold on the territory to where it soon became little more than a return to a previous "Soviet Socialist Republic" satellite status under the direct control of Russia. The Russian objective, of course, was a continued and guaranteed access to and control over the valuable Black Sea year round warm weather port of Sevastopol, where the bulk of the Russian Navy has been stationed for over a 100 years and is still mostly based, a full 25 years after the break-up of the old Soviet Union. Without the guaranteed possession of the port of Sevastopol and access to it through the adjacent Crimean region, the Russian Federation is destined to be nothing more than a "seasonal" ocean power, even with the modern submarine pens at Murmansk and Vladivostok since both tend to be iced over and closed to operational use much of the time during the cold winter months of the year. Access to this region and its year round entry to the world's oceans through the Mediterranean Sea has been one of the constant uninterrupted pillars of Russian foreign policy for well over 300 years, whether the government in Moscow is imperialist, communist, or nationalist.

The fact is that the entire Crimean region has been under either direct or indirect Russian control ever since the Russo - Turkish war of 1792 when the area was first annexed following the defeat of the Turkish Ottoman Empire, and has only been under supposed Ukrainian administrative control since 1954, thus the reason for the dispute. Control over the essentially valuable region and its seaport which has long held critical strategic importance to the defense of Russia (and the old Soviet Union) has never in fact been a part of the Ukraine or is it populated by a majority of ethnic Ukrainians, and was only turned over to the Ukrainian Soviet Socialist Republic as a reward for their important role in the modern "Socialist Federation" state by her communist masters in Moscow. Little did the Soviet Commissars realize at the time how much their fellow Russians would ultimately regret what was seen in 1954 as nothing more than a simple but really not significant change in administrative management decision, and that in 1989 with the unforeseen collapse of the Soviet Empire which resulted in the strategically critical region suddenly under the control of a competing power, the new independent country of Ukraine. And, the real and more important problem is that there is a long established ethnic dislike and historic suspicion between the old Russia and the old Ukraine which never actually went completely away during the 70 year Soviet era, and which immediately raised its ugly head once again when the shackles of control were lifted following a renewed independence in 1989. Not surprisingly, a new government is elected in the Ukraine with a decidedly suspicious and even with a somewhat anti-Russian pro European attitude in Kiev in 1991. Suddenly, the Russian leaders in Moscow wake up and discover that direct and guaranteed control over one of their country's most valuable resources has been lost, so they aren't at all happy, and so aren't the ethnic Russian population in the Crimean region who now find themselves under the complete control of the long hated and distrusted Ukrainians to the west. We should fairly note before we move forward that Moscow did in fact receive mutually agreed upon "guaranteed" access to and continued to maintain operational control over the Naval Base in Sevastopol by a formal signed agreement (1992) with the newly elected Ukrainian government in Kiev and still does today where it continues to base the vast majority of its Russian naval warm water blue ocean fleet. In 1993 a "bi-lateral" command of all naval assets stationed in the Black Sea was established between the new Russian Federation and an independent Ukraine. But, as would be expected from their long contentious historical relationship it has been and still is a very tense situation where both competing parties play their roles in making things difficult to say the least.

By the turn of the new century (2000) an active and highly organized resistance movement was born outside of Odessa and Sevastopol who immediately began to argue for a return of the entire Crimean region to direct Russian control with Russian and not Ukrainian citizenship for all those who lived in the area, and when they were immediately harassed for their "traitorous position" and suppressed by the government in Kiev, the ethnic Russian resistance movement set up militias (freedom fighters they were called by their supporters) and began to take up arms which their current allies and former Russian masters were only too willing to provide. In quick response to these activities, the Ukrainian government in Kiev moved additional military and security forces of its own into the region, which of course only added to the potential for violence and even more instability in the entire Eastern Ukrainian region. So as a result, what amounts to an on again off again rural and urban guerrilla war festers in the region for almost 15 years completely off the radar of the rest of the world for the most part until two significant things happen. First, a Russian nationalist named Vladimir Putin takes power in Moscow in 2005, and second, the Ukraine starts making overtures at about the same time to become a member of the European Union and even NATO, the American and West European military alliance born out of World War II with a historical anti-Russian intent and strategy. As an admitted and unapologetic Russian nationalist, one of Putin's highest priorities from the very beginning of his regime is to both reinstate his country's rightful influence on its borders to the west and also recover the loss to his country the international prestige held by the previous Soviet regime before its unexpected sudden collapse in 1989. And not surprisingly, a key part of both is the reincorporation of the Crimea region with its critically important Black Sea port of Sevastopol back under direct Russian control where it rightfully should be. An important thing to note here is that Putin's expansionist desires may begin with the strategically important Crimean region and its critical warm water port, but most observers of the situation in the region are in full agreement that they certainly don't end there. So, by 2009 and 2010 every East European and Baltic former Soviet Satellite country (Belarus, Estonia, Latvia, Lithuania, Poland, Romania, Ukraine) is either nervous about the immediate future with the waking giant to their east or feeling forced to make accommodations with the increasingly aggressive government in Moscow.

And then, the situation suddenly explodes out of control in 2013 as if a lid has blown off the pressure cooker, which it in fact has, when the decades long tension and underground guerrilla activities expand into open fighting and what amounts to open civil war by late 2014 between the Ukrainian military forces and the pro Russian separatists. Who did what first, and who supported who to make matters worse, will be an argument that analysts and historians throughout the world will battle for eons to say the least. But, without doubt, both Kiev and Moscow played their own direct and indirect roles in supporting and arming their allies in the region, which in fact has played the biggest part in fueling the increasingly bloody fight now taking place all across east Ukraine. Russian regular Army and Ukrainian troops face off in the area by early 2015, and there are in fact incidents where fire fights and even full scale artillery barrages risk open warfare between the two countries. The Ukrainian government places the blame squarely on Moscow by claiming that the fighting is the result of illegal destabilizing actions taken by Putin's Russian forces and her disruptive allies in the Crimea, while Russia counterclaims that it must support the plight of the ethnic Russians in the region who are being wrongfully suppressed by the Ukrainian regime. By the middle of 2015, there would be a total of well over 10,000 deaths and many more thousands of injuries on both sides, an untold destruction of property will have taken place throughout the region, and even the shoot down of an unarmed Malaysian commercial airliner in the skies above will have been experienced, along with the deaths of over 250 innocent civilians. The long festering situation is by mid 2015 spinning completely out of control and has now become not just a regional hot spot but an international problem for all. The Ukrainian government is screaming for help from the West, the other recently independent countries on Russia's western border are increasingly nervous, the European Union sees a potential return to the bad ole days of the Cold War with a Warsaw Pact block of countries to the east and a NATO block of countries to the west, and the United States fears a more powerful and aggressive Russia that will become a thorn in her side on the world stage once again.

As such, tensions between the West and Russia continue to increase between 2013 and 2016, and they increase especially between Moscow and Washington D.C. in particular. The situation quickly becomes a "tit for tat" back and forth set of actions and reactions, including increasingly stringent sanctions against the Russian government and economy applied by America and her closest allies. Diplomatic pressure is put on both regimes in the growing dispute to come to a negotiated settlement, led by Angela Merkel in Germany and David Cameron in Great Britain. In a public response to the increase in western supported sanctions, Russian Federation President Vladimir Putin threatens to ban American astronauts from shuttled missions in their Soyuz capsule to the International Space Station (Russian capsules provide the only access to the station for the USA since the retirement of its space shuttle fleet in 2011), while the Americans threaten in return to lock the doors on the station to Soyuz crews (by agreement the U.S. manages the ISS while Russia supplies the bulk of the transport to and from it). Russia refuses to help with the UN supported negotiations to prevent a nuclear Iran, and also refuse to stop supplying the brutal Syrian regime with weapons against a so called "democratic" insurgency that continues to fuel a civil war that's killing and maiming millions of innocent civilians and driving a migrant crisis of hundreds of thousands of refugees all across Europe. They also sit on the sidelines in the growing battle with Islamic terror groups throughout the Middle East, which in itself is counterproductive given their own increasing problems with home grown Muslim radical militants in Russia's own southern border republics. And, something not seen in almost 25 years since the fall of the old Soviet Union, Russian military aircraft once again begin to test the borders of places like the Baltic states, Scandinavian countries, Poland, Great Britain, Canada, the Caribbean, and even Alaska. The United States threatens, in turn, to reestablish discussions about an American designed anti-missile complex and forward bases in Poland as they too begin to prod the edges of Russian territory with their own ships and aircraft in a way not seen in the two and a half decades since the end of the old Cold War.

Worst of all is that through 2015 and into 2016, both Russia and the West (mostly the United States) are supplying increasingly more sophisticated and deadly weapons to their respective proxy allies in and around the eastern regions of the Ukraine. Heavier and more powerful anti-tank, anti-aircraft, anti-personnel, and field artillery weaponry are all being provided and used on both sides in the growing conflict, which not surprisingly is increasing even more the violence and death taking place throughout the region. And even worse yet, is the fact that the United States is putting heavy and very public pressure on the European Union to admit the Ukraine into full membership, and are even suggesting they be immediately brought into NATO itself, the once and now again anti-Soviet and anti-Russian alliance.

Altogether by the end of 2015, these increasingly violent and destabilizing actions and reactions are contributing to an ever more dangerous atmosphere that not only suggests a return to the very worst days of the Cold War, but could realistically actually lead to another ground war in Europe if some way isn't found to make both sides come to their senses before it's too late. Worse still is that the situation will continue to fester throughout the rest of 2015 and all through to the political campaign season of 2016 where the American Republican and Democratic candidates for President (Jeb Bush and Hillary Clinton) argue back and forth about the merits of the previous Obama policies and how things should move forward in regards to the situation in the Ukraine and the Russian Federation.

10

In the Situation Room

There's no denying the hard tension all around the big conference table in the White House situation room located in the basement of the West Wing. Sitting around the table are the President, the Vice President Mia Love, the President's Secretary of Defense, Robert Natter, the Secretary of State, Roger Noriega, John Negroponte the CIA Director, and Cameron Alexander, the President's new National Security Advisor. Hot steaming coffee and delicious looking croissants are being served all around by a most attentive White House staff.

Given that it is the White House for a fact, the not small room with its plush wall to wall carpet and enormous solid walnut conference table surrounded by leather bound solid walnut chairs is somewhat surprisingly spartan in a classic American corporate business office sort of way. There are pictures on the walls surrounding the room of the 44 previous Presidents of the United States, the last one being of Democratic President Barrack Obama whose picture has just been added to the gallery. Out of tradition, the current President isn't added until he or she leaves office. Placed in between the pictures are old style clocks with the current times of major cities around the world. In the middle of the large table itself is of course a most up to date telephone conference calling device with 4 speakers that are stretched out the entire length so that all in attendance can hear the person or persons on the other end. Unlike the commercial models seen in most corporate offices, this very special model has a very secure capability that inhibits anybody not invited from listening in on the conversations being held.

"Crap, what I really need is a damned cigarette," complains the National Security Advisor.

"Not allowed here Cameron, besides I keep telling you those cancer sticks are going to be the ultimate death of you," chides Jeb Bush who has known the man for nearly 20 years now.

Everybody else in the room is waiting expectantly for what the new President has to say, mostly because this is the very first meeting of his National Security staff since being elected into the office of President 2 weeks ago. As such, laying in front of each individual sitting around the table is a most professional looking and bound document labeled with "Vladimir Putin: President of the Russian Federation."

"Okay everybody, this is simple. Given the increasingly difficult and dangerous situation in the Ukraine we need to get up to speed as fast as possible. So, to do so, I want a clear understanding of the man I'm dealing with in the Kremlin, and before you is a most up to date document as crafted by the CIA and State Department," explains the new President. "But, here's the deal folks. We know and can see what it tells us about the man's public background and experience in government. We know he's a playboy of sorts who loves to show off and in fact is an undisputed "rock star" with women all across Russia. We know he's amassed near dictatorial powers in the office of President of the Russian Federation, and as such has recreated some of the methodologies of the Kremlin's Soviet era. We know he's smart, and we know he's ruthless. What I want to know is what we don't know and what's not written in these reports. I would like to know what makes the man tick and how he really thinks. So, with that I will open things up for discussion," says the President who is looking for information about a man he knows is to be a thorn in his side, and possibly even more.

"Well Jeb, the man is an absolute contradiction. He can be so darned accommodating and collaborative at times, but then at other times or even at the very same time the bastard can be

104

the most deceitful and devious son of a bitch you ever saw. That report is right, Putin is really smart like a fox, who knows how to expose and exploit every weakness in his adversaries, and more important he's absolutely willing to take advantage of them. More worrisome still is the fact that the man really is a rock star who enjoys great popularity not only because of his well crafted image but in the minds of most Russians, Vladimir Putin has returned a sense of honor and importance to the county not seen since the fall of the old Soviet empire," says the Secretary of State Roger Noriega.

"Thanks Roger. I agree with you, especially the popularity part. We best remember that in dealing with this man," says the President.

"Well, and we better also remember that Putin doesn't act like the typical Russian government apparatchik who can be counted on to be cautious and play it same when the chips are on the table. He's a risk taker who's willing to take advantage of those weaknesses he's identified in his adversaries.   You gotta remember the true significance of his growing up professionally in the old KGB instead of in the halls of government," offers CIA Director John Negroponte.

"Tell me what you mean by that John?" responds a curious Jeb Bush.

"It's simple Jeb. The man's sneaky and is always looking for ways to wiggle into and exploit the other guy, whether it be out in the open or in the depths of behind the scenes where you can't see him coming. It also means the guy is ruthless in a direct way that most government hacks shrink from. He doesn't mind leaving a few bodies on the ground if they will provide him the results he seeks," adds Negroponte.

"Interesting and a little scary," muses the President.

"You're damned right it's scary. The dude's absolutely cold blooded. But, here's the deal. Being cold blooded can play both ways. Yes, he will certainly kill to get his way, but on the other hand he understands like few classic government apparatchiks when the game is up and when to back down," says John Negroponte.

"The meaning?" asks Bush.

"The meaning is simple Jeb. The man can be counted on to press and wiggle and risk to the point of pushing the envelope almost to the level of disaster, but at the same time he can be counted on never to go too far. He's not a man we have to worry will press the button like some crazy," states a CIA Director who's confident in his analysis.

"Can we be sure of that John?" wonders Mia Love who knows Vladimir Putin only by the little fearful reputation she's heard and read about.

"I'm pretty damned sure Mia. The man's an absolute Russian Nationalist, something that he's in fact unapologetic about. He's a man who believes Russia should play great and significant role in not only Europe but the world. He's a student of history, so is committed to Pan Russianism throughout Eastern Europe and the former southern Soviet republics. He has a natural classic Russian fear of China, which we can take advantage of. But, the man won't push the button. I'm sure of it," explains Negroponte.

"Let me ask this John. The man's a playboy from what I understand. Can we take advantage of that in some way? What if we somehow got him into a compromising or publically humiliating circumstance of some sort?" wonders the President.

"Wouldn't work Jeb. Don't get me wrong, the man likes his women, but he's careful. No chance we could do a "honey trap" or some other entrapment strategy to set him up. From my understanding it's been tried several times in recent years and he never once has fallen for the bait," promises a pretty confident John Negroponte.

"Okay, that's all great John, but what's it really all mean as we look at what's going on in the Ukraine and the way Putin's flexing his muscles in places like Syria and elsewhere," wonders President Jeb Bush.

"What it means Mr. President, is that the man is pretty much unimpeachable and we can't expect Putin to back down in the Ukraine. He means what he says when he tells us it's an internal Russian problem and that East Europe is in the Russian sphere of influence in the same manner we claim Latin and South America is in ours. It also means that he will be willing to flex his muscles in places like Syria because he wants to be seen as a great power with influence in the course of world events. But notice how carefully he is using that power in the air war over Syria, Mr. President. He's careful not to over step his bounds and makes sure we know what he's doing so there isn't the risk of an unnecessary mistake. But, here's the deal with Putin Jeb, you better be ready for him to not only push and press us at every opportunity, but we had better be ready for him to do the unexpected at some point," points out John Negroponte.

"I agree with John," says Roger Noriega.

Both Cameron Alexander and Bob Natter also agree with the assessment of the Russian President, while Vice President Mia Love simply nods her head. So, with a unanimous consensus on the nature of their Russian adversary, President Bush thanks everybody for their valuable input and closes the meeting by suggesting that they all keep their eyes and ears open at the same time they all consider the most likely scenarios for future actions on Moscow's part.

(11)

State of the Union Address

It's going to be John Ellis Bush's first State of the Union Address to a joint session of Congress as the newly elected Republican President of the United States. It's a cold winter evening in Washington D.C. but frankly it's a not at all surprisingly warm setting in the refurbished capital building, given that a Republican President will be speaking to a Republican dominated Congress for the first time since the Reagan administration over 30 years ago. Men like Cory Gardner, Mike Coffman, Ted Cruz, John Ryan, Rand Paul, Mich McConnell, and John McCain literally can't wait to get started on a new conservative agenda that they have reason to hope a Republican President will fully support. More to the point for our discussion, the House and Senate Republicans are excited and nervous to hear what the new President will have to say about the worsening situation in Eastern Europe, with the Russian Federation, and the continuing civil war which is escalating in the Ukrainian Crimean region in particular. All have been frustrated for years now by what they see as an intransigent and dysfunctional policy towards Putin's Russia and throughout the region by the previous Democratic administration of Barack Obama and a non-combative legislature led by the now gone John Boehner. None have felt that the former President's policies or the work of either of his Secretary of States, John Kerry or Hillary Clinton, has done anything to encourage the Ukrainian's newfound pro western outlook or discourage the Russian aggressors under the leadership of Vladimir Putin with real actions on the ground. The fact is that in their conservative opinions our policy in recent years has looked more like a one step forward, then two steps back, or at other times two steps forward, followed by a large and quick step to the rear as things have continued to ebb and flow in the region with ever increasing violence and death. In real essence the Congressional Republicans feel that the Cold War has in fact returned with impunity in recent years, but the Democratic administration chose a position of denial rather than face the threat directly as they feel it should have been. The irony is that, contrary to conservative Republican perceptions, the severe sanctions currently in place against the Putin regime in the winter of 2017 have all originated with or at the behest of the previous Obama administration. During his Presidential campaign Jeb Bush stated repeatedly that the Ukrainian situation would get much more attention in his administration than the Obama administration has chosen to give it (emboldening Putin to act as he has they think), mostly because the new President and his advisors see renewed Russian expansion as the danger to that part of the world that it is. Most are aware that both Paula Dobriansky (national security advisor) and Roger Noriega (secretary of state) certainly see the world that way. Comparatively, the new administration according to the signals it's relayed so far, has every intention of downsizing our role in the Middle East by more and more relying on our "Arab allies" in the region as they continue to take the lead and play a much larger role in the fight against Islamic extremism and the growing regional power of Iran. Fortunately, the situation with Iran is in the best shape it's been in for decades with what appears to be the semblance of a workable nuclear agreement in place (although Jeb Bush has promised to take a close look at the agreements involved as President) and what amounts to an increasingly closer (never admitted) American and Iranian partnership in the continuing battle against ISIS in Iraq and Syria. Jeb Bush has also made it quite known that he intends to reach out to the Chinese with more of an olive branch of regional and international partnership as compared to the previous administration who openly talked for 8 years about a "an Asian shift of US military strategy" which was frankly nothing more than political speak for "we are going to look at China as our primary adversary and threat in not only the Pacific but throughout the entire world." Not surprisingly at all, not every Republican congressional colleague is in agreement with the new President Bush concerning China and a proposed shift in regard to our relations with that country, but the new President responds to their concern by simply stating that an aggressive Russia is a far more immediate and dangerous problem and that we need China's help to keep them and Putin's regime in check. So, with so many pressing issues at stake the Republican leadership of Congress is most interested and eager about what the President has to say tonight in regards to a proposed new foreign policy, and the increasingly serious Ukrainian situation in particular; a subject they all have been told in advance by the President's speech writers will get much attention tonight in his first State of the Union Address.

(The following is a paraphrased description of that part of newly elected President Jeb Bush's first inaugural State of the Union Address as it applies to the current situation in the Crimea, the Ukraine, and towards the Russian Federation.)

President Bush is speaking...

"The people of the United States of America, ever since the days of our Founding Fathers and the Declaration of Independence 240 years ago in 1776 have always stood for and supported the right and desire for freedom and democracy by people wherever they may be in the world. This has always been the case and as such is the case today throughout an independent Ukraine and the eastern region of that country commonly referred to as the Crimea." (hearty applause) "Some in certain sectors of the world want to make a claim that those fighting the Ukrainians in the Crimea are modern examples of freedom fighters battling their oppressors for independence, just as our ancestors did over 200 years ago in our own country against the British Empire and King George III. Nothing frankly could be further from the truth." (more applause) "What has gone on and continues to

110

do so is nothing more than a "cold blooded" Russian sponsored and funded illegal insurgency designed to undermine the legitimately elected Ukrainian government in Kiev's control over the area and region. Rather than wanting nothing more than an autonomous status for the region as proclaimed by the so called rebel leaders, the real objective as directed from Moscow is to pry away the region from its legitimate government in Kiev, including its valuable commercial center in Odessa and the critically important warm water naval installation located on the Black Sea in Sevastopol, and hand it over to their supporters in Moscow who covet it even now over 25 years since the fall of the Soviet empire in 1989." (applause again) "Russian President Putin's statements to the contrary, this is the current situation in the Crimea and this administration will not stand for it." (heavy applause) "Let me say that again, the United States will not stand by as a legitimate country is raped by another under the guise of a so called fight for independence." (this time every Republican in the room stands up to applaud as even do many of the Democrats in the chamber) "Our intelligence services have provided this office indisputable proof that the insurgency in the Eastern part of the Ukraine and the region called the Crimea is in fact being provided military leadership, intelligence information, weapons and ammunition, and even front line soldiers from Moscow and the Russian Federation's Army. The Russian Air Force has gone so far as to establish what amounts to a no fly zone over the region and the Russian Navy has forced its Black Sea Ukrainian counterpart to stay in port through outright and blatant acts of intimidation."

"So long as this situation continues, it will be the policy of this President to keep in place and even expand the sanctions and trade restrictions started and implemented by my predecessor, President Obama. (a few boos can be heard coming from the Republican side of the chamber in reference to the former Democratic administration) "No, no, just a moment. Let me say this right here and now, I am in total agreement with and applaud the strong sanctions put in place by President Obama and his administration. These sanctions already in place have hurt the Russian cause severely and I plan that they keep doing so until the Russians return to their own borders and pull their support for the illegal Crimean insurgency." (strong applause)

"So, in response to the growing violence perpetrated by the Russian regime in Moscow in the Crimea, I am announcing tonight that I will send a bill for approval to this Congress in the next few days that will include additional sanctions and trade restrictions, especially in those areas that have any possible military use, such as high technology digital equipment. I am also announcing that the United States Army and Air Force will be conducting "joint maneuvers" with our NATO British, French, German, Italian, and Polish allies on the ground and in the skies over East Germany this coming spring. Negotiations have also been restarted with our Polish friends about new forward bases for NATO aircraft and the potential construction of the long proposed NATO operated anti-missile installation that will serve as protective a shield from attack for all of Europe. I would in fact invite President Putin to join this effort instead of seeing it as a threat."

"Let me be clear tonight that we Americans and this President are determined and resolved to stand beside and support the freedom and independence of our Ukrainian friends, and will continue to stand with them against the illegal aggression sponsored and perpetrated by their Russian Federation neighbors, no matter the excuse from Moscow."

(this final statement of the State of the Union speech concerning the Crimean crisis in the Ukraine is quickly followed by an enthusiastic two minutes of uninterrupted applause by especially the Republicans in the room as they stand in support of their President and his newly stated policy and commitment)

Following the State of the Union Address, it will be Republican Senator John McCain who will be asked for his thoughts about the statements made by the President concerning the situation in the Crimea, and he unequivocally stated not only his total support but the support of the entire Republican caucus for what the President has laid down for his policy in the region.

Conversely Nancy Pelosi, the sitting Democratic minority leader in the House of Representatives, says that she fears that the strong statements made by the new President concerning the situation in the Crimea will serve only to make matters worse in the region with its unilateral actions rather than making a commitment to the negotiating table with a broad range of regional participants.

At a morning White House news conference held two days after the State of the Union Address, President Bush restates his resolve to give more direct support to the Ukraine, and when asked the question about the reported nature of the insurgency reiterates that the so called freedom fighters are nothing more than paid thugs hired by Moscow to foment chaos and instability in the region.   He further says that there is substantiated proof that Moscow has provided the insurgency with heavy and sophisticated weapons, including additional mobile units of the SA-9 missile system that shot down the Malaysian commercial airliner back in 2014. When asked if his administration would ever support providing more sophisticated weapons, such as F-35 fighter jets, mothballed F-111 fighter /bombers that could be sent at a deep discount, and our most modern anti-tank and anti-aircraft weapons and missiles, President Bush says that "we aren't" quite ready to go there as yet, but haven't entirely ruled doing so out at some point in the future if things don't improve with a Russian retreat under UN supervision. When asked about potential B-2 missions to take out specific rebel targets, the President immediately discounts doing so, and adds that for the foreseeable future no American military personnel will be directly involved in the Crimean fight.

In Moscow, in response to the speech and its aftermath, Russian President Vladimir Putin immediately and strongly discounts the claims made by the new American President about Russian interference in Ukrainian affairs, and once again describes the Crimean insurgency as nothing more than an honest rebellion of

"Ethnic Russians" against a repressive and illegal Ukrainian regime. Putin goes on to claim that the elections held both in 2014 and 2016 were ripe with illegalities and that the sitting government in Kiev is in fact illegitimate in the eyes of Moscow. And, he calls the NATO support for this illegitimate government despicable and an unwarranted interference by both the United States and her Western European allies. Putin then states that, of course, Russia must support fellow Russians in the same manner that he's quite sure that the United States will always support fellow Americans wherever they may be, and will remain committed to doing so regardless what the rest of the world might think or do. President Putin goes on to dismiss with a quick wave of his hand the additional sanctions and trade restrictions announced by the newly elected American President, and announces that in response he and his Kremlin advisors will determine the appropriate responses.

In the Ukrainian capital city of Kiev, the pro western Ukrainian President thanks the new American President for his continued support, and stresses that never will the Ukraine back down from the Russian bullies no matter how many arms and men they bring to the fight. He further states that the Ukraine remains committed to democracy and free expression while disagreeing with any attempts to create an autonomous Crimea as suggested by Moscow and her ethnic Russian "surrogates." Lastly, the Ukrainian President announces that he and his advisors will be taking the NATO suggested membership invitation into serious consideration for later discussions with the Ukrainian Parliament.

(12)

Secret Meeting in the Kremlin

It wasn't long (the very next day actually) after the new Republican President's state of the union message when an angry and determined Russian President Vladimir Putin calls a very secret meeting of his most loyal inner staff to discuss what options they have to respond to the continued American meddling into Russian and Eastern European affairs. The setting for the secret planning session in the Kremlin is in fact much like any corresponding meeting in Washington with the only exception being that the room where the meeting is being held is far more ornate and old world than the comparatively spartan White House basement situation room. In total comparison, however, to the Washington counterpart is how effectively the room is protected from those uninvited "guests" who could be listening in on the conversation by way of a hidden modern listening devise. The long conference like table the half dozen men are sitting around is the very same highly crafted table used by Tsar Alexander and Tsarina Alexandria centuries ago, and only the overstuffed padding on the high backed solid wood chairs has been replaced and upgraded since those far in the past days. Posted around the ornate room are no fewer than another one half dozen very serious looking men who, while dressed in business suits, are clearly paramilitary types, made obvious by the large noticeable bulges just inside their jackets where their easy to reach Markov automatic pistols are located. The room itself is just as ornate, if not even more so, than the 300 year old table and chairs with the heavy custom woven wool carpet like rugs on the floor that are so soft and easy on the feet they are almost like walking on a plush golf green, and the brilliantly painted walls with their highly crafted sculpted wood trim cornices, all painted with thick coats of 24 carat gold leaf paint. On the walls themselves are some of the same well crafted wool rugs, and in between them are painted portraits of past Tsars and Tsarinas. Interestingly enough, not a picture of any of the Soviet era leaders are to be seen amongst them. Off to the side in the not very small room is a gold plated and jeweled Russian Samovar tea service with solid copper, brass, and silver appointments, and in front of each of the important men sitting at the table is a just as ornate crystal glass with solid silver and gold handled tea cup along with a personal serving dish of traditional Russian sugar, English lemon, and fresh made cream. Along with the tea service is a pure white dressed male server in white gloves and hat. There's not a woman in or near the room, even in a service capacity, a clear indication that the western liberalization of women in a direct or even indirect role in Russian politics is still a distant dream. A well known teetotaler, the Kremlin staff knows from past experience that Vladimir Putin will not condone the presence of Vodka or any other alcoholic drink in the room.

President Vladimir Putin opens the secret meeting by first welcoming his associates and then doing a quick and angry review of what was said by the American President in his state of the union message the day before. He makes it clear that in his opinion, to no surprise of any sitting around the ornate table, that the words spoken by President Bush are nothing more than continued American meddling into an issue (the Ukraine and the Crimea) they have no business concerning themselves with. He goes on to compare their doing so in the same vein as if "we in Russia would be so presumptuous as to instruct them on their Negro problem or their century old claim to hegemony in the Western hemisphere of the Americas."

Also in the room with the Russian President is Prime Minister Dmitri Medvedev, Foreign Minister Sergey Lavrov, Defense Minister Sergey Kuzhugetovich Shoygu, Chief of Staff Valery Gerasimov, and Naval Chief of Staff Viktor Chirkov. Frankly,

116

Mikhail Fradkov, the standing director of the SVR is not at this quickly called meeting because he's currently not in very good standing with his President, and more than a few are predicting that we will soon be sacked in favor of another. To the uninformed or non-observant the room and session would seem to appear pretty casual with a conversation being held among relative equals, but a closer observation would show that first of all President Putin always speaks first and never is he interrupted while doing so, and then the second observation would be that there's almost always a total and unanimous agreement with everything he says, and even if not readily agreed with any comments are unquestionably tactful and even furtive in nature. Most of the discussion is in fact nothing more than a rubber stamp of agreement for what the Russian President thinks and says. All at the table know for a fact that not everything about the old dismantled Soviet government is past history, and that either "counting or feeding the trees" is one of them - meaning that any who go too far in disagreeing or arguing with the boss could end up in a gulag with no more to do than count the hundreds upon hundreds of trees or finding themselves as fertilizer for the same. General Shoygu, one of Vladimir Putin's longest associates going all the way back to their years together in the old KGB during the Soviet era, makes a derisive comment of his own about the arrogance of the American President as well as Americans in general in support of what his mentor and protector is saying.

"For sure Comrades the Americans do not nor do they care to understand the true politics and history of what is happening in the Crimea," offers Dmitri Medvedev, the Prime Minister. "They don't know the Ukrainians they way we do, and actually think of them as freedom loving democrats, something we all know better than to believe," he adds.

"You're correct in what you say, Dmitri, but being stupid or unaware of reality doesn't give a country the right to tell others how to conduct their own affairs," points out President Putin.

"True enough Mr. President. The fucking Americans think that just because they are so rich and so powerful that they can dictate their desires to any they wish to. Look at what they continue to do in the Middle East - complete nonsense," offers Sergey Lavrov and longtime student of the United States and its foreign policy.

This comment brings about a unified snuff of derision around the table as they all consider the continued arrogance and inexplicable stupidity of the foreign policy of the United States. Lavrov goes on to point out the constant missteps experienced by the Americans, regardless who's in power in the White House or Congress, because their only interest is the short term economic benefit they can provide their capitalist benefactors from their policies around the world. Just look at the insane do, then confuse, then repudiate, then undo policies that Washington has conducted in Iraq for 30 years since the Shah fell in Tehran. They put Saddam Hussein and his Sunni Bath party in power in Bagdad as a break against Iran and supply him in a decade long war with the Iranians to keep Iraqi oil flowing, then further confuse him by turning their backs when he gets aggressive with both his neighbors and his internal enemies (the Shiites in particular) so long as the oil continues to flow, and then out of the blue they take him out when oil production slumps and he threatens to sell his oil to the Chinese and create a massive power vacuum by having no effective plan for who to replace him with so that the very Iranians they worry about move in and strengthen their position. And all the while in the chaos that gets created in a broken down Iraq, ISIS suddenly appears and takes over the oil fields for themselves, causing the Americans to lose them after all. No Russian, whether a Tsarist, a Commissar, or a Nationalist, would ever do such a stupid thing against the interests of our own foreign policy, says the Foreign Minister.

"Thank you for the history lesson, Sergey," offers a pleased Vladimir Putin, who then begs the question of what should be done in the face of American meddling and increasingly difficult U.S. supported sanctions against the Russian economy.

Nobody around the conference table is willing to go out on a limb with any suggestions until they hear what their leader thinks, so being safe Viktor Chirkov, the Naval Chief of Staff simply suggests continued support for the Russian separatists in the Crimea while voicing concern about doing anything that might lead to further confrontation with the Americans or NATO. Both Dmitri Medvedev and Sergey Lavrov agree with his comments. Only Chief of the General Staff Valery Gerasimov is willing to say that something needs to be done to get the arrogant Americans to quit stirring up the international pot against Moscow.

"Thank you, Valery, I agree. We can't just sit back and let the Americans decide the framework for the rest of us. Frankly, they can't do a damned thing to stop us in the Ukraine and they know it, and we certainly should know it. But they can make us really look bad in the house of world public opinion. We need to do something that upsets them and throws them off guard and off their game," says President Putin.

"What are you recommending Comrade?" wonders Sergey Kuzhugetovich Shoygu.

"Here's what I think we should do. While the Americans are so focused on the Ukraine and too arrogant to think we would dare do so, we should launch a surprise attack and occupy their island of St. Lawrence located at the southern entrance of the Bering Strait. I've had some folks do some quiet investigating, and they don't even have a single combat unit or defensive system on or near the island, so we could take it with a quick assault by elite forces..."

"For God sakes, Vladimir, the Americans will go crazy if we do such a thing! It could even lead to nuclear war," nearly cries out Dmitri Medvedev.

"Never mind Dmitri, you're wrong, and here's why. We will take the island quick because there are no defensive forces to stop

119

us. And, we will occupy the island as benevolent friends rather than plundering invaders. I have just the man in mind to lead the invasion assault and occupation to make sure that is the case. So long as we simply take the island then do no more as we avoid any loss of life and in fact make attempts to make life better for the 1500 people who live there, I'm quite convinced the Americans will do nothing except make plans to take it back at some future point, which in fact we should be ready for since the only thing I want to do with the action is upset them and make a point," offers a President who knows for a fact that none at this table will dare actually go against his proposal. "Besides comrades, I have spent some time studying their President and his imperial family, and have decided that regardless what they might say in public they are pragmatists and will do nothing so dangerous as you suggest," he adds with tremendous assurance.

Soon, with all of the tactful and dismissive questions answered around the Kremlin table, Russian Federation President Vladimir Putin gives both his Chief of the General Staff (General of the Russian Army Valery Gerasimov) and Chief of the Naval Staff (Admiral Viktor Chirkov) their respective marching orders to get an assault invasion plan put together and on his desk in 10 days.

13

Things Begin to Heat Up a Little More

The situation heats up even more during the early spring months of 2017 following the State of the Union speech made by President Bush and after additional sanctions are implemented against the Russian government at the same time the United States not only begins the promised NATO maneuvers in Germany, and starts the threatened discussions about a new anti-missile installation in Poland, but the United States Navy also announces that a 9 ship "squadron" that will include the Ticonderoga class guided missile cruiser Gettysburg has been "invited" to make a "friendly courtesy call" visit to the northern shores of the Black Sea where it will call on the "Ukrainian" port of Sevastopol. Moscow, and Russian Federation President Vladimir Putin in particular, are enraged at the brazen affront and blatantly in your face nature of the U.S. Naval visit, which they of course call a completely unnecessary provocation. And, when the United States Navy squadron does in fact enter the Black Sea in April they are immediately over flown and harassed continuously by Russian Mig-35 and Su-31 fighter bombers, Hind helicopters, and are even over flown by low flying Russian Tu-95 Bear and Tu-160 Blackjack bombers. And of course as can only be expected, they are constantly monitored by Russian patrol boats and "fishing trawlers" the entire time after they cruise east past the Bosporus Straits of Turkey and while they are in the Black Sea, then continue being so all the way until they pass back through the Dardanelles to return to the international waters of the Mediterranean Sea. Even more ominously, while in the Black Sea the squadron has to take note on their sonar screens the presence of a submarine lurking in the vicinity, which all rightly assume from the electronic signature on their sonar screen is a Russian Federation attack sub. In truth, the Black Sea is also considered international waters like the Mediterranean, but for well over a century it's been treated more like a Russian lake, so from their point of view the incursion of the American Naval squadron is indeed a serious provocation to be met in kind by their own naval and air forces.

By the summer of 2017 Putin goes so far as to bring up a long forgotten territorial claim and actually threatens to occupy what he now refers to as the disputed island of St. Lawrence (rightly claimed by the United States as part of US territory due to the Alaskan purchase all the way back in 1867) located just south of the mouth of the Bering Strait in retaliation for the recent U.S. Naval incursion into the Black Sea. Of course, no one who truly understands what's going on between the United States and Russia really takes the threat seriously at all, or even think there is a remote possibility of a real attack or imminent invasion of the island. So, even though the specific threat is made from the Kremlin, still no actual measures are taken or even considered by the United States to make any attempts to firm up the nonexistent defenses in the region, since only about 1300 people live on the entire island, and 671 of them live in its tiny western coastal village of Gambell. The only other population center on the entire island is the village of Savoonga located on its eastern coast, with a population of 643 mostly native Americans. As it were, Gambell has always served as and is still in the second decade of the twenty first century the island's primary commercial center with what amounts to a regional governor in residence.

It would be in late August of 2017 when Vladimir Putin makes a trip to the United Nations in New York City where he gives a speech to the General Assembly that proves to be quite inflammatory in his claim that not only is the eastern region of the Ukraine known to the world as the Crimea a historical part of Russia, but so are the islands off his country's western

Siberian coast, Japan and Alaska. He even goes so far as to say that there should be immediate negotiations between Russia and the United States regarding the rightful return of what he once again refers to as "disputed territory" that's been taken from the Russian Federation based on the illegality of the transaction that wrongfully put Alaska and the Aleutian Islands under American control all the way back in 1868.

While the Bush administration and his advisors don't really take Putin's claims or the less than subtle suggestions made at the United Nations all that seriously or even begin to think he might think or dare to act on them in the Alaskan region or the Bering Strait, additional surveillance aircraft are sent to the region to keep a closer eye on things, primarily high flying U2 surveillance and Boeing P-8 Poseidon marine patrol and reconnaissance aircraft as well as the jet powered RQ-4 Block 40 Global Hawk drones. At the same time the Russians were increasing their military presence over the Bering Strait and off the coast of Alaskan territory with their own remote drones as well as a stepped up series of over flights of the region by the venerable Tu-95 Bear 4 engine turboprop reconnaissance bomber. These enormous aircraft frankly haven't been seen in the skies off the coast of Alaskan territory since the collapse of the old Soviet Union and the end of the cold war in the late 1980s. Worrisome is the fact that the skies in the region are getting pretty crowded with the various surveillance and military aircraft from the two countries patrolling and keeping a close eye on each other by the fall of 2017, which not surprisingly results in a few incidents from time to time that threaten to blow up in everybody's faces. One in particular is scary when a Russian Su-35 and an American F-18E fighter get a little too close to each other while playing "chicken" off the coast of Kamchatka, and actually touch wingtips causing both to return to their respective bases with some significant damage. Harsh messages pass back and forth as a result, but thankfully both sides do agree to ask their pilots to be a bit more carefully when in close proximity to each other in the crowded skies.

In late September of 2017 President Jeb Bush makes his own appeal at the United Nations, not a speech to the General Assembly as his Russian counterpart had done earlier in the year, but to the 21 member Security Council, to whom the Russian Federation is a founding member with the power of the veto like the United States. So, as such, when President Bush offers an American sponsored resolution to the Security Council expressing the democratic desires of the Ukrainian nation and government, and that all outside parties should in fact immediately withdraw from the disputed territory, the Russian representative vetoes the effort before it even has a chance to come to a vote. This, of course, comes as no surprise to the American delegation since they both expected and knew it would happen. President Bush simply wanted it on the record with the UN Security Council that the United States officially supports the Ukraine in their dispute with the Russian Federation. What does surprise the President and the entire American UN delegation is a resolution forwarded by the Russian Federation delegate that calls for the immediate return to Russia of St. Lawrence island (a known U.S. possession and part of the state of Alaska) and the Kuril islands (an internationally recognized Japanese possessions since before World War II) located off the northern Japanese coast. Both the United States and the Japanese security council members immediately speak out against the proposed resolution before both vote against the resolution along with the majority of the council's members when it finally comes to a vote, making a veto unnecessary in this case.

And then, in a continuing tit for tat back and forth military demonstration of "international competition" not seen on the high seas in over 20 years, both the Russian and American Navies get involved in the gamesmanship. As a follow-up to the port visit made by the US Naval squadron in the Black Sea at the end of last year, the Carrier Strike Force 7 with the nuclear aircraft carrier Ronald Reagan and its compliment of F-18E fighters and support ships at its center makes a call in and just outside the harbor in Hanoi, Vietnam, a traditional Russian ally ever since the end of the Vietnam war in the mid 1970s. Not only does the US Naval squadron make the call (the Ronald Reagan itself even entered Hanoi harbor itself) to Hanoi, but while doing so it's announced in Washington D.C. that new extensive trade agreements are being negotiated between the two countries. And, of course, these actions further anger Putin and his government in Moscow.

At the end of the summer the Russian response to the in your face Naval visit to Hanoi is a visit to Havana's harbor in Cuba by a Russian Naval squadron that includes the steam turbine powered assault carrier Admiral Kuznetsov with its inventory of Su-33 multi-role fighters and Kamov Ka-27 anti-submarine helicopters. This particular demonstration, in fact, is significant because never even during the darkest days of the cold war have the Russians dared bring such a public display of naval air power to the traditional American waters of the Caribbean Sea. Like the Black Sea, the Caribbean is officially considered international waters where all can navigate freely, but traditionally they've been recognized by most as waters exclusive to the United States Navy for strategic purposes for over 100 years since the end of the Spanish American War in 1899. At the same time both Moscow and Havana announce that they too are conducting important trade and security talks of "mutual interest." While Washington is in fact bothered and concerned by the public display of Russian naval power in our "own waters" we won't become truly concerned about the talks between the Castro and Putin regimes until their nature become clearer sometime later in the year. There's reason for the current American lack of concern given the recent thaw in relations between Havana and Washington which has quickly led to much interchange of goods and people between the two countries in the past few years and there's even been preliminary talks of an eventual security agreement between the two longtime adversaries, so nobody in Washington or in the Bush administration really think that Raul Castro would put all that's been accomplished in recent years between the two countries at risk by being too cozy to the Russians.

There's even more concern, however, when Russian nuclear attack surveillance submarines are discovered to be positioned off the coast of Washington state just outside the Puget Sound to the northwest and not far off the coast of Groton, Connecticut to the east. In each case it's an Akula Typhoon class attack submarine found to be cruising not more than 2000 feet under the surface just off the coast not far from two of America's most important naval installations, and both are home ports to our Trident and Seawolf submarine fleets. The defense departments response is quick and immediate as a Seawolf attack submarine is launched to shadow and keep tabs on both of the unwelcomed Russian intruders, and in both cases Naval Boeing P-8 Poseidon maritime search planes armed with torpedoes are put in the air to harass the Russian submarines with sonar buoys and other detection devices dropped in the water to chase them off. Closer to shore both harbors and harbor entrances are patrolled day and night by Navy MH-60S Seahawk helicopters around the clock to discourage any potential breach of perimeter security, and a decision is made that if any more Russian incursions happen both harbor entrances will be mined as a further defense measure for our strategically critical submarine fleets.

Things really begin to heat up even more when off the coast of Connecticut an American Seawolf and Russian Akula attack submarine collide as they are "playing a dangerous game of tag" under water and are both forced to surface. The Seawolf has a control wing fin that has been almost entirely ripped off while the Russian sub has severe damage to its sail. The commanders of each of the subs can be seen by their crews shaking their fists at each other as they peer over the sides of their damaged boats. Both ships will be forced to limp home for immediate repairs, but the incident does cause the two naval adversaries in Moscow and Washington to take some pause and quietly agree behind the scenes to back off just a little in their increasingly dangerous tit for tat activities under the world's ocean waters. The Americans suggest through their representatives in London that they withdraw their Los Angeles and Seawolf class subs

126

away from the coast of Murmansk while the Russians agree in response to do the same off the coasts of Connecticut and Washington in the United States. The Russians still aren't aware that the United States does in fact have an ultra quiet specially equipped Seawolf armed with a full complement of water to shore and cruise missiles that they've snuck into the Black Sea that is at that very moment sitting on the bottom listening and waiting just in case.

In general, tensions continue to remain high between the American and Russian governments throughout the latter part of the year in 2017, as they struggle to find common ground on any issue military or economic for the most part, as they both continue to engage in a series of act and response reactions that are serving to increase those same tensions as the months continue to go by. While there are a few cases where agreements are crafted, such as the one following the air collision in the north Pacific and the submarine incident off the US eastern coast, there remains a troubling amount of teeth bared standing off against each other by each country's naval and air forces, especially in the north Pacific and Bering Strait. In an attempt to alleviate tensions and get the two sides talking, Germany's Chancellor Angela Merkel offers to step in as a third party facilitator where invited, and even offers her own offices in Berlin as a location for negotiations. To her frustration, neither side in the growing dispute between Russia and the United States seems in the least interested in her offer or proposals.

Also behind the scenes and far away from public view at Whitehall in London, there are infrequent but ongoing negotiations between representatives of the State Department in Washington and the Foreign Ministry in Moscow, where tacit "off the record" discussions are being held between those with clearer heads in hopes to insure that the current crisis between their two countries doesn't somehow spill over into a more serious military incident or even a nuclear exchange. Both sides do in fact manage to agree in principle that far too much is at stake and way too much work had been done by previous administrations in their two countries to risk allowing their current differences, regardless how severe they may appear to be, to reach a level of atomic war. Unfortunately, these off the record discussions fail to come to any sort of functional agreement outside of the simple mutually stated desire to prevent the unspeakable from happening, something that in itself is an accomplishment in fact during the increasingly tense situation.

What the United States naval and air intelligence apparatus is only vaguely aware of and completely ignore in terms of its obvious significance for reasons that are entirely inexplicable given the current circumstances, the Russian Federation Moskva class amphibious assault and helicopter carrier Leningrad with no other ships in attendance quietly slips off its dock to leave the port of Petropavlovsk Kamchatskiy in the dead of the night to head south east on an undisclosed secret mission.

14

A Shocking Assault From the Sea

Even though hardly a single American or their President take a bit seriously the repeated claims or threats made by Vladimir Putin towards the end of 2016 and all through 2017 concerning the Bering Strait, and St. Lawrence island in particular, military planners in Moscow do take their outspoken President quite seriously and have in fact been asked by the Kremlin to create an immediate plan for a surprise assault on the American territory just in case for when the choice is made to do so. And, contrary to what some in the West might think, the Russian armed forces, especially its military planners and elite units, are still a significant force to reckon with in 2017, especially since President Putin has spent much of the last 5 years bolstering their capabilities once again following years of neglect after the fall of the old Soviet Union. In addition, the Russians have traditionally been and continue to be some of the best at thinking outside the box when it comes to tactical military strategy, and no one who is familiar with their thought process should have been surprised at the development of a daring plan to invade and take over a neighboring territory once the decision has been made to do so. But for some reason, those in the furthest reaches of the U.S. Pentagon or American intelligence services who have actually been tasked with watching the Russian forces closely and knowing them intimately for over 60 years ever since the opening days of the Cold War all the way back in the late 1940s will be quite surprised on this day at least.

Highly skilled and trained Russian Speznet special forces troops will be used as the main force for the proposed sneak attack on St. Lawrence island, and the strategy will be a simple one with the Moskva Class Helicopter Assault Carrier Leningrad serving as the base of operations with its specially designed 16 stealthy radar evading Mi-8MTV-2 high performance transport helicopter gunships that can fly at near 250 miles per hour with a range of well over 500 miles with their specially made auxiliary fuel tanks and can fly at an altitude as high as almost 20,000 feet. For this attack they will be asked to fly at an altitude of no more than 100 feet, but will be asked to fly at the very maximum of their 250 mile an hour capability. The Russian sneak attack plan calls for the Leningrad to sail from its base at Petropavlovsk Kamchatskiy (located on the southern end of the Kamchatkan peninsula) during the night to a remote southern location not more than 200 or so miles off the Gambell coast of St. Lawrence island where it will launch its assault helicopters with their complement of more than 300 Speznet troops. Each Mi-8MTV-2 can carry 24 troops, so the first assault will include 4 helicopters with their 96 assault troops who will sweep in and secure the town of Gambell while the citizens sleep during the night. And then, to gain further control over the island before the Americans can respond, an additional 400 troops will be transported to the island from the Leningrad using the same Mi-8 helicopters in addition to 12 others as they fly back and forth to deliver their precious cargo of men and supplies. It will be a middle of the night set of landings, and according to the Russian plan, the entire island should be secure and fully under their control no later than 0600 hours in the morning by the time the islanders wake up.

At exactly 2300 hours (11:00pm Gambell time) the 4 Mi-8MTV-2 helicopters lift off from the deck of the Leningrad for their fast 200 mile flight over the black ocean waters to Gambell. The night is clear with only a little cloud cover here and there (the Russian planners had actually hoped for more of a cloudy sky but had also feared the possibility of an ocean so stormy and choppy they wouldn't be able to launch their helicopters) so the choppers are able fly at a low 50 to 100 feet above the ocean's waves to avoid detection by American radar located at far off Nome and Anchorage. It appears from the lack of activity in the surrounding seas and skies that the Russian special forces strike force has in fact accomplished their mission of surprise as not a single warning message leaves the island as they approach. The 4 helicopters will be careful not to use their terrain mapping radar during the flight to avoid any chance of detection by the same American radars to the east. There are no such radar detection facilities for the Russian attackers to worry about on St. Lawrence island itself. In fact, there will be no need to worry about any military resistance at all on the island according to their most up to date intelligence.

At 2356 hours the Russian assault helicopters with their compliment of heavily armed Speznet special forces troops (each soldier is armed with a grenade capable AK-74 short barrel assault rifle and plenty of ammunition) land just outside of town and using their sound suppressed low velocity ammunition the troops quickly dispatch the few dogs who dare bark in the night as they quickly secure the town while the majority of its citizens continue to sleep completely unaware that they are being invaded. Interestingly enough, the dogs will end up being the only casualties this night, and more interesting is the fact that the Russian government will end up compensating their owners for their losses. The assault troops are in fact discovered by 3 citizens who are out in the night, but to the relief of the Russian commander general, they were able to immobilize and silence each of them without the need of a single shot or unnecessary violence. Not at all a classic example of traditional blood thirsty Speznet leadership, the Russian general in charge of the operation has warned his troops that any unnecessary violence or death perpetrated against the unarmed citizens on the island will lead to quick and severe punishment.

Elizabeth Quviariatukuluk, like all of her Gambell neighbors, will wake up the next morning to discover that they are now supposedly part of the Russian Federation instead of being

131

Americans as they were just the day before. Not only is it proclaimed that they are now part of Russia, but the Russian commander claims that there is nothing for them to fear and that there will be no reprisals or unnecessary violence perpetrated by his troops so long as the citizens cooperate as needed and required. He insists that nothing will change in their lives and that his forces will mostly retire to a base installation they will build in the coming weeks to be and stay out of their way. The commander also insists that there will be no reason for the citizens to be concerned or rebel against their presence, and that in fact he hopes they can become friends over time. He strongly encourages the citizens in both Savoonga and Gambell to come to him with any concern or complaint regardless how small, and promises to act on them accordingly when they do. The general did announce that some additional defense measures will be taken by his forces to prevent any American interference, and over the next several days the citizens watch as a very serious looking mobile anti-aircraft tank is brought onto the island along with a most capable looking anti-aircraft missile battery. And, in the coming weeks, the only real sign of the Russian presence are the occasional moving around of the 2 Mi-8 choppers assigned to the island.

Over the next six weeks, ever since the Russian Speznet special forces suddenly appeared in their Mi-8 assault helicopters and literally took over the small town without a fight on that shocking evening while they slept, the sudden Russian occupation of American soil has frankly not been so nearly difficult as one might have predicted with barely any violence at all taking place. Not even one person was injured or died that night or in the weeks afterwards, with the only incident of reported abuse by the Russian occupation soldiers taking place against a native woman, or any citizen for that matter. And this reported incident resulted immediately as described below with the Speznet perpetrator being executed by firing squad on the spot following a quick and public military tribunal conducted in front of the citizens as promised by the Russian general.

The reported incident was a simple one, but was at the same time a clear test of the Russian general's promise. Sitting at his desk doing the all to be expected paperwork always demanded by his superiors general Arkady Islonovich Kamanisky looks up to see one of his Lieutenants walk in with a girl who could be no more than 13 or 14 years old who has a tear stained face and a dress that's been clearly torn. When asked by the general what this was about, the Lieutenant informs him that this young woman claims that she has been raped and she and the villagers are insisting it was by one of his soldiers who snuck into her room last night and forced her to have non-consensual sex with him repeatedly through the night. The general could clearly see when he looked closer at the whimpering girl that she had dried blood on her upper legs and some light bruises around her face, so he immediately ordered a lockdown of the entire Russian base and a check of each soldier to find the culprit. It didn't take long during a careful search to find bloody underwear hidden under the bed of a Major Sergeant Rishikoff who finally admitted to the crime during his interrogation following a bit of hands on encouragement from the general's personal security force. Once the dragged out admission was received and the native girl herself tearfully verified that it had in fact been Sergeant Rishikoff who entered her bedroom and raped her repeatedly the general ordered an immediate gathering of the town's citizens in the town square. With the prisoner in handcuffs and 3 very serious looking Russian soldiers armed with their AK-74 assault rifles standing behind the general he loudly read the charges against the Russian soldier, announced that he's been found guilty by a fair and impartial investigation, and that the penalty for his transgression against the citizenry of St. Lawrence island and the native teenage girl would be death by firing squad. And, as the gathered citizens watched in shocked but curious silence, Sergeant Rishikoff was tied to a lamp post at the edge of the town square, his badges of unit and rank are ceremoniously ripped from his uniform, a blindfold is put over his eyes, and he's immediately shot dead by a volley of shots fired from the 3 man firing squad standing only 10 meters away. With that general Arkady Islonovich Kamanisky simply states that it should be a lesson to any Russian soldier who doubts the seriousness of his nonviolent policy, then turns and leaves the square with a set and very troubled look on his face as the dead body of the Russian special forces soldier is untied and taken away. The general has reason for concern since his army has a long history of abusing and raping women under its jurisdiction in occupied territories and he worries that it could easily get out of his control if strict discipline isn't maintained. To further make his point to the rest of his soldiers in his unit general Kamanisky holds a stand at attention meeting of his entire force where he demotes the Lieutenant in Rishikoff's unit to Corporal and announces that any further actions of the sort will result in the same death sentence and demotions. As stated earlier, there would be no further problems of the sort while the Russian soldiers were in residence on the island. As for the native girl who was raped that night, she would give birth to a bustling baby boy nine months later who would be heartedly welcomed into her family and by the Gambell community as a whole without one bit of stigma concerning how or who by he was conceived.

The interesting part of the Russian occupation of St. Lawrence island is the reaction, or more to the point the lack of it, of the native American population as a whole, and there are a few things to consider in analyzing it. First of all it's not as if they aren't loyal Americans, but not in over a 150 years of being officially American citizens of the United States have the people of St. Lawrence island really felt like they were a close part of their supposed brethren in the "lower 48" or even the state of Alaska for that matter. They were expected and required to pay their taxes, but tax collectors rarely showed up if an islander was remiss in doing so. More than a few commercial fishermen on the island have in fact never paid taxes, nor ever have they been investigated by any individual or individuals from the IRS for the remiss or refusal. In addition, over those same years not more than a few dozen young men from St. Lawrence island have ever been called to serve in the United States military, mostly in

World War II and only 3 in Vietnam. And frankly, during that same 100 or so years the United States government has done little of significance to welcome the island to their family or offer any real assistance in growing the local economy, not that any on the island actually resented any of the above missives by any means. The fact is that even though St. Lawrence island has long been considered part of Alaska and the United States, it's realistically such a remote and isolated outpost as to be either commercially or strategically irrelevant. Another important factor in the relative lack of concern or complaint for the forced change in governmental allegiance of their island is the very nature of the islanders themselves, who have for hundreds of generations lived a truly independent life away from the normal daily hustle and bustle of outside world activities that would require an understanding of or strong loyalty to a governing authority. The native islanders of St. Lawrence island have literally lived on their own by way of their own devices for so long that who governs them or flies their flag above the lighthouse is essentially irrelevant to them for the most part, so when the Russians show up and announce that nothing of impact will change in their everyday lives with their arrival, they naturally take the truth of what they are told for granted and simply shrug their shoulders and go on with their lives as they have for thousands of years. The fact that the new Russian military governor, as he soon calls himself, acts as promised and has a ship full of Russian beer and vodka, fine caviar and smoked fish, and succulent garden potatoes and beets for a huge celebration to be held all across the island sure doesn't hurt his cause at all. And, when another ship shows up loaded with new coats, scarves, hats, fishing and hunting equipment, and huge supplies of clothes making materials, his status as a new friend instead of an occupying enemy is pretty much sealed with the local population for the most part, especially since not a word is being heard from Washington. In another move that would help ingratiate the commander and his soldiers to the local population he quickly made known that many of his soldiers have skills in home and vehicle repair, and that any citizen need only apply to have services rendered, including even free materials supplied by the Russian government. And to the surprise of some, in the coming weeks Russian soldiers could be seen working side by side with Gambell residents on homes or cars while using materials delivered by ship from Vladivostok at the behest of General Kamanisky himself.

In more ways than not General Arkady Islonovich Kamanisky of the Russian Speznet is a classic Russian. He's a loud and outspoken man of 56 years who has the stocky build of a soldier who has seen nothing but a desk for his battlefield for quite some time, meaning that his jowls are fleshy and his belly hangs over his overextended belt just a little too much. Kamanisky is a jovial man unless unnecessarily provoked, which the executed rapist discovered with a quick and efficient death, who makes every effort while on the island to gain allies and make friends instead of enemies. He speaks English well and is truly open and friendly as he makes almost daily visits to the streets of Gambell, and even spends time for a shot of vodka or two with the "boys" down at the bar on many afternoons. You see, even though a classic Russian in so many ways, the elite Speznet forces General is a man who has closely studied military history who knows that the best way to prevent or avoid a rebellion from any citizenry is not to use force or intimidation as is so often the case but to make every effort instead to win their hearts and minds to his cause.

And, most important as the general claimed from the very beginning of their arrival, except for some appreciated home and car repairs things really don't change all that much for the people of St. Lawrence island except for Emma Vonderlinden, a chunky 48 year old woman who has been widowed twice by the time the Russians show up on the island in 2018. Emma, like most on the island, is a combination of native Indian and Russian heritage and her fleshy big boned body and friendly easy going nature reflect the fact. Emma not only is a friendly and well liked member of the Gambell community, she's a neighbor who receives much compassion for her sad loneliness at the loss of not one but two husbands to an early death. And more than a few men around the area have made an effort to help "alleviate" her sadness in a most mutually agreeable manner from time to time. As such, Emma comes to the quick attention of the Russian commander at one of the first social gatherings of the town folks with their recently arrived occupiers, who immediately sees a woman who fits his outlook for a potential mistress perfectly. General Kamanisky has in fact been happily married to the same woman for over 25 years, who has also had what he refers to as "affairs of the heart" in virtually every place he's been stationed in since. By his own admission the general not only loves his wife, but he loves all women of beauty, and in Emma Vonderlinden he definitely sees a woman of beauty.

"Let me make a toast to beautiful women everywhere," shouts the Russian general who is already on his sixth shot of vodka and who has been informed that the handsome and stocky large breasted woman in the crowd is quite possibly interested in him.

"Hail to beautiful women," shouts the crowd back in response to the Russian general's toast.

As things are settling down in the room for the moment and the general is getting his shot glass refilled with more Russian vodka, a man comes up to him with his sister (Emma) in tow and introduces her to him as the person he had told him earlier wanted to make his acquaintance.

There's no way to miss, nor does he try to hide, the appraising look that general Arkady Islonovich Kamanisky gives his new friend's sister who is now standing before him totally silent with a seemingly shy demeanor. And of course, the low cut scoop necked blouse Emma has put on especially for this occasion in hopes that she can get the Russian general's attention draws the man's eyes to the huge fleshy mounds of her enormous bosoms and the deep crevasse like cleavage they create which are fully exposed with the rise and fall of her breathing. It's almost as if the man would reach out and put a hand on her, which in fact the general is wishing he could do, as he continues to stare while he licks his lips in obvious rapture at the image he sees standing before him.

Emma would sleep with the general that very night, and would continue to do so with great relish for as long as he stayed on the island, even though she knew he was married at home by his own admission and that she had no other hope than to be his mistress. The two of them actually became a couple and most in town were pleased to see Emma so happy once again, even if for only a while since like most military men the general could expect to be reassigned to another mission much sooner than later. She would always say afterwards that the general was a great and gentle lover who cherished her, and she would in fact sleep with him again when he visited the island years later, even though his wife had been with him.

General Arkady Islonovich Kamanisky's wife of 25 years was herself a woman of thick stature who could clearly at her choosing satisfy a man in the bedroom. Christiana Rovanovich was in fact a regal looking and acting woman with her own undeniably handsome looks even at her age of near five decades. She claimed with honest reason a connection to Russian royalty and even a remote tie to the Romanov family who had ruled the Russian Empire for more than a century before being brutally killed by the Bolsheviks during the Civil War after the Russian Revolution of 1917. The truth is had she known about her husband's affair with Emma Vonderlinden, she would have simply scoffed that it's only to be expected, and of course she would have had little complaint given her own recent activities with the family gardener in Vladivostok. In fact, when the Kamanisky's did visit the island in later years Mrs. Kamanisky would respond when introduced formally to Emma that her husband has always had good taste in women in a merry voice that all could hear.

But, of course, even amongst the apparent silence outside of their public complaints there's no way the United States will ever put up with the takeover and occupation of any of its territory, even if that territory is in fact a small, remote, and mostly ignored couple of frontier towns on some island that many folks across the country don't know even exists. Nor does it matter at all that the United States has mostly paid little attention to the island and its people for most of the 150 some years it's been under its jurisdiction. It also becomes immediately clear and is in fact assumed that it will more than likely take a huge and destructive fire fight to take the island back since the Russkies have in fact set up what is appearing will soon be a strong defensive perimeter around the outskirts of town (as they have also in the island's other village of Savoonga) and in the town square itself, in addition to the military outpost they are building not far away, and the assumption is that they will continue to build up their defenses even more in the coming months.

And regardless how unconcerned most of the islanders appeared, there were of course, some who were more than willing to help on the island itself who would make it a little easier for the Americans to eventually take it back from the Russians regardless how kindly or friendly they acted. It's true that for the most part the vast majority of St. Lawrence islanders simply shrugged their shoulders and went on with their business as usual after the Russian soldiers arrived, much like they had over 200 years ago when the first Russians showed up on their shores in 1792 and they had once again when the Americans took over not a century later. But, there were a small and understandably quiet minority of folks, made up mostly of the few men on the island who had once served in the United States military who weren't so enamored with the Russians or willing to live under their jurisdiction. Their numbers were few, far less than 2 dozen actually, and they knew they had to stay quiet and under the radar so not to cause themselves or others any undue harm while the occupation was in place. Only a few suggested they undertake some guerrilla actions to inhibit the Russian soldier's ability to function, but the majority insisted that doing so would only undermine the apparent benevolence of the Russian general and most likely lead to a more difficult existence on the island and even likely some injury or death. But, what they could all agree to do is keep a close eye on what the Russians were doing on the island and use a most interesting method to communicate the gathered information to mainland sources to be furthered to American government agencies. They would meet on a weekly basis at a secret location where they would discuss and list what they saw or witnessed, then use a archaic teletype machine to send the information to Nome by Morse code in a manner not easily detected by the Russian occupiers. Ironically, in a modern day and age of ultra sophisticated communications methods, strangely forgotten is the realization that such archaic but virtually undetectable methods can be used against them. The biggest problem had been in fact finding a receiver of their communications on the other end, but they finally did when a Morse code hobbyist in Anchorage answered one day and put them in touch with the proper authorities. In this way the members of the "underground" as they called themselves could feel that they were doing something to overturn the Russians at some future date without unnecessarily risking themselves or their fellow villagers. The men and 2 women spent their time monitoring and watching the Russian soldiers come and go, listing the various types of equipment they saw brought to the island, the progress on the military installation being built, while making daily attempts to identify and write down the Russian aircraft seen over the skies of the island with their binoculars that they were careful to use only when nobody was watching. What they collected was then sent by Morse code to their contact in Nome. While the information itself wasn't entirely that useful or even very helpful to the eventual recapture of the island, even though it did verify what the drone pictures were telling them, just knowing that there were those on the island who wanted to resist the invaders was a much appreciated positive indication for the planners in Washington. Most on the island, in fact, would be surprised later following the Russian departure to learn that there had been an active resistance movement right in their midst. What's interesting about the short history of the St. Lawrence Underground is that the Russians did in fact quickly discover and know who they were and what they were doing almost from the beginning, but mostly due to the Russian commander's insistence and the mostly benign and insignificant nature of their activities they simply watched the men and women without interfering so long as they didn't commit violence or inhibit their own activities in any negative manner. This was all so as a matter of fact since the strategy from the very beginning as determined by no other than President Putin himself for the Russian invasion and occupation was to both be benevolent occupiers and freely give up the island eventually when the Americans finally decide to take it back.

(15)

A Six Month Negotiation

Just like the estimated 1296 unsuspecting citizens of St. Lawrence island President Bush discovers to his great surprise during the middle of what was to be a typical work day in the life of a modern American President on April 2, 2018 that a piece of U.S. territory has been ripped from our control in spite of our belief it could never happen, and in spite of the clear warnings that had proceeded the unprovoked invasion. In his case President Bush finds out during a whispered conversation from a member of his security team who rushes into the room while he and his advisors are in the middle of a cabinet meeting at 1:00pm in the afternoon Washington D.C. time (6:00am Gambell time) following the overnight Russian assault. The cabinet meeting is immediately suspended as the President quickly calls his national security staff to an emergency meeting in the secure White House west wing basement situation room.

It's 5:10pm eastern standard time in Washington D.C. and New York City, when all 4 television networks break into their normally scheduled evening newscasts for what they describe as an unscheduled announcement coming straight from President Bush's Oval Office, pointing out to their viewers that even they don't know as yet what the subject is or what the President plans to say to the American public.

"Fellow Americans, it's with great concern and sadness that I must inform you that Russian forces, without provocation or warning, have invaded and occupied American and Alaskan territory on St. Lawrence island, a place located at the southern mouth of the Bering Strait, during the past 24 hours. According to the information we have to date, the Russian forces arrived on the island by assault helicopter late last night and quickly took control with little or no violence. I must tell you that the Russian commander involved and in charge has been in communication with us and has insisted and promised that our former citizens will be treated with respect and kindness, and that there were fortunately no casualties involved with the exception of 2 dogs during the attack. We can only hope that this actually is and will continue to be the case. Folks (and with this statement the President leans forward towards the camera with a set and very determined look in his eyes) I have to tell you that this happened because your government and this administration failed to take President Putin's threats made last and this year seriously, and as a result we've gotten caught with our pants down. That's my mistake, I admit it, and I take full ownership of it. But, let me say this both to you, my fellow Americans, and especially to our Russian friends in Moscow; we will not take this action lying down. Let me repeat that, the United States will not sit back and accept the illegal invasion and occupation of our territory no matter the claimed excuse or reason. We demand that the Russian forces immediately withdraw and will be making a formal request to the UN Security Council and General Assembly to pass a resolution to that effect in the coming days. Trust me when I say that your government will react appropriately to this illegal assault and occupation of American territory and citizens, and we can only hope that Mr. Putin and his people understand this simple fact and react accordingly before we are forced to take further action. I also ask that you all keep the fine people of St. Lawrence island in your prayers. Good night, and we will keep you all abreast of the situation in the coming days and weeks."

That same evening, Jeb Bush puts in a call to Vladimir Putin to speak to him directly about the situation and our concerns, but to his dismay the call goes unanswered when his staff claims the Russian President is unavailable.

Thirteen hours later a RQ-4 Global Hawk reconnaissance drone launched from Elmendorf Airbase in Anchorage, Alaska, overflies St. Lawrence island to take pictures that show a newly positioned missile battery and anti-aircraft weapon, and the beginnings of construction on a probable Russian military installation of some sort. The drone also notes much Russian air and sea activity surrounding the island, although they do nothing to interrupt or stop the drone's presence. Daily drone and U2 flights over the island and region will both start and in fact will continue for as long as the crisis continues, as do the continued presence of the Russian air force and navy in the region. The biggest fear of the American administration and military planners is that the Russians will move quickly to militarize the island with more capable anti-aircraft missiles, fighter and bomber aircraft, and additional troops that will make the island that much more difficult to take back. From the sketchy reports being received from Gambell and Savoonga, it appears that approximately 400 to 500 Russian special forces troops are currently on the island. While keeping a close eye on the Russian military installations on the Kamchatka peninsula and at Vladivostok, a warning is sent to Moscow about the dire consequences that will result if they do in fact further militarize the island over the coming days and weeks. The biggest concern to those who continue to watch Russian military activities on St. Lawrence island is that offensive capabilities will be brought to the island, such as an airstrip to handle modern fighters and bombers or medium and long range missile silos. And, not unexpectedly, there is nothing but silence from Moscow and the Kremlin.

Three days after the announced invasion and occupation, the German Christian Democratic Chancellor Angela Merkel once again offers to mediate the growing crisis, and again suggests an emergency private conference among the interested parties for deliberations to be held in Berlin at a future date in a concerted effort to find a peaceful solution. British Prime Minister, David Cameron, also offers his assistance to co-sponsor such a meeting in support of Ms. Merkel to relieve the crisis, as does French

President François Hallande. It comes as no surprise to any that not a word about the crisis is heard from the Chinese government in Beijing. More disturbing is the short and very to the point announcement that comes as a response from Moscow that from their point of view there's nothing to either discuss or negotiate and nothing that can be settled or accomplished by a conference in Berlin, so they "respectfully" decline the German offer at this time. In response the Bush administration in Washington D.C. makes a terse one sentence statement saying that while they appreciate Ms. Merkel and Mr. Cameron's attempts to mediate and might be willing to attend such a conference at some future time, that since the Russians have declined to do so, they respectfully will as well for the time being.

In the weeks following the occupation by the Russian special forces troops there's a huge increase in over flights and outright incursions by Russian military aircraft in the skies around Alaska and even the northwest coast of the continental United States itself. These flights include Mikoyan and Sukhoi fighter bomber aircraft, Tu-95 Bear reconnaissance and Tu-160 Blackjack bombers, and Ilyushin May surveillance aircraft. The United States Airforce and Navy respond in kind as once again both air and sea reconnaissance and surveillance assets are quickly returned to the north Pacific and north seas. Additional Global Hawk and Predator drones are sent to Alaska, as are another high altitude U-2 spy plane. In addition the F-22 fighter force at Elmendorf Air Base just outside of Anchorage is beefed up with a squadron of F-16C Block 40 fighters, a squadron of F-15C fighters, and a brand new F-35A stealth fighter squadron. And, without fanfare, 4 B-1B Lancer bombers are moved to the Anchorage base to be in a forward position just in case, and both the B-52 squadrons in Louisiana and the B-2 Spirit squadron in Missouri are put on an round the clock alert status.

A conference which does in fact include the Americans who finally agree to participate is in fact held without the Russians in Berlin 4 weeks after the assault and the resulting veto by the

Russians of the American sponsored resolution condemning it at the UN security council.   But unfortunately the Berlin conference immediately breaks down into a meaningless series of complaints by the Americans who demand that all present not only take their side in the dispute but demand that any signatories insist on an immediate Russian retreat from the island. In frustration after only 2 short days, those attending the conference go their separate ways with no stated or written agreement to the pleased satisfaction of the non-attending Kremlin and displeasure of the American delegation. Chancellor Merkel and Prime Minister Cameron are left to announce they will continue to work on getting the two sides together as soon as possible since it's their greatest hope that the current situation won't lead to an outright shooting war between the United States and Russia which would be devastating to the rest of the world.

Six weeks after the invasion and occupation of St. Lawrence island by the Russian Speznet forces, the President of the United States once again takes to the air for an important announcement to the American people and the rest of the world.

"Good evening fellow Americans. And good evening as well to you who are listening outside of the United States. I want to take this time to update you all on the situation in the Bering Strait and on St. Lawrence island. Here's where we currently stand. Six weeks ago Russian special forces landed without invitation or cause to occupy what is American territory and part of the state of Alaska. Since that time a formal resolution has been offered by the United States at the United Nations to both condemn and reject the invasion and occupation which was immediately vetoed without explanation by the Russian UN Ambassador in the Security Council. Direct warnings have been sent by this office to the Russian President making clear that we don't accept the status quo on St. Lawrence island and that there will be dire consequences if they fail to withdraw their occupying forces. And, as you know, German Chancellor Merkel,

British Prime Minister Cameron, and French President Hallande all made a concerted effort to mediate the crisis to no avail in Berlin a few weeks ago where the Russian government even refused to attend or explain themselves. And let me say this before going forward, it is with heartened relief that I can tell you that the Russian occupying forces appear to be conducting themselves according to all existing modern agreements and it also appears that the citizens of St. Lawrence island are being treated with respect and professionalism. I salute the Russian commander on the scene for his actions and I also salute the Russian government for allowing it to happen.   That said, I stated the day after the unprovoked invasion and occupation of American territory that your government and this President wouldn't stand for what the Russians have illegally perpetrated, and we won't do so. So, tonight I announce to you an official ultimatum to President Putin that if Russian forces are not removed from St. Lawrence island and the people freed and returned to the jurisdiction of the United States that we will take the appropriate actions to make it so. A formal signed letter to this stated fact is being at this time hand delivered to Mr. Putin's office at the Kremlin in Moscow."

And once again, President Jeb Bush leans forward and looks directly into the TV camera with wide unblinking eyes as he adds the following:

"The United States of America did not initiate this crisis, but if our Russian friends refuse to withdraw from American territory as requested by this office we will finish it. I thank you for listening and God bless America, God bless the American people, and God bless the fine people of St. Lawrence island. Goodnight."

The very next day a copy of the announcement speech along with a copy of the letter delivered to Moscow was provided to all of the networks that included the details and a specific deadline date for the ultimatum which was given as October 1, 2018. The ultimatum simply states that the invasion as well as the following occupation of the island by Russian forces was both unprovoked and illegal, and that all Russian forces and influences must leave the island and the surrounding skies and 12 mile territorial waters by the date indicated. The ultimatum states clearly if this doesn't happen, the United States will take whatever actions might be necessary and appropriate, including the use of military force to take back the island.

16

Cyber Warfare Goes Wet

It all starts with a not entirely unexpected but still surprising and disabling Russian sneak hack attack on the most secure NSA (National Security Agency) mainframe computer systems. It's been long known that the first opening gambit in any truly modern 21st century war would more than likely be an organized concerted and highly secret attack on the computer based digital infrastructure of a nation's adversary, and that will certainly be the case between the United States and the Russian Federation in 2018 when suddenly the lights blink and go completely off on virtually all of the computer screens in the huge Fort George G. Meade complex in rural Maryland. The same problem is taking place also at the CIAs Langley headquarters in McLean, Virginia. For years (decades in fact) it's been known throughout the American security community that hack attacks on CIA (Central Intelligence Agency) and NSA capabilities are a key and essential part of the Russian operational plan in the event of a potential shooting war between their country and the United States, so its arrival does in fact come as no real surprise at all, and as such the NSA is fully prepared to respond accordingly as well and as fast as they can.

The hidden sneak attack is really a comparatively simple but highly effective one designed only to send a clear message, interrupt, and disable a few essential capabilities during the outset of any fighting between the two countries. The problem lies in the fact that any digital attack within the ultra sensitive multi layered firewalls of the widespread NSA computer network must be by its very nature a complicated and sophisticated one, which means that any considered response must also be a complicated and sophisticated defense. The first problem is that while it's surely known that the source of the hack comes from and at the direction of Moscow and their highly capable SVR digital intelligence division, the attack itself is routed through a complicated multi layered maze of international transfers, relays, and hidden trapdoors circling the globe that the NSA responders must first identify and unfold before they can even begin to deal with them. And, only after completing this highly detailed and time consuming task can the defenders even begin their difficult task to search for the deeply hidden code within literally 100s of millions of lines of code that make up their network to find the introduced trojan malware that's causing the myriad of frustrating power interruptions and chaotic error messages blinking on and off on just about every one of the thousands of computer screens in the building. It actually only takes a short few minutes for the NSA searchers to investigate and correctly identify the hidden transfers, relays, and trapdoors that lead them directly to the SVA (Sluzhba Vneshney Razvedka) or Russian Foreign Intelligence Service computer center in a 4 story windowless concrete block building smack in the middle of Moscow. However, a few minutes in the modern information rich microsecond world of digital computers might as well be hours or days, even weeks, in comparison to a now forgotten past just a short few decades ago. And as such, it only takes an additional 5 minutes or so for the arrayed Cray super computers at Fort Meade to search out and identify the corrupting code within the NSA programming which is causing the problem so they can block or remove it, which of course they immediately do as the Russian hackers have expected they would do. But, in the not more than several moments that it takes the NSA defenders to identify and correct the problem with their computers all of the lights go out and the information feeds disappear on the vast network of signaling devices our entire intelligence network relies on to keep an eye on things, so what happens is that the 16 ship Russian assault helicopter force can deliver its cargo to St. Lawrence island while all of the American observers and analysts are effectively blind and have their attention engaged elsewhere (mostly the Ukraine and along the Eastern European border), which is the exact reason for the SVR hack attack in the first place.

Our own response is a simple, immediate, and sneaky one, which is triggered automatically by the Russian hack as we not only seek to remove the offending malware in our system but conduct our own responding hidden entry into the Russian Federation SVA (Sluzhba Vneshney Razvedka) computer network in a manner that surreptitiously inserts our own almost impossible to find deeply hidden malware "trojan horse" into the Russian network that simply will sit benignly in place ready for an electronic signal that will activate a series of our own hidden trapdoors who in independent concert will take over the host system in a very specific manner when the proper time comes.

And, that time will come in approximately 6 months when a signal flashes out of Fort Meade that tells the deeply hidden malware in the Russian network to activate and come alive which will then quickly interrupt the signals from specific Russian satellites in orbit that normally allow them to see what's taking place in the Bering Strait and seamlessly replaces those same signals with what we want them and they expect to see. We will want them to see a north Pacific ocean whose southern entrance to the Bering Strait is free of non-Russian naval vessels, specifically a specially equipped American carrier battle group that will be tasked with heading in that direction. And, we'll also want the pictures downloading from the satellites above to show that there is no atypical out of normal activities taking place either at Elmendorf Airbase outside the city of Anchorage, Alaska or at the airfield located outside of Nome to the northwest on the far western coast of Alaska. We certainly won't want them to see the unscheduled arrival of the C5 Galaxy and C17 Globemaster III cargo transport planes bringing their massive loads of equipment and supplies to the region, or the 2 squadrons of F-35 Lightning stealth fighter bombers (1 squadron of F-35As and 1 squadron of Marine F-35Bs) arriving at Elmendorf. Most important of all, we won't want them to see the specially designed V-22J Osprey tilt rotor troop transport aircraft being flown into Nome and hidden in hangers in readiness for a specific purpose.

And as always is the case where the Russians are concerned, both the CIA and NSA has to concern themselves with the undisputed potential of the likely wet operations they will undoubtedly conduct against our country at some point during the conflict, since without question the Russians are still the very best at doing so, in spite of what Chinese intelligence might wish to think. In days past the task of being on top of and fighting the "black ops wet operations" conducted by Russian or Soviet intelligence had been the job of a super secret off the books joint NSA and CIA taskforce created in the 1970s innocuously called Treadstone. However, after the unexpected collapse of Russian Communism and the old Soviet Union in Moscow at the end of the 1980s it was decided to decommission Treadstone since the cold war was apparently over and won by the United States. But, as the new Russian Federation grew in power and began to increasingly flex its muscles with her neighbors and beyond during the first decade of the 21st century under the leadership of President Vladimir Putin, a true Russian nationalist whose greatest wish was to return his country to its rightful position as an undisputed leader in the world of nations, it was decided in 2012 that a new just as secret joint task force between the CIA and NSA was needed to combat renewed Russian intelligence efforts around the world. The new "off the books" taskforce would be called by yet another innocuous name, the Stonehouse Hedge Fund strangely enough, and it would be managed by the former governor of Connecticut, George Rafferty, an old trusted friend of the American intelligence community. And, when the cyber war between Russia and the United States finally begins, the highly skilled folks at the Stonehouse Hedge Fund are fully ready to respond as required.

The Stonehouse Hedge Fund's secret operations center is located in a 6 story nondescript and a bit smudgy around the edges red brick and mortar building just off of downtown Baltimore, Maryland not far from the docks. Their main "corporate" offices are just down the street from Wall Street in New York City since the well conceived and even somewhat real cover story for the fund is that it's a player in the pension fund markets throughout the country. In fact, those who work on the first 18 floors of the fancy NYC downtown office building with the bright neon name on its roof mounted marquee, have no idea that on the windowless 19th floor between them and top executive management who are located in their own offices on the opulent penthouse 20th floor there's a very secret hidden staff with a much different set of objectives than what they do to monitor and manage the funds under their stewardship and control. Unbeknownst to any but the most observant, the so called 19th floor listed on the public elevator banks that move employees up and down the building is actually the building's 20th floor and it takes a couple of seconds longer to get between the 18th and 19th than it should have. Interestingly enough, buried deep in the archives of city newspaper reporting is a small article written at the time the building was being refurbished in 1998 how interesting it was that there appeared to be a not explained wide windowless gap in floors between the 18th and top floor of the building, but to the relief of the secret managers of the building nobody took notice and the issue immediately died without any further discussion. And of course, during all of the near 20 years since the building was redesigned to its current configuration, those managers on the top floor pay close attention to any public or private interest in that before mentioned gap between floors. Those very few who have access to and do use that secret unmarked and windowless floor also have their own secret elevator to take them there and back down that's located far out of sight of any other employee in a locked away secret back hallway of the office building which takes a special numbered key to enter or operate. It's on this hidden ultra secret 19th floor where Greg Jones, Randy

153

Robertson, and Jillian Henderson have their offices when not present in the operations center in Baltimore, where in fact they do spend most of their time as the primary "wet agents" for the fund when not out on an assigned mission in the field.

Gregory James Jones is a former middle linebacker for the San Francisco 49ers who is without any element of doubt a most intimidating bald headed black man at just over 6'3" tall with a highly sculpted body that's a still hard and well conditioned 245 rock solid pounds. After retiring from a 6 year injury plagued career in the NFL (National Football League) in 2004, Greg (he literally hates his full name Gregory James since it's the name his mother always used when he was in trouble as a kid) decided to go back to school -he had been an All American at the University of Colorado where he did graduate with a Social Science masters degree - to major in criminal science and was immediately hired as an FBI agent in 2006 upon graduating with near perfect grades. From the time he joined the FBI Greg was seen as a promising "up and comer" and in 2012 when the newly founded Stonehouse Hedge Fund was created Greg Jones, the once all American linebacker, was quickly tapped to be the leader of its "wet operations staff." Those who played with or against Greg or even coached him called him one of the most intelligent and dedicated football players they had ever seen and a man who's absolutely driven to succeed in everything he does.

Randy Robertson is the very counter opposite of his former college and pro football partner and longtime mentor at a sliver over 5'8" tall and a slight 155 pounds soaking wet on the scales. Randy and Greg Jones have been close friends ever since the two of them went to high school together in southwest Denver, Colorado back in the early 1990s. While Greg went on after high school to play college and pro football Randy Robertson went to school not 15 miles away at the University of Denver (he graduated from the school with honors) where he would eventually become a highly skilled computer geek who specialized in sneaking undetected into operational computer programs. There were more than a few times while still in college when his undetected sneaking by Randy's own admission were not fully authorized which resulted in some free movie tickets here and there, as well as a few other perks, along with a quiet misdemeanor charge which was what got the FBIs and NSAs attention about his special skills in the first place. Greg Jones describes Randy Robertson as literally the smartest and absolutely cleverest dude he's ever met anywhere. Randy Robertson calls Greg Jones the most capable and loyal man he's ever come into contact with.

Jillian Henderson, the only female on the Stonehouse wet operations team, is the quintessential picture of modern sexy cool with her 5'9" 127 pound 40 year old body with womanly curves in all of the right places. Jillian was a onetime San Francisco 49er cheerleader where she first met Greg Jones and where the two of them had a blazing year long affair. The second she openly admits to with some pride, while the first is something she wishes for the most part to leave in her past. After leaving her position as a 49er cheerleader in 2002, Jill entered training to be a secret service agent, where she became an astonishingly good one with surprising weapons skills that belied her glamorous looks. Any who know her in the "service" call her one of the most accomplished and dangerous men or women they've ever seen with either a knife or gun in her hand. Of note is that both Jill Henderson and Greg Jones move on from their love affair to eventually become happily married husband and wife to other people than themselves. Greg is now in fact close personal friends with Jill's husband Dan. Greg Jones loves to describe Jill Henderson as the most beautiful and toughest smart woman he's ever known. Jillian Henderson always teases that Greg Jones is the best piece of ass she's ever had besides her husband, and is also a very good man to have along in a bar fight. Jill's husband always readily agrees with his wife's assessment of his friend Greg - the bar fight part, not the piece of ass part.

The roles played by the 3 Stonehouse wet opts team are simple, functional, and effectively clear: Greg Jones is their undisputed leader who networks with their various intelligence agency and defense establishment partners and provides some much needed muscle during their missions, Randy Robertson is the computer systems smart guy who makes things happen on the job and keeps them always in contact when in the field, and Jillian Henderson is the very deceptive and most seductive weapons expert for the team whom they all rely on to use her variety of special talents to get them into places where they usually would be welcome or invited. The Stonehouse Hedge Fund wet ops team has a simple chant that they love to use when discussing their opposition, which is "we will intimidate (Greg), we will beguile (Jill), we will outsmart you (Randy), and we will always win in the end (All Three). Together, they form a most formable adversary to any who get in their way, but in any case Jillian Henderson does in fact dislike it when she has to play the role of the seductive tart during any of their assigned field missions, which is often. To alleviate her dislike, Greg Jones constantly encourages his longtime friend and one time lover to embrace the role for the importance it plays when needed, and to simply look at it like an accomplished actor using available assets and spitting out lines in a movie.

Today, Greg Jones, Randy Robertson, and Jillian Henderson have just deplaned from their long transcontinental across the ocean and economy class commercial American Airlines flight from New York City's Kennedy International Airport to Sheremetyovo International Airport just outside of the Moscow city limits. The CIA and Stonehouse in particular have a "special" arrangement with American that allows them to fly under false names and carry some atypical normally disallowed pieces of equipment so they can appear like just another typical group of 3 passengers wherever they go. The 3 of them have flown commercial specifically in this case because they frankly want to keep their arrival and presence in the Russian capital city completely off the radar that would show in "bright neon like flashing lights" if an unscheduled private flight arrived especially from within the United States in these troubled times. Their objective is to find a man named Arkady Kamorensky, one of Russias most capable computer hackers, and a man they know is currently under the secret employ of the SVR intelligence agency with a portfolio to create havoc for the American intelligence computer network. And, when they do find Mr. Kamorensky, their job is to interrogate him about the things he is doing and then "neutralize" him and get out of Russia before they are discovered. Their plan is a simple and classic one called the honey trap, where once the man has been identified and located, they will set it up where Jill will hopefully seduce him with her looks and charm, then "neutralize" him at the first opportunity after finding out all of what he knows and can tell them.

"For God's sakes, don't these airlines people know that their passengers have legs longer than six inches," complains Jill Henderson.

"Sorry Jill. I thought it was important that we keep an image of just regular folks in economy this time," says a Greg Jones who is clearly struggling with the lack of leg room in economy class.

"Okay, I've located where Kamorensky lives, and I've also discovered that he likes to imbibe in a bit of fine Russian iced Vodka after work and before going home to his wife at the end of a long work day like all good Russians," announces Randy Robertson as he continues to stare at his computer screen.

"Perfect," suggests Greg Jones before he turns to Jillian Henderson, who immediately responds by saying with just a touch of a frown that she knows it will be her role to meet the man at the bar and seduce him.

"How do we know he will bite and take the hook?" wonders Robertson.

"Come on Randy, who could ever resist these?" says Jill Henderson with a self deprecating laugh as she lifts up her impressive chest with her hands.

"Good point," muses the computer geek with his own chuckled laugh.

"I'll have to grab some clothes and make a few changes to my appearance but neither will be a big deal at all. I'll make myself look a bit haggard in the typical Russian fashion, sexy in the way that makes me seem on the lookout, but clearly a local citizen in everything I wear and how I act," says Jill.

"Okay it's a plan, but Jill I think you should probably spend a few days in the bar flirting with a few other guys before you make your move so it's not quite so obvious that Kamorensky is your primary target," suggests the wet ops team leader.

"I think you're right," offers Ms. Henderson. "I actually was thinking about pretending to be a high class street hooker, but I'm not so sure that would work with either the area or with Mr. Kamorensky, so I've decided instead that I will pretend to be an underappreciated and unhappy wife of a government apacharik on the lookout for some action," she adds.

"Sounds good to me," responds Greg Jones.

"Sounds kind of catty but effective if my opinion means a grain of salt," adds Randy Robertson with just a little smirk.

"Randy, you had better handle the observation part of the program, since there aren't a whole lot of black folks in this part of the world, and my presence might be unduly noted and remembered," suggests Greg Jones.

"Right about that chief, but given that the surveillance will be for several days, I better do some disguising of my own from day to day," responds the wet team's computer geek.

"Oh boy, I can't wait to see this," murmurs Jillian Henderson as Greg Jones simply laughs at the suggestion.

It's late afternoon in the dimly lit and somewhat seedy neighborhood bar where Jillian Henderson who is now calling herself Sonya Restinovskovich (she has actually gone so far as to look up the name in the register at the Russian Ministry of Finance across town - thinking that it was far enough away that her ruse wouldn't be discovered before they can complete their mission) walks in wearing a sexy, alluring, but typically Russian

158

dress that nicely highlights her seductive features. It's a black cocktail style dress with just the right amount of smudgy edge to it that purposely shows off her womanly curves, her long legs, and her impressive not quite covered cleavage. It also goes well with Jill's pale skin, almost shoulder length dyed black wavy hair, brows, and long eyelashes. Her bright maroon red lipstick adds accent to the alluring over painted image she presents as she walks up to the bartender to order herself a glass of iced potato Vodka. As she knew they would, all of the male eyes in the room immediately turn to look in her direction, as even do a few female eyes who recognize her with frowns mostly as some serious competition. Today, she openly flirts with a guy also standing at the bar as she drinks her two drinks, going so far as to lean in and tease him with the near protruding tips of her breasts as her dress falls open while she tells him her sad story of an unhappy marriage to an under appreciative government apacharik. She will soon take him outside where she then offers the momentarily stunned and confused man more money than he's ever seen in his entire life to go back into the bar in a couple of hours and brag about the gorgeous piece of ass he's just had. The money comes with a not so subtle threat that there will be serious consequences if the man doesn't do as asked and nothing more for the obnoxious amount of money he's being given. As Randy sits on the other side of the bar later that same night in his disguise (tonight he's dressed as a local construction worker) while watching their ultimate target, he can only smile to himself as the marked man Jill had left the bar with earlier comes back in and loudly proclaims his manhood in graphic terms over several more drinks with his friends. Tomorrow she will do much the same with some other unsuspecting target wearing the very same dress, with whom in this case she will actually leave the bar with once again, only to this time instead of bribing him to return and brag to friends, she lets him feel her up and kiss her just a little before suddenly dropping him, leaving him to wonder how a gal who seemed so hot one moment got so cold and disappeared the next. His complaints afterwards to his friends about the unacceptable

159

treatment will only serve to add some mystery to her image with the neighborhood bar patrons. Dressed today as an office worker in a wig, tinted contacts, a fake mustache, and a cane, Randy watches it all from his seat in the bar. On the third day Jill openly seduces yet another patron in the bar, this time taking him to the ladies room where she brazenly removes the top of her dress to let him feel her up before announcing that she will pay him 15000 rubles in American dollars if he will go back into the bar and tell everybody that she'd given him a blow job, then just as casually leaves the bar after the agreement is made and the money passes hands along with yet another no so subtle threat before the man can return to his spot at the bar and also brag to his friends about his conquest. Again, Randy Robertson is in attendance, wearing a different disguise this time as a local cab driver, to witness the charade and see that their target is also in place to witness all of the action.

On all three days Jill and Randy have both seen Arkady Kamorensky come into the bar and sit by himself at the same corner table where on each day he throws down 3 glasses of ice cold spiced Vodka before getting up and leaving without saying a single word to anybody else in the bar. The man's apparent aloneness will actually serve to benefit her mission since Jill won't have to worry about any distracting entanglements with her target. Today, the fourth day, Jill / Sonya is back in the bar once again dressed this time in a blouse that's so low cut that it seems as if her boobs are about to fall out if she leans over too far, which in fact they would, and she's again flirting openly with a guy at the bar to whom she suggests that he buy her dinner, making it clear that if he does so, there will be a reward that needs no further description in his immediate future. Randy watches it all dressed again as the same construction worker as that first afternoon. Jill actually does sleep in the same room and bed with the man that night in a close by hotel room, but through only a night long effort of beguiling strategy does she avoid having to have sex with him (something that she would have in fact been regretfully forced to do if mission success had absolutely demanded it of her) while only letting him see but

160

not touch her hardly at all with his groping hands while only dressed in her underwear as she lay in bed with him. To the contrary, Jill has to fully disgust herself by outright fondling the man's various grubby assets as they lay together. She's pretty sure the joker actually cummed in his pants at one point during the night. She explains herself by softly purring to the near inebriated man that he will need to properly earn her favors before she lets him fully enjoy them, letting him of course assume that there will be the indicated "another" day.

To Jill's great relief the man from the long night in the hotel room is not in the bar when she arrives on the 5th and final day of her mission the very next afternoon, but as she expected and hoped Arkady Kamorensky is yet again. Also present in the bar is a very inebriated Polish businessman (Randy in disguise) who makes a drunken attempt to pick up Jill but is outright rejected to his disappointment. Today Jill's purposely worn a much more conservative business like suite with an open jacket over a sheer white blouse that readily allows her bra to show through and a matching almost knee length skirt that still shows off her long legs and highlights her full bosom to great advantage. And, after brazenly walking up to his table after brushing off the drunk where she takes a seat without being invited across from where Kamorensky sits in open mouthed surprise, Jill casually takes a filtered cigarette out of her purse, lights it, and takes a long draw on it before letting the smoke drift out of her nose and mouth and saying that she's frankly looking for some companionship that's a bit above most of the men she's so far seen in the bar, letting the thought hang in the air that what she's observed or experienced so far isn't all that very impressive. The surprised man seems to get the point she's making that it's he who is that suggested step above, and with even a smug look on his face offers to buy her a drink as he notes how he's seen her in the bar these past few days with some of the other men, giving Jill the opportunity to tell the man her sad tale of unhappy marriage woe and just how absolutely unsatisfactory those other men have been these past few days.

161

Arkady Kamorensky does in fact still love his not un-pretty wife of 15 years. But, the romance has long disappeared from their marriage bed, and it's been some months since the two of them have been intimate. More to the point, Arkady is more than a little sure that his wife has been having an affair and sleeping with a young neighbor man on their apartment floor who can't keep his eyes or hands off her every time they pass in the hallway. More than once he's come home early from work only to hear the unmistakable sounds of sex going on in the man's apartment and to find his wife strangely not at home, only to have her come into their apartment not long after smelling of sex with some lame excuse about where she'd been with friends. Suddenly, a man who has led a mostly colorless life up to now who knows for a fact that he's been cuckolded by a cocky snot nosed neighbor and can't even tell his own wife about the important secret work he does is completely enamored by the totally unexpected attention he's receiving from this wonderfully beautiful and sexy woman. At the very moment these thoughts are roving through his head the seductive woman casually undoes three of the top buttons of her blouse to allow a peek at her deep cleavage, and all Arkady Kamorensky can do in bug eyed response is dream about bragging to her about his important work after they make passionate love. In his mind he has sudden visions of being a Russian James Bond as he quickly tosses down a large mouthful of iced Vodka with little notice of the burning as it goes down his throat. By now the earlier drunk appears to be dead out and snoring at a nearby table.

And of course, it doesn't take long for Jill to successfully convince the not bad looking but clearly uninteresting man that he is a man of interest to her, as she bats her long dark eyelashes above her hooded eyes and opened burgundy colored lips that simply scream without saying so that they wish to be kissed, at the same time she seems to mindlessly fiddle with the opened buttons of her blouse in a manner with her fingers that does nothing more than highlight her impressive but still somewhat hidden bosom underneath the jacket. The fiddling of course isn't mindless at all but designed to bring the man's attention to two of the most important assets Jill possesses to help her complete her despicable task. Finally as she casually brushes a painted fingernail across Arkady's cheek, Jill / Sonya asks the man if there might be someplace they can go where they can "have a little more privacy," and after a moment of silent hesitated consideration, Arkady Kamorensky suggests the very same hotel she and her earlier mark spent the night last night. She wonders if there's an alternative, not wanting to chance being recognized so soon at the hotel. She tells him frankly that she doesn't want to risk that the manager at that particular hotel might turn her in to the cops as a prostitute. Arkady, entirely intent not to lose this stunning and unexpected opportunity, offers another hotel further down the street, and one the lovely Sonya Restinovskovich, sad wife of a most unappreciative husband, hurries to lead the now eager man out of the bar as the disguised Randy Robertson watches from across the room as he appears to be sleeping off his drunkenness. It comes as no surprise really, but Robertson is still always amazed how easily his female partner can pick up and seduce men. Kamorensky worries on the way to the hotel about it's higher cost, but Jill scoffs and tells him that her pathetic over paid but under appreciative husband can easily afford it as she reaches into her purse to pull out a pile of 100 ruble bills so she can hand them to her companion. Robertson waits only a few minutes after the couple leaves to stumble himself out of the establishment and disappear around the corner. Greg is watching it all from a hidden location across the street.

In the not fancy but nice enough hotel room it doesn't take very long at all for Jill to fully seduce the eager man by taking off her jacket first, then her blouse, and finally her black lacey bra, and get him to take all of his own clothes off so that Randy and Greg can storm into the room from where they're waiting outside when she loudly excuses herself to go to the bathroom and snap the incriminating pictures of the man with his pants down to his ankles with a full hard on in a hotel room. They quickly make clear to the shocked mark how easy it will be for them to photo shop the necessary images into any scene they choose, not only with a gorgeous woman as his unseemly partner but with some young stud of a man with his own clothes removed (which in today's Russia is the far more dangerous threat), before showing them to both his wife and work supervisors as Jill casually returns to the room and puts her clothes back on as if it were just another business meeting. Their suggestion is easy, either tell them what they need to know about the SVR network, or the doctored up pictures will be given to both his wife and boss, causing him to lose both his high paying job and his family, and possibly even his freedom or life. And, of course, it doesn't take long for Arkady Kamorensky to make his not quite impossible choice, and so after a mere hour of interrogation the Stonehouse Special Operations Team have all of the information they've come to Moscow for.

"Well, all we need to do now is tidy things up a little before we head home to Washington (clearly the man isn't even concerned about telling his victim where they come from)," suggests Greg Jones while looking directly at the distressed and totally submissive Russian sitting before him who still frankly has his pants and underwear down at his ankles since he's never been given permission to do otherwise and is simply too scared of the men with guns not to leave them so.

"Yep, all we need to do is tidy up a little," says Jill Henderson who just not an hour before had been Sonya Restinovskovich (she has all of her clothes back on now) as she casually reaches into her large purse and pulls out a Glock semi-automatic 9mm pistol and perforated tube like silencer that she begins to slowly screw on to the end of the gun's barrel. All Arkady Kamorensky can do is stare in stunned wide bug eyed sudden and retched fear as he watches his entire life pass before him while Jill carefully and expertly prepares the gun for use, obviously on him.

"My God, you can't be planning to kill me!" the now completely desperate Russian says in a near gasping shout.

"What else do you suggest we do Arkady?" responds Greg Jones as if it's the most normal of conversations to be having.

"I'll do anything!" cries out the Russian as Jill completes the task of installing the silencer and is carefully cocking the awful looking gun by pulling its slide back and letting it go to ram a bullet into the chamber after making sure it has ammunition properly loaded in its fifteen shot clip. It's clear to the man watching her, that Jill has obviously done this before, so must surely not be some poor sad and unhappy housewife, which of course he's known from the moment the 2 men came busting into the hotel room with their flashing cameras.

"Well, I don't know Arkady, it's just so much easier to clean this all up by simply eliminating the problem," further suggests Greg Jones with a simple and casual shrug of his shoulders.

"I'll do anything, I'll spy for you, I can help you know what the SVR is doing, I have access, I can even load malware into their programming that they will never find," moans the soon to be killed and now very desperate Russian computer scientist.

"Too complicated I'm afraid," muses Jones without further comment.

"Please, it's not complicated at all really, we can use the laptop your friend has to do it, I can trick the network into thinking it's all coming from a different IP location so they will never know the source if they discover it which they won't I can assure you," Arkady Kamorensky hurries on to say as the now loaded gun points in his general direction in the practiced hand of his soon to be assassin who only a short hour before he was dreaming of having as his lover.

"Hmmm... Randy do you think he can really do it?" Greg Jones seems to be saying with great question in his voice.

"Oh sure it can be done Greg, but I'm not convinced this guy can do it at all," responds Randy Robertson simply to drive up the tension with the scared Russian just a little bit more.

"Oh God please, I can, I can, I promise that I can do it!" nearly screams a now completely desperate Arkady Kamorensky.

"What do you think guys?" Greg Jones muses on as if trying to decide while looking at both of his two associates in turn, one with a gun still in her hand and the other with a very sophisticated laptop in his.

"I'm not sure, it would still be easier to just kill the guy, fill him full of drugs, and put him in a dumpster back in the alley," murmurs a seemingly decided Jill Henderson as she continues to stare with cold calculating eyes at a wide eyed and sweating Arkady Kamorensky.

"Oh my God!" gasps the pleading but nearly defeated Russian as he uses a hand to wipe the beading sweat from his forehead.

"You know Greg, this just could possibly work," offers Randy Robertson in a sudden olive branch of glimmered hope, designed to be exactly so.

"Oh it will, it will, it certainly will I promise!" pleads a slobbering Arkady Kamorensky.

"Well okay, let's give it a try," offers Greg Jones with a shrug after a long two incredibly stressful moments to the trapped Russian computer expert. "And by the way, put your damned pants back on," adds the wet operations leader.

"Oh God, thank you, thank you!" literally coos the Russian in relief as he pulls up his pants and underwear.

"Just so you know, Arkady, if this doesn't work or if ever you say anything to anybody about us or what has happened, this is what you can expect." And as Jill Henderson is talking to the man sitting before her, she pulls a two foot long braided wire garrote from her purse with a metal ring on each end for her fingers to hold and tells him that if he talks to a soul she will personally hunt down and find him, slit his throat in the bed where he sleeps next to his whore wife, so she can find his detached and blood soaked head at the foot of her bed when she wakes up. Arkady's eyes are nothing if not bug eyed in response to her gruesome but somehow very believable threat. Arkady Kamorensky, the unquestionably talented computer programmer hacker, literally pees his just put back on pants on the spot.

During their long flight home, on Aeroflot this time having left their hardware at the hotel for the embassy to pick up, Jillian Henderson turns to Greg Jones and Randy Robertson while they sit together in an almost empty first class cabin after sweeping the entire area for bugs and murmurs just how much she hates playing a tart. Her hair and eyebrows are back to their normal blonde colors, having had the black dye bleached out of them. Randy kids how she's so heavenly good at it though in a manner that a younger brother would an older sister, but Jill simply scoffs at the comment by saying that she had been simply disgusted when she felt she had to strip all the way to her waist for the lecherous bastard, and had actually feared that she might have to fuck him to get what she needed. Greg smiles in sympathy towards his friend as he muses that in some ways she has the toughest roles of all on their team, having to not only shoot some of their customers but seduce and screw them as well at times. Jill just laughs as she relaxes just a little, and says, fuck Greg I would far rather shoot the son of a bitches than let them see me naked or sleep with them. "God, I don't know how Danny stands it, knowing what I do, whispers Jill Henderson."

"How does he stand it Jillian?" asks Randy in all seriousness.

"Well Randy, I have to tell you that he seems to really get off on it mostly when I give him the blow by blows and literally responds by screwing me blind he gets so horny," giggles Jillian to her younger associate.

"What the hell, maybe I should try that with my wife when I get home," offers Randy Robertson.

Randy has recently married his life partner in the state of Oregon where such single gender marriages are allowed. "You know Randall, I don't really think trying to tell your wife about some fake mission sexual escapade would likely lead to an amorous experience, but more likely would lead to a black eye if I read Robert correctly, puts in Greg Jones to end the conversation on a funny note, causing everybody to laugh before sitting back to get some sleep while the commercial airliner cruises over the Atlantic Ocean towards its destination in Miami, Florida. As a side note, Danny Henderson really does get off on what he hears about his wife's acting role and experience in Moscow, so much so that he suggests they go to a very nice restaurant and pretend to be doing what she did in Russia, then come home and consummate their pretended roles in a most intimate manner.

Arkady Kamorensky does in fact introduce a very clever piece of malware code of only two seemingly innocuous words and no more than 3 nondescript numbers into the SVR computer network hidden so deep that it will allow the Stonehouse Hedge Fund programmers in Baltimore to monitor their activities without them knowing or even suspecting they are doing so. And, Arkady would never say a thing about the incident that frightful day in the hotel, but he did in fact have to live in constant fear, especially when one day he received a plain brown package in the mail with a video of the movie the Godfather with a note to take a peek at scene 23 where the detached bloody horses head is discovered on the end of the bed. Message sent and understood, except for his wife to whom he can't find a plausible explanation that solves the mystery in her mind of who would send her husband such a movie and why. Frankly, the man who for 15 years has been almost boring in his lack of emotions has become a basket case of nerves lately, to the point that she recently had a private detective follow him and watch what he does at that neighborhood bar he stops at almost every day. But, nothing was discovered and soon the Kamorensky family returned to an almost normal state of nervous boredom as they watched the on goings of the growing tension and short war fought between their country and the imperialist and arrogant United States. Arkady, lost in thoughts that he could never admit to his wife, knew for certain what role he had played in the war between the two countries.

For his wife's part, she simply went back to screwing their youthful neighbor every chance she got without one bit of inkling still what her pathetic husband did for a living or the role he had played or almost played in recent events.

Back in the hidden or nondescript hallways of Baltimore, Fort Meade, and New York, the very special malware that their involuntary Russian agent helped them insert into the Russian intelligence computer network, compared to the automatically triggered malware installed into the NSA system which was only designed to disrupt, would allow American intelligence to first deceive the Russians about the goings on in the Bering Strait and then to spy on what the Russians knew and better yet know what they were planning now and into the future. Frankly, it was nothing more than a listening device rather than anything intended to confuse or obstruct its target. Best of all, the Stonehouse Hedge Fund was able to remove the incriminating malware from the Russian network once the fighting was over and before it could be discovered simply by sending a prearranged signal to their secret agent.

Arkady Kamorensky never did hear again from the 3 strange Americans who had so brutally treated him, but in spite of the worrisome memory of the mind numbing threats of that day, he did dream now and then about what it would have been like to experience the lovely and exquisitely beautiful Sonya Restinovskovich's favors in the bedroom. He also continued to be frustrated at his wife's obvious amorous activities with their cocky neighbor who barely bothered to hide his cuckolding actions. And, a full 3 years after the fact another DVD video of a movie called Flicka showed up in his mailbox, and the very next day he secretly removed 2 simple words of computer code from the SVR network. More strangely, Arkady suddenly fell over at his table in the bar one afternoon after work while drinking his iced vodka and died right on the spot from a massive heart attack. No one would ever know for sure if it was the last act in the Stonehouse strategy, an act of revenge or reprisal from an ever suspicious SVR, or simply the odd coincidence of a frustrated man leading a sad and tortured life. For her part, his wife would simply move next door full time after the funeral.

17

Things Heat Up Even More

As would be expected the surprise assault on St. Lawrence island and its shocking takeover by Russian forces immediately ups the ante between Moscow and Washington over an already stressful relationship because of the Ukrainian and Iranian situations, and very quickly the tension between the two capitals shows a great and problematic risk of things spinning completely out of control if the two sides aren't careful to prevent it from happening. The unforgettable truth and reality is that each side still (even decades after the SALT disarmament treaties) have thousands of devastating nuclear warheads sitting in silos, on launchers, or cruising under the ocean's waves in submarines targeted mostly at each other.   And, over the months following the invasion and occupation several things do in fact happen in relation to each other to verify that dangerous fact in addition to the unequivocal ultimatum announced by President Bush.

Only a week after the invasion and takeover of St. Lawrence island, a fishing boat named the Delta Star based out of Nome, Alaska which is on its annual crab fishing expedition in the Bering sea is commandeered by a Russian Naval Patrol Boat and forcibly directed to the Russian Naval Base at Petropavlovsk, Kamchatskiy to the southwest. To their stunned surprise the Alaskan fishermen were approached on the high seas of international waters by the Russian naval patrol ship and quickly fired upon by a mortar like grenade launcher before boarding when the crew quickly and understandably surrendered. There was an immediate and loud protest from Washington D.C. and the State Department, but the Russians simply claimed that the crab fishing boat had intruded on Russian territorial waters and was actually an American spy boat not a fisherman as claimed. Not a soul in the world knew this to be anything but Russian blustering and nonsense, but few were willing to step up and call it such. The Russians then announced that they were placing a "protective screen" around the waters of the Bering Strait because they now considered them as territorial waters under their direct jurisdiction rather than the international trade route or fishery it's long been considered by all of the countries who fish in its well stocked waters.

In immediate response to the kidnapping of the crab boat, President Jeb Bush recalled the Ambassador to Russia and suggested that if the fishermen and their boat weren't returned asap the American embassy in Moscow would be vacated and closed. He also rejects in entirety the Russian claim that the Bering Strait is under their jurisdiction and that access would be anything but unlimited.

In response, five days after the kidnapping of the Alaskan fishing boat a Russian "fishing" trawler sitting not far off the coast of Norfolk, Virginia was approached by a United States Navy destroyer and told that if they failed to follow them into the harbor they would be sunk, and as the shocked Russian seamen watched two M48 torpedo launchers were turned and aimed in their direction as was the multi-barreled 50mm Gatling gun rotating cannon located on the destroyer's forward deck. Just as the Americans had before, the near defenseless Russian trawler's crewmembers quickly surrendered their boat and their government loudly complained about the act both in the public media and at the UN, and threatened dire consequences if the boat weren't immediately freed. The State Department simply said that the Russian trawler had moved within the 12 mile zone of American territorial waters and would be released only if and when the illegally kidnapped Alaskan fishing boat was allowed to sail home from Kamchatka. The interesting part of this incident is the American claimed 12 mile territorial zone, because the

172

entire rest of the world only recognizes a 5 mile zone, including Russia, so the trawler had in fact been within its "internationally" recognized rights to be anchored where it had been. A week later the Russian trawler was allowed to depart from Norfolk after the Alaskan crab boat was quietly released with its crew from Petropavlovsk Kamchatskiy.

At the height of the fishing boat and trawler incidents, both countries did in fact recall their ambassadors and announced that their embassies in both Washington D.C. (Russians) and Moscow (United States) would be temporarily shut down and all staff workers would immediately vacate their respective host countries. In the case of the Russians in Moscow, they reacted to the announcement from Washington by announcing themselves that the Americans were in fact being expelled from the country as foreign spies, even though nobody believed it to be the case. There was also talk of closing trade offices in New York City, San Francisco, New Orleans, St. Petersburg, Vladivostok, and Smolensk. For the time being the only indirect communication between the two countries would be through a third party, which would turn out the be the British, so for the coming months messages would pass back and forth between Washington and Moscow that were routed through London in a manner that kept the barest of conversation alive.

While this was all going on there was a parallel military buildup by the United States Navy and Air Force at both Pearl Harbor (South Pacific Carrier Strike Group) in the Hawaiian islands and at the air base at Elmendorf, Alaska (fighters and bombers). The US Navy Aircraft Carrier Strike Force Ronald Reagan was being readied with a full complement of aircraft and weapons to depart for the north Pacific. At the same time a squadron of B-52J bombers were moved from their base in the Philippines to Joint Air Operations Base Pearl Harbor on the island of Oahu, Hawaii. While this was going on 2 Seawolf and 1 Los Angeles class attack submarines left their pens in Washington on a route that would have them patrolling the north Pacific waters within the week. In addition a squadron of B-1B Lancer bombers is moved from its base at Ellsworth Air Force Base just outside of Rapid City, South Dakota to Elmendorf Air Force Base in Anchorage, Alaska. And, while the Americans are making their military moves to strengthen their presence in the north Pacific and Alaska, so do the Russians as they strengthen even more their Naval and Air Force presence in both Vladivostok and Petropavlovsk. And an additional Guided Missile Cruiser squadron is on its way to the north Pacific from its normal Black Sea port in Sevastopol, and the Russians have moved their own Akula and Zulu submarines from their base in Murmansk to be on patrol to watch and keep an eye on the American subs headed to the region. The Russian Air Force is also strengthening their presence in the region with additional squadrons of Tu-160 supersonic bombers, Su-31 and Su-35 fighter bombers, and Tu-145 turboprop Naval surveillance aircraft. The strange part of the build up in the region is that the Russians make no attempt to bolster their presence on St. Lawrence island itself, aside from the 500 Speznet troops and 2 anti-aircraft units already on station. The Americans can only assume that the reason is that they either fear a military response if they attempt to do so, or aren't doing so in order to keep the situation under control. The truth is actually a combination of both.

While all of this is going on throughout the north Pacific region and the surrounding areas the continued daily over flights by the American U2s and Global Hawk drones are showing the operational completion of the SA-21 Growler anti-aircraft missile battery and the new almost competed military installation with an unknown purpose on St. Lawrence island. The SA-21 missile battery is of primary concern with its 15 highly accurate rocket launchers that have a range of almost 500 miles and can reach an altitude of 50,000 feet from its position. This means it can reach almost all of the way to the airspace over Elmendorf Air Force Base outside of Anchorage, Alaska, and can certainly cover the airspace over the Bering Strait and surrounding area, including Nome on the Alaskan west coast. Washington is also very concerned about the ZSU-57-2 mobile anti-aircraft artillery vehicle brought onto the island and made operational, which is a fearsome and very effective weapon against low flying aircraft.

Washington and the defense department reacts to the updated information by publically warning Moscow not to use either the missile battery or the rapid firing cannon against American aircraft while at the same time the most up to date and modern Patriot anti-aircraft missile batteries are moved to both Nome and Anchorage for defensive purposes. In addition immediate actions are taken to beef up the F-22 fighter presence in Anchorage by moving 2 additional squadrons of brand new F-35A stealth fighters to the Air Base from their home base in Utah. And, to both send a clear message to the Russians 4 F-15C fighter bombers and 4 A-10E ground attack fighters were also sent to Elmendorf. By now Elmendorf with its many squadrons of fighters and bombers has become a very, very busy place in what is now the busiest forward Air Force base operated by the United States Air Force anywhere in the world.

At the same time that the buildup of US naval forces was taking place at Pearl Harbor, Hawaii where the aircraft carrier Ronald Reagan and its Carrier Strike Force 7 is being prepared for departure for an unannounced north Pacific patrol, the aircraft carrier George H. W. Bush is also being readied for departure from Norfolk with its own unannounced but obvious destination. The George Bush carrier group is equipped with 3 squadrons of the new F-35C stealth fighter bomber.

What isn't foreseen or expected by the Bush administration or by the State Department is what takes place in Cuba. While the recent Russian naval visit to Havana had been an embarrassing slap in the face, the agreements that came afterwards between the Russian government and the Castro regime were totally unforeseen and unquestionably disturbing. It's announced that a Russian naval battle group would be based in Havana, Russian frontline fighter and bomber aircraft would be dispatched to the island, and the Cuban President made a demand that Guantanamo Bay be closed and returned to Cuban control by the end of the year. The very next day a squadron of Tu-95 Bear reconnaissance bombers and a squadron of Su-35 fighter bombers land at the air base just outside of Havana. Immediately, over flights by Russian fighters and bombers were seen throughout the Caribbean Sea and off the coasts of Florida, Georgia, and South Carolina. It would be some time before the Americans discovered that the improbable and unpredicted agreement was due to the massive bribe of Russian oil to the Cubans, but just the same having such a powerful adversarial military installation only 90 miles from our Florida coast was troubling to say the least, and something that had not 50 years before brought the world to the brink of nuclear war. And of course, as expected, the Bush administration complained vehemently about the newest Russian actions at the UN and in Geneva.

The most visible result of the most recent actions taken by the Russians in the Caribbean was the immediate expulsion of what few remained of the Russian embassy staff from Washington D.C. and in New York City, who were told that they would be invited to return only when the military presence in Cuba came to an end and St. Lawrence island was returned to American jurisdiction. The Russians, of course, reciprocated by throwing out of their country what remained of the American embassy staffs in both Moscow and St. Petersburg, and warned that any Americans left in the country should leave immediately or be considered possible spies and arrested. In a quiet message out of the public eye, Washington warns Moscow that any mistreatment of American nationals within her borders would be met by the most "severe of retaliatory actions."

Soon after it was announced in both Warsaw and Washington D.C. that the United States and Poland had reached a formal agreement for the immediate construction of the MEADS anti-missile battery on its soil to be "operated" by NATO. Much is made of the fact in the announcement that the "shield" isn't targeted at any particular country, but is instead designed to protect the "entire continent" against an unprovoked rogue missile attack. Of course, especially given the timing of the announcement, there is no question in any European capital who the real target of the new installation actually is. And, the Kremlin makes no bones about the threat they think the missile battery represents and accuses the United States of plunging the world into an even deeper second cold war which puts everybody at risk.

Two days later the Russian Federation announces that they too would construct a new anti-missile battery on their western border next to Poland. In comparison to the Washington and Warsaw announcements a few days before, the Russians make no claim that their system will be anything other than a counterbalance to the American missile battery. They also announce at the same time that they are suspending shipments of Russian made rocket engines used on the American Atlas and Delta rockets. This comes as no great surprise to any in Washington, and is a situation in fact that has been prepared for with the development of the new American BE liquid methane fuel rocket engines. However, the NASA space agency, responsible for managing the American efforts surrounding the multi-national International Space Station, announces that while no efforts will be made to deny entry to the station my Russian Cosmonauts, visitors holding Russian visas would no longer be invited to or allowed inside the American modules on the station. Moscow quickly reciprocates with their own denial of welcome and visitation to the modules they manage. Unknown to only the parties involved, an ugly fight breaks out among 2 American astronauts and 2 Russian cosmonauts on the International Space Station during a supposed previously scheduled joint maintenance project that results in some fairly severe injuries and a complete shutdown of any further interactive activities between them. More seriously, when a Russian Soyuz cargo capsule arrives at the station with much needed supplies, the Americans first refuse to allow access to the docking unit by the capsule, and then when they finally relent the Russians refuse to share the much needed supplies with their American associates even though the International Space Station agreements demand that they do. In response, the American astronauts refuse to complete the spacewalk to repair the solar array on the Russian habitat module as promised by the international treaty and won't even allow them to have the replacement parts in their possession to do so themselves. Fortunately for the American astronauts an emergency shipment of supplies is sent to the station by Space X, but the real concern is whether the Russians will allow the Americans to fly home in their Soyuz capsule in a month as agreed upon.

Two days following these public statements the Russians announce a total ban on all Vodka shipments to the United States, causing President Bush to suggest a "drink Kentucky Bourbon instead of Russian Vodka campaign." The highly publicized campaign is immediately successful as the consumption of Russian Vodka in the United States drops almost overnight by a staggering 80%. However, the campaign also brings an immediate howl of displeasure from representatives of the California wine and regional craft beer industries who both complain about the favoritism shown the Kentucky Bourbon industry during the campaign. As a result President Bush amends his campaign to include all American alcoholic drinks as a substitute for Russian Vodka, which of course makes everybody happy except the Russian Vodka distillers who have long relied on the profits from their loyal and thirsty American consumers to help pad their bottom lines.

The final tit for tat comes when the Russians officially announce that they will no longer honor the longstanding SALT I and SALT II nuclear arms agreements with the United States that have been in place to provide nuclear stability to the world for nearly 25 years. The truth is that the Putin regime has been for some years cheating on the agreement with new cruise and ballistic missile technologies disallowed by the agreements, as in fact has the United States in response to the Russian actions. However, regardless what the realities are behind the scenes, it still comes as a concern to the rest of the world that two of the three (China is the third) largest nuclear powers are now at odds and the security blanket of the long in place agreements appears to be disappearing right before everybody's eyes as the United States immediately responds by saying that they are disappointed but will act "according to our interests" to the Russian announcement.

The reality is that over a five to six month period things are truly on the verge of spinning completely and entirely out of control between the Russians and the Americans over the Bering Strait and St. Lawrence island issue, there's no direct or functional communication between the two parties taking place except for the few messages that pass back and forth through London, an increasingly confrontational and dangerous military buildup is taking place especially in the upper regions of the north Pacific, and there continues to be a tit for tat back and forth action and reaction set of events that only serve to increase the tension in what amounts to a high stakes poker game that could lead to war on a wide scale if common sense doesn't step in at some point sometime soon.

Throughout the increasingly stressful and dangerous situation German Chancellor Angela Merkel and the British Prime Minister (David Cameron) make continuous but fruitless efforts to get the Kremlin and White house to sit down together, or at least get their negotiators together, to defuse the situation and move to some sort of less dangerous future accommodation that all can live with. Over a six month period Chancellor Merkel will put on an astonishing one third of a million air miles in her private plane by flying back and forth between Berlin and Washington D.C. and Berlin and Moscow in her repeated attempts to make the warring leaders come to their senses. She would say later that it had been like living out of a small suitcase for a full 180 days. Likewise, David Cameron would literally burn the phone lines to Moscow, Berlin, Brussels, and Washington D.C. in his continuing attempts to help Ms. Merkel craft a solution acceptable to both parties in the dispute. The only silent party in the international dispute is Beijing, whose leaders offer nothing by either comment or support at any point along the way to help find a solution. Frankly, as is so typical of the Chinese in these sorts of situations they seem happy just to sit back and watch as their two most serious contenders on the world stage continue to fight each other and self destruct.

One of the odd and truly interesting parts of the growing dispute between the Russian Federation and the United States is what's happening, or more important what's not happening, in the skies over Syria and on the ground. Where Russian and American military assets are mostly in a direct confrontational mode throughout the world and more often than not playing increasingly dangerous games of tit for tat like on a chess board, none of this is happening in Syria where the Russians are engaging in their own air and ground campaign against Syrian rebels and Islamic terrorists while the Americans are doing the same with their allies in the very same skies. Strangely in a place highly crowded with military aircraft of all sorts, armed with a wide array of extremely capable weapons, there have been few incidents and not a single shot fired at each other in anger. More surprising to some, but not others in fact, is the manner in which the Russians, and President Vladimir Putin in particular, seem committed to keeping the American military staff planners in the region informed about their intent and activities in the region. Putin has even gone so far as to suggest joint planning and missions against the Islamics through intermediaries, something that of course won't happen, at least in the immediate future.

(18)

Strange Bedfellows

The oddest part of all in the increasingly nightmarish arguments between the United States and the Russian Federation are those areas where the two countries appear to continue to work together in spite of their differences in the Ukraine and in the Bering Strait, the tit for tat sanctions and economic penalties being levied back and forth, as well as their growing military competition in other areas throughout the world. As mentioned earlier, the Russians are purposely staying clear of and even cooperating with to a point with the Americans in the skies and on the ground in Syria, and visa versa. And the fact is in Syria that there's becoming a strange but un-admitted alliance of sorts between the two countries with a mutual objective to destroy the growth of Islamic based terrorism as represented by ISIS and its allies. Of course, there's still much friction and contention how the Russian intervention into the civil war is designed to help prop up and save the beleaguered government of their longtime ally, Bashar al-Assad, as one of their primary objectives. Conversely, the American administration wants to see the brutal and dictatorial Assad government removed and replaced by something far more acceptable. But, interestingly enough, these differences have been placed on the back burner in this specific situation where surprisingly given their differences the Russians and Americans are finding a way to work in concert with each other for mutually acceptable objectives for the most part.

Even more surprisingly, especially given their support for the Assad regime in Damascus, is how the Russians have provided significant if not openly public funding to help relocate and settle the many hundreds of thousands of Syrian refugees who have been displaced by the decade long civil war in their country. Oil riches coming from the oil fields in Siberia and the still all Russian southern fields are supplying the millions of Rubles that the Putin government is quietly offering to its western European neighbors as an aid to their efforts to help the desperate refugees looking for a safe haven from their torn apart country and place to settle in the future. This circumstance is especially interesting, given how few funds the Americans have made available to their supposed European partners to aid in alleviating the impact of the influx of refugees from the Middle East.

Almost as surprising is the cooperation that begins to happen in the increasingly open Arctic waters (the result of recent climate change and melting of the ice pack) where virtually every nation has been preparing for the eventuality of mineral and oil wealth as a result. The Americans, Canadians, Chinese, and the Russians have been particularly active in this regard in recent years, causing some frictions and a few incidents here and there. Long a playground of the super secret ballistic missile and attack submarines of the great powers (Russia and America especially) the Arctic ice sheet has been a place where more than the occasional confrontation takes place, and because that is so a quiet and very unpublicized message travels from Moscow and Washington that proposes not only a truce in this area of potential disaster, but that the two countries use the opportunity to find common ground as partners, and shockingly given how they are fighting in so many other venues they do respond with an announced agreement that they will remove all military assets from the region and form a cooperative partnership for future exploration.

The Russians, at the urging of their President himself, even go so far as to send a relief team to the United States when the states of North and South Carolina are devastated by a category 5 hurricane and the resulting floods that have literally hundreds of thousands of Americans living without roofs over their heads or electric power. Conversely, the United States sends its own relief team to Smolensk when a 500 year blizzard covers the region in 10 feet of drifting snow which puts millions of Russian citizens at desperate risk since hardly a train or plane can get into the area.

19

What Options Do We Have to Consider?

Sitting around the long 8 sided three quarters of a century old conference table in the very tense basement situation room in the west wing of the White House are President Bush who's now been in office for well over a year now, his Vice President Mia Love, National Security Advisor Paula Dobriansky, Secretary of State Roger Noriega, Defense Secretary Robert Natter, and CIA Director John Negroponte, along with what staff they need to provide the necessary back-up information for the meeting as well as keep careful detailed notes of the undertaking.

The subject today, not surprisingly as it has been for many days and weeks in this very same room, is what to do about and how to respond to the Russian assault and takeover of the island of St. Lawrence at the southern mouth of the Bering Sea, an admittedly remote island, but without question a part of the American State of Alaska by treaty, which makes it American territory which must be taken back. However, every person in the room is and has struggled with how to do so without risking a devastating confrontational war with the Russian Federation that without question would be destructive with much loss of life and might even lead to a much bigger worldwide or even nuclear problem.

Comfortable that they can't be either overheard or spied upon since the room is subterranean, lead lined, and wired with a network of electrical grid work that makes stealing a signal from outside a near guaranteed impossibility. And of course, and as such, everybody knows that what is said in this room stays in this room, with the exception of those notes taken from the room and stored in lock sealed office safes.

"Without doubt Mr. President, as we've discussed numerous times over these past weeks the Russian action is a flagrant act of war that can't go ignored," presses Defense Secretary Natter.

"Without question it can't be ignored and it won't be as we all know, but what to do is the more important issue we must resolve as soon as we can," responds the irritated President.

"I don't suppose there's even the remotest possibility that we might accept the status quo, after all the Russians do seem to be treating the population so far with what amounts to a professional and even friendly kindness according to our sources," puts in an obviously hesitant Vice President Mia Love. The truth is that Mia Love is the true outsider in this tight knit group so really doesn't know or feel confident in her role quite yet even after a full year in office, but does feel that the most unlikely or unpalatable of options must be put on the table if there is to be an honest discussion.

"Really, you really think we should just sit back and let Putin run rip shod over part of American territory!" gasps an astonished National Security Advisor Paula Dobriansky.

"No, not at all Paula, I'm just throwing it out there because it needs to be said and rejected," responds the now contrite but still a little intimidated Vice President.

"Good that you did, Mia, because whether despicable or not, it is an option we should and even must consider," points out President Bush, then asks the group as a form of dismissal, what the other more realistic options there might be that should be on the table for them to consider? "And folks," he immediately goes on to say, "here's another option that won't be on the table when all is said and done, which is an increase in readiness of our nuclear forces, they will stay at DEFCON 5 on standby status, because I in no way want to send the wrong message to the Russians so this thing gets entirely out of hand and leads to a damned nuclear holocaust," explains the President.

"Jeb, are you sure you want to take that off the table so quickly?" wonders CIA Director John Negroponte.

"You're damned right I do John, no chance am I taking that any such thing can happen and I plan on contacting Mr. Putin yet today to inform him of the fact and that I expect him to take the same position, 'nuff said," says the determined President to end this part of the discussion. "One thing I do want to do is move two of our aircraft carrier battle groups closer to the Russian landmass to send a clear and unmistakable message that we take this seriously, and the Secretary of the Navy has informed me that the Carrier Strike Group 7 with the CVN 76 Ronald Reagan can be moved immediately towards the North Pacific to sit off the coast of eastern Siberia and that the Carrier Strike Group 2 with the CVN 77 George H. W. Bush can be moved from Norfolk to head to the North Sea off Murmansk after it finishes resupplying in South Hampton Great Britain. We can then start flight and patrol operations as soon as these two carrier strike groups get into position. The instructions to make these happen have already gone out to the on ship commanders, so what else do we need to do to put a full court press on the Russians and Mr. Putin?" wonders the President who is clearly in charge. "Frankly guys and gals, I want that fucking bastard to feel the pain from what he's done, but we need to do it in a fashion that doesn't risk getting even more out of control causing an unnecessary loss of life than we already have," he adds in what amounts to a long speech.

"Well, more sanctions and trade restrictions are the obvious choices to tighten the screws even more on the Russian economy to start with," says CIA Director John Negroponte.

"I think that's a given John," responds the President, then says doing exactly that will be action #1 as he writes it down. "Honestly, here's how I look at it - if we're selling it to the SOBs I want it stopped and if we're buying it from them I want another source found asap!" adds the President in a tone that makes clear it's more of an order than suggestion.

"I know there was the cyber hack attack that the NSA conducted against the FSB (Federalnaya Sluzhba Bezopasnosti or Federal Security Service) last year, is there some other cyber attack we can launch?" wonders Paula Dobriansky.

"Surely, we can and are in fact already doing some of that, but the risk we take if we aren't careful is that the Russians will undoubtedly respond in kind with their own attack," inserts CIA Director Negroponte.

"Mr. President, I strongly recommend that we avoid any damage to their satellite array. Making them blind just might push Putin over the edge and result in what none of us want," offers the NSA Director.

"I think we should do something of that order and am glad to hear that we are already working to do so, but make sure John that your people and the NSA are confident that what we do both leaves their satellites undamaged and can't be traced back to us," points out President Jeb Bush.

"How about something   like putting a hit on their RT international   television   network   that   interrupts   their programming or even inserts some confusing or embarrassing misinformation" offers the increasingly confident Vice President Mia Love.

"Very good idea Mia, let's add that to the list," responds the President, "can that be done John.?"

"I'll check with my people but from what I hear there are hacks all of the time on networks everywhere where folks are playing havoc with content, so my thought is that doing so to the Russian RT network should be a cakewalk for our people," offers John Negroponte, the CIA Director.

"Anything else folks... now look, it's obvious that the one thing we need to do is take the damned island back, right?" throws in the President. He then adds take the island back to the growing list of options. "So what else can we do, like I said before I want to put a serious hurt on Putin once and for all that might even get him to withdraw without an invasion that will undoubtedly cost lives," says the President.

"We could always conduct carefully targeted surgical strikes against the supply and airbases in Kamchatka that are supporting the invasion and occupation," suggests Defense Secretary Robert Natter.

"Not a chance Bob, too doggone risky that it might start a real serious shooting war," responds Jeb Bush. "If we did that my guess is that they would respond immediately by hitting Nome or maybe even Elmendorf itself next to Anchorage, and besides it does appear as if the Russians are taking care not to add any more military assets on the island if my information is correct."

"According to our intelligence Mr. President, your information is in fact correct and the Russians appear to be satisfied with the 500 or so special operations troops they now have on the island," puts in the Defense Secretary.

"Thanks Bob, so let's drop that option for now but we will keep the Ronald Reagan battle group on station just in case and let the Russkies know we have that option in our back pocket," finalizes President Bush.

"We could always send troops or advisors to the Ukraine as they've been requesting from Kiev for months even though I have to admit that I don't like the idea at all," puts in Secretary of State Roger Noriega.

"I don't like it at all either Roger, again too risky since sending more troops into an already tense situation will only serve to cause things to escalate further out of control and widen the dispute," responds the President again. "Frankly, there's virtually no support for it in the Euro Zone for doing so and if we did do it I think the Russians might use it as an excuse to interfere in the Baltic's who are already worried enough," points out the President to his advisors. "But, we'll also keep that in our back pocket just in case it becomes necessary at some point in the future," he adds.

188

"Hell, we could always invade Cuba and overthrow the damned Castros," throws in the Defense Secretary almost jokingly.

"How I would love to, Bob, just to put the screws to the nuts of that tyrant Raul Castro and is brother," offers the President. "The fuckers have screwed us with this new so called agreement with Moscow and deserve to be taken out. But, why don't we do this, not invade or attack, but send a very clear message both behind the scenes and publically that we aren't happy one bit about what they are doing and might even consider beefing up our presence at Guantanamo at some point in the future," suggests the President.

"The word on the street is that Moscow bribed them with a trillion dollars of free oil to get them to give them access to the naval facilities and airfields the Russians are using on the island," points out CIA Director Negroponte.

"I don't give a hot damn why they did it, John, the fact is they have put a finger in our eye in the world's opinion and the bastards are going to pay for it," spouts a now angry President Bush. "What's down there so far, by the way?" asks the President.

"There's currently a Naval Cruiser battle group anchored in Havana, at least one missile sub and a couple of attack subs floating around the island in the Caribbean, a Tu-95 Bear surveillance bomber and two Tu-22 Blinder medium range and two Tu-160 long range heavy bombers have been sighted by U2 over flights at the airbase outside of Havana, and it appears that a squadron of Su-31 fighter bombers are on their way to the island," says Defense Secretary Robert Natter.

"Shit, that's a lot of hardware," muses the President with what amounts to some concern in his voice. "Missiles?" he wonders with real concern.

"No missiles thank God, and none of the rest frankly is that big of a deal or even all that much out of the ordinary except for the bombers and fighters, which are in fact still in small numbers meant to send a signal more than be any real threat is my opinion, and we have a Seawolf and a Los Angeles class submarine keeping tabs on the Russian subs," says Secretary of State Roger Noriega.

"Good point Roger," says the President. "But, here's the real deal, if the Russians send ground to ground missiles to Cuba the American people will never stand for it since it would remind them too much of the Missile Crisis in 1962, so I'm going to send a clear and easy to understand message to both Putin and Castro through London and Berlin that that's the God damned tipping point relative to Cuba, and if they do so we will without question take them out," points out President Jeb Bush.

"Understood Mr. President," responds Defense Secretary Natter.

"Are you sure Mr. President that those kinds of messages even in private might not inflame the situation unnecessarily?" wonders the Vice President.

"It could without question Mia, but I heard enough from my dad what it was like in 1962 that I don't want to chance a return to that situation by any confusion or misunderstanding on anybody's part," offers the President.

"Good enough sir," she responds.

"So, an immediate shutdown of the removal of restrictions of Cuban economic and social interaction between our countries with maybe even putting them back on the list of countries who support terrorism, and a clear message to both Putin and Castro what the end game will be if offensive missiles are introduced, that about it?" summarizes President Jeb Bush.

"That's it," responds Roger Noriega, the Secretary of State.

"Good, make it happen," finalizes the President. "So what else?"

"You know, oil has in the last decade or so become a big part of the Russian economy and their foreign policy," muses a thoughtful Vice President.

"So, I get that since they're already using their damned oil wealth so effectively to get their way in Cuba," responds Jeb Bush?

"Well here's my thought, using oil as a tool or weapon of foreign policy can play both ways," adds Mia Love in a voice that's now become instructive to the rest of the group.

"How so?" asks the now curious Defense Secretary.

"What if we were able to pull away one of Russia's most profitable customers right at a time when they've committed hundreds of millions of barrels of non-profitable free oil to the Cubans, somebody like say the Europeans?" again muses Vice President Love as if she's trying to put the scenario together in her own mind.

"Interesting, how could we make it work? We sure as hell don't have the reserves to fill that big of a market ourselves," wonders National Security Advisor Dobriansky.

"I think Mia's on to something. What if we went to our Saudi friends and offered to subsidize cheap oil that they could use to undercut the Russians in Europe? Their cost of production is so low and they always have a huge glut of reserves to fall back on that could be used if we can get them to agree. And, we could privately pressure our European friends to accept the deal which I can't imagine would be hard at all given how upset they are with the situation in the Ukraine and Russia's aggressive policies, and taking the Euro oil market away would surely put huge crunch on the Russian Economy if not drive it into deep depression," offers Secretary of State Roger Noriega.

"I like it, great idea Ms. Love and Mr. Noriega, I think you both earned your pay today," gushes a now truly excited President.

"Just a thought Mr. President, somebody will need to get on the horn and convince the Chinese and Indians not to buy the overflow of oil that the Russians will soon have and be willing to sell for a cheap and attractive price," points out Director Negroponte.

"You're right John, I will do that," responds President Bush.

"Good. So, we're going to bump up sanctions and trade restrictions, launch a quiet and indirect cyber attack against RT, take back the damned island, go after Raul and his gang, then work with the Saudis to flood Europe with cheap oil that will undercut the Russian supply to her customers. One last question, can you be sure the Saudis will play Roger?" says the President in review of their discussion.

"Oh Mr. President, just the chance to stick their thumb in the Russian eye will have the King slobbering with anticipation after how they've been so cozy for years with the Iranians and screwed things up so much in Syria in recent years, I can assure you," responds Roger Noriega.

"Good. Now let's get to work and set up working groups for each of these actions we've decided to take. Obviously time is of the essence. Some of these actions we can implement overnight or in a few days, but Bob I want you and your team to get a plan put together to take back that island in no more than 180 days, and 120 would be a whole lot better," throws in the President to the group.

"I'm afraid Mr. President that it will take every bit of 180 days to get that island back," says the always frank Robert Natter.

"I'm afraid you're right, but make it happen as quick as we possibly can, there are Americans out there who need their freedom back," responds the President.

It would be the very next morning when the Defense Secretary met with his assistants and the members of the Joint Chiefs of Staff to begin putting together a plan to take back St. Lawrence island from the Russians. They would decide how they were going to accomplish the assault, what methods they would rely on, what Army, Airforce, Marine, and / or Navy units to use, and how many troop assets would be needed to complete the takeover. It was quickly decided that they would use Marine Special Forces as the main body of the strike force with support from both the Navy and the Air Force. Not surprisingly

192

disappointed with the decision, the Army would be left out of the party. It would be a highly coordinated effort that would rely on well orchestrated timing of all of the assets involved. The President has made clear that he wants as little loss of life as possible, including the Russian soldiers on the island. For that reason, the decision is made that the Russian government of President Vladimir Putin, will be given a warning and promise before the assault takes place. Over the next three days, the Joint Chiefs with their staffs put together the details of the operational plan that they then submit to Secretary of Defense Natter for approval, who then takes it to the President for his signature. By the end of that very week everything is decided and the assets needed to accomplish the mission begin to move to either begin their training or be in position when the time comes, which is decided will be 120 days from now.

The very same day that Defense Secretary Natter was first meeting with the Joint Chiefs, inexplicably the Russian international news reporting network, RT, started having unexplainable glitches in its signal around the world. One glitch would be patched in England only to have the lights go out in Taiwan or Tokyo. And, this seemed to be going on repeatedly as the day went on. Also inexplicably, strange reports would appear here and there that required fixing and explaining by the Russians, and in one case in the very traditionalist Indian television market XXX rated movies with naked men and women engaging in some of the most astonishing of acts began to play that took well over an hour to get off the air, causing a sensation of complaints and threats that RT would be banned from the country if promises of a recurrence couldn't be provided. Even in Russia itself, even worse XXX movies began to appear with men and women engaged in homosexual acts in a manner designed to anger a society that has in recent years put a huge taboo on them. Every bit as maddening to the management at RT, out of nowhere an obnoxious and most unflattering cartoon representation of President Putin and his government started showing up on the air throughout Russia and the world.

193

On Wednesday that very same week, President Bush announces during a White House press conference that in response to the unwarranted invasion of American territory by the Russians, newly established and even more stringent sanctions and a total trade embargo would be in place by the end of the week on all Russian trade goods. No American licensed ships or planes would be allowed to deliver goods to Russian territory, regardless of their source, and no Russian ships or planes would be allowed to dock or land on United States territory until the Russians left St. Lawrence island and returned it to U.S. control. Air service would also be suspended between the two countries, and the American Ambassador to Russia is being called home for "consultations." While he lacked the authority to press the issue, President Bush strongly recommended that Wall Street and American investors quit doing business with Russian companies and even divest themselves of their holdings where it was appropriate. The next day the value of the body of Russian holdings on the exchange fell a full 32% as more investors than might have been expected to do so sold off the stock, more due to a fear of loss of value than any form of patriotic duty of course. By the end of the week those same companies would lose over 60% of their total value on the exchange to Jeb Bush's great satisfaction.

On Tuesday Secretary of State Roger Noriega began negotiations with the Saudi government and oil industry managers, and by Thursday there was an agreement to increase production of Saudi oil by a full 15% so that they could offer to supply the western Euro-zone a "very attractive" competitive price that would undercut the Russians who were currently supplying them. On Friday, the Saudis publically announced plans to the world that they would be increasing production by 15 to 20% so they can become even more competitive on the world market. The plan frankly is a simple one, while the Saudis can actually make money on oil sold at $10 a barrel believe it or not, the Russians must receive no less than $38 a barrel to break even. They are currently selling their oil to the European Union countries for $55 a barrel, so the Saudis plan is to offer the same product to the Union members at the astonishing low cost of $25 a barrel, a staggering 55% decrease in cost. Noriega has agreed to subsidize the sales to the Euro Union at a level of $10 a barrel as a reward to the Saudis for their loyal participation. The move, if accepted by the Europeans as it will be for the simple reason that it will be so profitable and for the second reason that the United States will be strongly encouraging them to do so, will cost the Russian oil industry well over 5 million barrels a day in sales overnight and deliver a crushing blow to the Russian economy in general. This will be "Eco-war" at it's best and most devastating.

At the very same time, Secretary Noriega met in a secret meeting with the Venezuelan Oil Minister to negotiate an agreement where the oil that they have been supplying Cuba will be sold to the United States at a higher profit for a period of 5 years. With the signed agreement in hand, Noriega then calls the Cuban "Cultural Attaché" in Washington to his office to inform him that under no uncertain terms does the United States accept the situation in Cuba where Russian military forces are streaming into the country, and that in response there will be enforced an immediate trade embargo of all American goods going to the country, including automobile parts and cell phones. All of the recently increased contact between the two governments will be cut off and none allowed by civilian citizens in either country until the crisis passes by Russians leaving the Caribbean. Cruise ships with American tourist passengers on their way to Havana will be asked and required to turn around, with a U.S. Navy escort if need be. On Thursday morning, a new oil agreement with the United States is announced in Caracas by the Venezuelan Oil Minister, when he also announces that the highly subsidized oil deliveries to Havana will be discontinued by the end of the year because of the new agreement. Unannounced but still true, the Bush administration has also contacted Canadian oil officials to let them know that "they would be highly disappointed" if their northern allies were to provide oil to the Cuban government during these times of crisis.

Oddly enough, in the middle of all of the continuing spiral towards a potential conflict, a message get's sent through London that both parties would benefit if an agreement were made to not interfere with or do damage to their respective satellite arrays. The response from Moscow is an immediate message back that says, "we concur." The fear of course is that any interference with space assets in orbit could lead to the space war and the weaponization of near earth orbit in a manner that's been feared for decades.

20

Lightning Strike

For several months now a combination of US Airforce U2 spy planes, MQ-1 Predator, MQ-9 Reaper, and RQ-70 remote drones have kept close tabs on the goings on of the Russians on and around St. Lawrence island, along with any number of other U.S. naval and intelligence assets that are all doing the same on a daily basis. Not only do the spy satellites, aircraft, and ocean going vessels allow the U.S. military the ability to know what's going on throughout the region, but their around the clock observations provide the much needed information that the American Marine assault force will use later in their mission to know the exact locations of the anti-aircraft missile battery, the mobile cannon, the Russian troop barracks on the island, and the locations for the electrical substations in both Savoonga and Gambell. One MQ-9 Reaper was in fact most likely shot down by a Russian SA-21 anti-aircraft missile on one of its missions (admittedly there could have been a mechanical malfunction that might have also explained the loss although it's unlikely since a missile launch from the Russian battery was in fact detected just before signal loss), but no other was lost and the Russians appeared to have only intended to send a message by shooting it down as there have been no attempts to shoot down any of the other drones or any of the dozens of manned surveillance planes or fighter bombers cruising the skies over and around the island. What the Americans don't know is that the missile officer who made the decision to shoot down the American drone was severely disciplined and sent home to Russia for doing so without prior approval from his superiors, after which the remaining missile operators were instructed to hold their fire until given permission to do otherwise.

Also in the air over the Bering Strait are a second U.S. Airforce U2 spy plane that's keeping an eye on things all the way from Nome to the east to the Kamchatka peninsula to the west and a United States Airforce E3 Sentry AWACS radar control plane that's not only preparing to use its sophisticated systems to jam all communications between the Russian air and naval bases located on Kamchatka and the Russian soldiers on St. Lawrence island, but is also prepared to manage any American air assets in the region, especially if there's an air battle. The U2 is flying a continuous circular route at just over 90,000 feet in altitude while the AWACS is cruising in a figure 8 race track pattern at 42,000, both in international airspace. The U2 has one pilot on board while the E3 Sentry has a crew of 11. Just off the screen, both are aware of a single Russian May radar control aircraft (the Russian version of the AWACS) that's cruising over the Kamchatka peninsula as it watches them from a safe distance.

At this very same time the Aircraft Carrier Ronald Reagan Battle Group has sailed to a position just outside of 200 miles south of St. Lawrence island where it stands ready to support the assault mission with its carrier based F/A-18C and F/A-18E fighters, as well as provide the first strike in the invasion with Tomahawk jet powered cruise missiles that will launch from the Port Royal, a Ticonderoga class guided missile cruiser. Part of the carrier groups job in the coming attack will to use its assets to further discourage any intervention from the Russian forces on Kamchatka. And we should note that while this is all taking place a few letters and numbers of malware do in fact activate on signal to create a picture of blithe inactivity of the carrier group at its docks in Hawaii.

In readiness at Elmendorf Airbase just outside of Anchorage, Alaska two 4 plane squadrons of F-22 Air Superiority Stealth fighters and a 4 plane squadron of F-35B Marine vertical take-off Stealth fighter bombers are at the ready. On signal the Marine F-35Bs take off for the one hour low level flight to Nome, where they will refuel and wait to be called into action over St. Lawrence island. One of the F-22 Raptor squadrons will fly a protective shield over the Bering Strait while the other 4 plane squadron will be held in reserve at Elmendorf in case they are needed due to any potential or serious interference by the Russian air force.

Sitting in a hanger out of sight at the Nome airfield are 5 ink black strange looking airplanes that are in fact highly customized Marine V-22J Osprey tilt rotor vertical take-off and landing troop carriers. Designed and manufactured by Bell Helicopter and Boeing Aircraft in partnership, the V-22 is one of oddest and most unique aircraft in the inventory of the United States military. It's a combination helicopter and airplane in one airframe that has the ability to take off, hover, and land vertically, while it can also fly at a speed of over 350 miles per hour (the exact figure is classified) during horizontal flight with as many as 24 soldiers inside, all accomplished by a maneuverable set of two powerful tilt rotor engines positioned on the ends of its stubby wings that rotate forward for flight and back above to vertical for taking off and landing as needed. These particular 5 aircraft, however, have been specially designed with a black radar absorbing coating on their exterior surfaces, have some strange angles to their outside aluminum and carbon skin designed to defect radar returns, and have an odd looking radar signal jamming pod on their underbelly. Also, the twin Rolls Royce AE1107C motors on the V-22J (the "J" is a special designation for the special ops version) have been redesigned to lower the sound volume of the aircraft by 55% as it approaches at low altitude at the same time their power has been greatly enhanced. Also newly installed on the chin of the V-22J is the 360 degree rotating rapid firing 5 barrel automated Gatling cannon that can fire 20mm rounds at a rate of 1000 depleted uranium armor piercing rounds a minute at a directed target on the ground. Attached to the 20mm gun turret is an auto feeding drum magazine that can carry an optimum load of 8000 rounds to use on their targets. In addition to the cannon on the chin, each V22J has a mount on each side of the forward cabin for a 7.62mm machine gun (the ship is also equipped with 4000 rounds of belted ammunition) to be used by these weapons for defense and to cover the landing zone if needed. Each V-22J will carry a crew of 2 pilot - gunners and a 24 man assault unit. For this mission, one of the V-22Js will land to secure the east coast town of Savoonga, two others will land in Gambell village to do the same, and the last two will land at the Russian military installation to secure it and neutralize or capture the Russian soldiers based there.

In full battle readiness also at Elmendorf in Alaska, just in case they might be needed, is an entire Expeditionary Brigade of Marines made up of over 14,000 fully equipped infantry assault troops, combat logistics support, light artillery, and fully equipped anti-personnel and anti-armor Humvees. All were ready to load onto their C-130J cargo transport aircraft for immediate delivery to Nome or to the remote battlefield itself if things get too dicey on St. Lawrence island.

On St. Lawrence island, just outside the perimeter fence of the Russian military installation under construction is a fully operational SA-21 Growler anti-aircraft missile battery to protect the occupied island from enemy fighter or bomber aircraft. The battery has 15 missiles already loaded and armed in their launch tubes (14 more are in a nearby trailer with one having been used by the missile operator sent home for firing it on the American drone to test the operational status of the system) and there is a control trailer 1/2 mile away with a full radar capability. The 3 Russian soldiers in the trailer van will receive a very strange unsigned all capitals message on their screens an hour before midnite that simply says: "IF YOU WANT TO STAY ALIVE DON'T LEAVE THE SAFE CONFINES OF YOUR VAN TONIGHT." The 2 Russian soldiers manning the ZSU-57-2 anti-aircraft mobile cannon located on the other side of Mt. Atuk will also get the very strange unsigned message on their computer screens.

(1:30am Washington time)

"Mr. President, all of the assets are in place and ready for their launch signal," says the Defense Secretary.

"Thanks Bob," says President Bush with a serious and even grave look on his face, tell them to be ready to move on my orders.

(9:00am Moscow time)

"Mr. President, I'm told that you should expect a direct call from the American President in one half hour," says an aide to the Russian President who's just sitting down to dinner.

(9:30am Moscow time - 10:30pm in Kamchatka)

"Sir, all contact with our people, aircraft, and Naval task force on and around St. Lawrence island has been disconnected by a problem with the uplink or jammed by what could be American E3 AWACS aircraft," announces the same aide to the Russian President as he continues to eat his evening meal.

(10:00am Moscow time - 3:00am Washington time)

"Mr. President, this is a courtesy call to inform you that American armed forces will be landing on St. Lawrence island in exactly one hour from now. You are probably aware that all of your communications on and around the island have been suspended and they will continue to be so. I warn you, Mr. President that there will be the most dire circumstances if you or your forces interfere with his operation in any way. I also promise you that we will take every precaution to prevent an unnecessary loss of life and that your people will be returned to you in good time when the island has been secured. Good day Mr. President." With that President Jeb Bush puts down the red phone that he's used to call Vladimir Putin without so much as waiting for an answer from the President of the Russian Federation.

Once the message has been received and understood, President Putin gives clear instructions that the American assault is not to be interrupted unless they receive the casualties he has been promised won't take place.

(3:30am Washington time - 11:30pm Nome time)

"Yes sir, we are fully ready and will launch within 5 minutes." With that the general in charge turns to his staff and tells them to launch the 5 MV-22J Special Ops Osprey aircraft with their 120 assault troops and ammunition load.

(11:45am St. Lawrence island time - 3:45am Washington time)

2 jet powered low flying cruise missiles armed with their one ton conventional warheads launch from their launch tubes in the north Pacific ocean just south of the south entrance of the Bering Strait, and nose over to begin their 200 mile wave high trip to their assigned target.

5 minutes after that, 2 more jet powered cruise missiles complete their own successful launch in preparation for their 30 mile low level flight to their own assigned targets on St. Lawrence island.

(12:00am St. Lawrence island time - 4am Washington time)

Following a 75 mile flight at less than 50 feet in altitude to avoid discovery, all 5 of the V-22J Osprey transport aircraft land at the same time without incident outside the town of Savoonga, the village of Gambell, and just outside the perimeter of the not yet completed Russian military installation. Using hand signals only the Marine special ops troops dressed in their low observable night uniforms with black smudge to keep their faces from shining in the dark, disembark from their aircraft with their night vision goggles to quickly secure the area. No noise flash bang grenades designed to stun have replaced high explosive or anti-personnel models, and low velocity high impact rubber bullets are in use instead of the normal 7.62 parabellum ammunition (the regular stuff is on hand in their battle harness if needed). In each unit also is a Marine responsible to carry the laser blinder (the assault troops have special goggles to be unaffected) and one to carry the ultra sonic sound generator (the assault troops have their own special ear plugs for the same purpose). Both are designed to suppress the opposition by incapacitating their eye sight and hearing. The combination of nonlethal grenades

202

and bullets, blinders, and sound generators are intended to limit the violence of the assault and hopefully prevent unnecessary casualties as well. The 3 squad assault force is also completely ready and well prepared with what they need if required to use deadly force where necessary.

(12:15am St. Lawrence island time)

Not 5 minutes after the two man Marine laser pointer team whose command leadership has yet to give their trust to an unpiloted drone to do the job are in position to properly set up and put their red dot pointers squarely on the Russian SA-21 missile battery located outside of the Russian military installation, 2 Tomahawk cruise missiles fired from the decks of the guided missile cruiser Port Royal soon appear over the small hill to the ocean side, pop up, then dive on top of the 15 missile battery with their warheads loaded with 4,000 golf ball size explosive shells that simply obliterate the battery (along with the close by trailer holding the 14 back up missiles) in a massive split second of explosion and fire that would remind you of the 4th of July. In an instant, the high altitude air space over St. Lawrence island belongs solely to the United States Airforce.

At just about the same time the other two man Marine laser pointer team sets up and puts their own red dot pointers right in the middle of the deadly self propelled Russian ZSU-57-2 anti-aircraft weapon located on the other side of the installation. In some ways the ZSU-57-2 is the more feared of the two Russian air defense batteries with its 4 quick adjusting radar operated 50mm rapid firing cannon turrets. And, just like happens on the other side of the Russian military installation, no more than a few minutes after the mobile tank has been "lit up" by the Marines, 2 more jet powered Tomahawk cruise missiles launched from the Port Royal arrive over the ridge to distribute their destructive golf ball sized munitions that in a wave of fire and smoke completely destroys the defense battery in another split second of fire and smoke. Fortunately for the Russians, the ZSU-57-2 battery is not manned (the two crewmen took the strange message they received at its word and got the hell out of Dodge in time as did also the men nearby the missile battery) when the highly sophisticated jet powered American cruise missiles arrive to take it out.

As soon as the Russian radar guided SA-21 anti-aircraft missile and ZSU-57-2 anti-aircraft cannon batteries are taken out the squadron of Marine F-35B fighter bombers arrive on location to provide a needed air cover just in case. Not 20 minutes later the squadron of F-22 fighter interceptors also arrived to provide a "protective" screen to the west in case Russian fighters show up, and two actually will. They were a flight of 2 Mig-35 supersonic fighters on a fast collision course with the Marine F-35Bs over the island even though in reality they couldn't really see them on their radar. The Russian pilots were simply flying blind in retaliation to the attack by the Americans, knowing that surely there would be enemy air assets in the region t support any impending invasion. From above, the United States Air Force E3 AWACS Sentry aircraft alerted the Russian fighter bombers that they would soon be intruding on American airspace and must turn around if they didn't want to be shot down. Not seeing any sign of American fighters on their 20 year old lookdown radar screens the Russian pilots simply continued on their 1200 miles per hour course that would put them over the island in not even 7 minutes. One more warning message comes from the American AWACS plane that also gets ignored by the Russian fighter pilots since their screens are still blank.

Not 30 miles away and about 10,000 below the Russian cruising altitude are the 4 U.S. Air Force F-22 fighters with their 6 AIM-120C medium range air to air missiles and 2 AIM-9 short range air to air missiles ready to engage the enemy. On signal from the E3 AWACS, the flight of 4 advanced 5th generation fighters separate into 2 groups of lead fighter and wingman who each target one of the fast approaching 4th generation Russian Mig-35s. Both immediately go to super cruise (the F-22 has no need for the classic gas guzzling afterburner of earlier fighter jets) as they close the distance at a speed of well over 1400 miles per hour and gain altitude at the same time that they arm their AIM-

120C fire and forget missiles to be ready for launch when their targets are acquired.

"Target one acquired."

"Target two acquired."

"Target one is showing green and ready to shoot."

"Target two is showing green and ready to shoot."

"Do we have permission to shoot?" speaks the American flight leader into his microphone in a voice that seems far too calm for the situation.

"Flight leader you have permission to shoot," comes the just as toneless answer from the AWACS standing high above and to the north.

"Launch one, we have engine ignite and missile is away," from the first F-22 flight leader.

"Launch one, we have engine ignite and missile is away," from the second F-22 flight leader.

"Launch two, we have engine ignite and missile is away," from the first F-22 flight leader.

"Launch two, we have engine ignite and missile is away," from the second F-22 flight leader.

"Both missiles have acquired their target, are tracking and locked on," says the first.

"Missiles have acquired their target, are tracking and locked on," says the second American fighter pilot.

Almost immediately, the Russian Mig-35 pilots detect the missiles in the air headed their way and begin to maneuver quickly and desperately in an attempt to lose them even though they have no idea who launched them or where they came from, which will be to no avail at such a short range of not even 20 miles. Both pilots are screaming into their microphones for the May to give them their targets. But, the American F-22s have in less than a moment opened their weapons bay doors, launched their missiles, then reclosed the doors to return them to undetectable stealth mode. While doing so the Russian May only got a momentary blimp on their screens that failed to give them enough information for location and targeting before it melted away once again. The Mig-35s didn't even receive that much on their obsolete radar screens. In the meantime all 4 of the AIM-120C missiles are squarely locked onto the heat signatures put out by the twin turbofan engines on each of the Russian fighters and are cruelly and relentlessly homing in at over 2500 miles per hour. In less than 3 minutes the robotic air to air missiles rapidly close the distance and the 2 Mig-35 fighters that even with all of their capabilities are no match for the fast flying robots headed in their direction disappear in an enormous explosive cloud of smoke and debris caused by their 100 pound high explosive warheads. Both Russian pilots died instantly without a chance to escape their cockpits, never having the opportunity to see the planes or pilots who killed them.

"One targeted bandit destroyed," announces the first F-22 flight leader in a toneless voice.

"Two targeted bandit destroyed," announces the other F-22 pilot, also in a none emotional voice.

"Confirmed, one and two Russian aircraft down and destroyed, no chutes detected," responds the AWACS control aircraft, "you can return to your patrol pattern blue flight."

"Roger that, skies are clear, no Russians in sight," inserts the flight leader of the second F-22 flight who have been watching the one sided air battle from a location that allows them to make sure they can support the other 2 plane flight if needed or necessary.

With that the first air battle fought directly between American and Russian pilots since the Korean War ended 66 years ago comes to an end with a clear victory by the United States Air Force and their much maligned 5th generation F-22 Stealth fighter aircraft. Air Force analysts would later determine that the Russian pilots never did detect the American fighters even though they were within 20 miles of their position, as also apparently had not their own radar surveillance aircraft. This had represented the F-22s very first air to air battle against a front line adversary with modern aircraft (although technically the Mig-35 is considered a 4th generation fighter in comparison to the American F-22 which is considered a superior 5th generation airframe), and the result has been more than pleasing to say the least to both the U.S. Air Force and Lockheed Martin General Dynamics, the builder of the fighter.

To the south about 200 miles away, a lone overly aggressive Russian Tu-95 Bear Reconnaissance bomber was successfully and to its good fortune forced to leave the vicinity of the carrier strike force when a 2 plane flight of F/A-18C fighters were scrambled by the aircraft carrier Ronald Reagan to intercept it. And, it did immediately turn away in a wide sweeping circle to head back towards the Kamchatka peninsula following a stern warning not to intrude on the 100 mile no fly zone around the battle group.

In Savoonga the first thing the Marine special forces assault troops do after landing and departing their V-22J Tilt Rotor Aircraft transport is go to the town's already located electric power substation to turn it off temporarily so they can rob the Russian defenders of the power they need. After doing so they go to a house on each side of the town to quietly tell the people why the power has suddenly gone off. They also asked them politely to tell all of their neighbors and to stay inside for the time being. They then turn their attention to the occupiers, and here in Savoonga there's only a small Russian guard force (no more than 50 troops billeted in a single barracks) who take only about 10 minutes to overpower (gladly, they don't put up much of a fight before surrendering to the Americans) and secure.

After landing just outside of Gambell another squad of Marine assault troops also go to the town's electric power substation to turn it off first thing after leaving their aircraft. And, after doing so they also go to a house on each end of the village to quietly tell the people why the power has suddenly gone off on a temporary basis and to ask that they too tell all of their neighbors and stay inside for the time being before they then turn their attention to the Russians, and in and around Gambell there are over 100 Russian soldiers in two barracks locations, so the two assault units will take 15 to 20 minutes to overpower and secure them, which they do with relative ease with their vision and sound suppression equipment just like their counterparts in Savoonga.

At the Russian military installation still under the final stages of its construction, the assistant to the commanding general (who is not in residence at the time but who is instead with his mistress in nearby Gambell and who will ironically know before his own security troops that they've been invaded by the American force) nearly welcomes the American assault force when they land in their V-22J aircraft and quickly fan out to take on any defenders who might be ready for them. And gladly, they don't even have to use their laser eye blinding device or ultrasonic sound suppressors against the just over 300 troops in residence who don't put up any but some sporadic resistance after seeing both of their anti-aircraft missile and mobile cannon batteries so easily go up in plumes of smoke and flames.

The night time assaults on the 2 villages and the military installation go so surprisingly well with so little of the expected violence and resistance from the Russian occupiers that the planners back at Nome remove the 2 Apache AH-64 Attack helicopters that were loaded on the 2 C-130 cargo transport planes being readied to fly to St. Lawrence island with the Humvees and supplies the recovery troops would need. In addition the 14,000 man Marine brigade was ordered to stand down back in Anchorage since their presence and participation will obviously also not be needed this night. They will be, however, kept on high alert just in case there is a Russian counter response to the retaking of the island.

The huge one after the other impossible to miss explosions on the island caused by the 4 Naval launched Tomahawk cruise missiles landing nearby immediately alerts anybody who has not already been alerted to the arrival of the American relief force by the dogs in the area, so soon there are more than a few curious citizens peeking out windows or even standing outside in both Savoonga and Gambell who are trying in vain to get a handle on what's going on in the dark of the night.

One of the more interesting incidences that takes place during the assault was when 2 Marine elite special forces troops approach a small house on the corner just off the town square where they find a middle aged woman dressed in what can only be described as a sexy nightgown and a rotund middle aged man in his pajamas standing on the porch. The buxom woman is Emma Vonderlinden who is desperately trying to undo the muss of her hair with her hands as she tries to decide how much trouble she might actually be in with the arrival of the Americans, and the man on the porch is none other than General Arkady Islonovich Kamanisky from the Russian military outpost who is gaily welcoming the Marines as if they are old friends while he stands on the porch with a noticeable bulge between his legs that makes clear that he and the woman standing beside him have been interrupted from something other than sleep.

(5:00am Washington time)

"Sir, we just got word that St. Lawrence island has been secured by the Marine Elite Special Ops forces and is now completely under our control," says Secretary of Defense Robert Natter to the President.

"That's great news Bob," says the President, "casualties?"

"None that we know of, the Russians didn't put up much of a fight as it turns out," offers Bob Natter.

"Glad to hear it, carry on, now let's all go home and get some sleep before I inform the nation tomorrow morning," adds a completely exhausted but very relieved Jeb Bush, "job well done everybody."

(2:15am St. Lawrence time)

The lights go back on in not more than 45 minutes in both Gambell and Savoonga as all in both towns look around with wonder and just a little concern before simply returning to their homes to go back to sleep.

(1:15pm Moscow time - 2:15am St. Lawrence time)

"Mr. President, St. Lawrence island is apparently back in American hands, and they are saying they will return our soldiers in a few days as soon as transport can be arranged," says an aide who nervously interrupts his superior from the late night reading he's doing.

In response, Russian President Putin who in fact expected the assault to take place and gave orders not to try and stop it simply puts his book down and slumps his shoulders in quiet but dejected acceptance of the reality of it, as in truth he now has much bigger problems on his plate with the sudden and continued deterioration of the Russian economy caused by the orchestrated loss of European Union oil business with the resulting massive demonstrations in Moscow, St. Petersburg, Smolensk, and a few other major cities. Ironically, the book Vladimir Putin has been reading is War and Peace by the greatest Russian author of all time, Leo Tolstoy.

Of course, like all of the other native citizens on the island Elizabeth is woken up in the middle of the night by all of the chaos, fireworks, dogs barking, and activity. Even she can't see much of anything except what appear to be some distant explosions near where the Russian defense installations are located from the 3rd story of her lighthouse home. And, like so many others she finally tries to go back to sleep with little success due to the unexplained anxiety of the situation. She can't help but wonder who these men really are, and feels that she can't just assume they are Americans or that they are here to help them. Frankly, almost 6 months of stress and anxiety are finally taking their toll and Elizabeth like so many others is frozen in fear and worry about what might come next on their once quiet and solitary island.

(9:00am St. Lawrence time, 1:00pm D.C. time, 8:00pm Moscow time)

"Ladies and gentlemen of St. Lawrence island let me announce to you that you are once again safe from your foreign occupiers and now under the protection of your American government in Washington D.C., and President Bush himself sends his personal welcome back and best regards. Let me publically say first of all that I greatly appreciate the professionalism of the Russian commander (the general has recovered from his night time interruption and is now standing and smiling in full uniform next to the American Marine commander) and all of his troops whose combined actions have gone a long way towards preventing an unnecessary loss of life or destruction of property, and I assure both you and his countrymen that he and his soldiers will be returned to their country just as soon as possible. For the time being let's all hope that things can return to normal also as soon as possible, and I'm announcing to you now that there will be a town meeting tonight to give every one of you further details about our plans as we go forward." This was the 5 minute announcement shared in both Gambell and Savoonga the morning after the successful assault to repatriate the St. Lawrence native Americans from their previous Russian occupiers.

That very same night a town hall meeting were in fact held as promised in both Gambell and Savoonga where more details of the American Marine assault and repatriation of their island were provided. The people were introduced to the squad commanders of the units involved who were all cheered for their brave efforts. Yet another message was read from the President welcoming again the islanders back to the bosom of their American family, and again he wished everybody Godspeed in their efforts to return things to normal while promising their full support from the U.S. government in both Washington and Juneau. There was also a message of welcome from Governor of Alaska, Bill Walker, who promised a personal visit to the island just as soon as it could be arranged.

21

Lighthouse Encounter

The target village of Gambell and the surrounding area appears to be completely secured by early morning with no noticeable hints or evidence of any sort of apparent resistance from the Russians anywhere on the island and not a single sign of interference from any detected Russian air or sea assets in the region, so Marine Captain Jon Anderson takes it upon himself to go to check out the lighthouse located just down the coastline several hundred yards so he can reconnoiter and check it out. He's told that only an unmarried woman lives there, but because it's still so hard to believe that the Russians gave up the island so easily there's still the real concern that there could be hidden Russian soldiers, their sympathizers, or even a few collaborators who could potentially be a problem to he and his men, as unlikely as that now appears to be, and the towering 3 story lighthouse would be a perfect location for them to perpetrate an ambush if they actually chose to do so. One of the first things that invasion troops are taught, especially elite forces, was to never assume anything and to always make sure the worst or unexpected can't happen to unseat your plans. But even with all that thought and said, for inexplicable reasons that nobody could actually recall if ever asked, not one of the members of his unit accompanied the Captain on his recon mission to the lighthouse.

When he first steps up onto the tiny and squeaky wooden porch of the tall 3 and a half story lighthouse Captain Jon Anderson quickly sees that the front entry door is ajar, which causes him to pause and listen carefully for a moment with his assault weapon poised to fire just in case. With his awareness and antenna on high alert he also sees what looks like still wet clothing on a clothes line flowing with the morning breeze in the small yard like area next to the building, and notes that besides a couple of solitary towels all of the garments appear to be women's clothing attire. Does make sense he thinks to himself given what he's been told about who lives here. Jon looks closer to make sure, but there doesn't look to be anything hanging there that could remotely be anything a man would wear. All he sees are a couple of bras, several pairs of what look to be cotton panties, some Capri like pants, some shorts, and 3 girlish tops, and nothing else. Maybe he should have brought along another member of his unit for support, he begins to wonder as his gaze returns to the bras and panties for a moment. Must not be a bad looking gal he thinks to himself also as he notes the healthy size of some of the underclothing. Not hearing anything outside or seeing anywhere anybody could easily hide Jon moves forward on the small deck like porch to take a look inside ever so slowly while staying on full alert as he silently eases the door open with a nudge of his elbow at the same time he points the short barrel of his 7.62mm HK MP5N assault rifle with its special rubber tipped bullets through the growing opening with his finger ready on the guns trigger before he enters into the tiny anteroom of the lighthouse. He cringes just a little when the porch boards creek once again when he moves.

It's still early in the morning with the sun just beginning to peek low over the eastern horizon, so there's little natural light as yet inside the building, making it hard for him to see among the shadows at first before his eyes have a chance to adjust to the even dimmer light, so the Captain hesitates for a short moment so he can take stock and regain his vision before moving any further into the room. That done and with his alert and sharp unblinking eyes roving across the area before him, Jon Anderson carefully notes everything he sees and hears as he carefully steps into the not more than six foot square room. Quietly but loud enough to be heard, he hails if there's anybody in the building at the same time he continues to move one careful step at a time through the tiny anteroom, taking special note of the

214

pair of women's hiking type shoes on the floor and the 2 closed doors that indicate that there are other rooms beyond and a stairway to the other 2 or so levels of the lighthouse. There's also a wide arched opening without a door to what looks like must be a kitchen in the back of the first floor level. Most likely a back entry door there, he thinks to himself. He pauses again to listen with his ear tilted to hear anybody that could be waiting upstairs or beyond the arch in the room behind.

She's in the kitchen after taking what had been a relaxing and soothing shower before getting ready to make herself some breakfast, and is still quite frankly a little overwhelmed with worry and some fear from the unexpected and still not understood activities during the night. Never before has the electricity gone out as it did, which had required her to use up much of the stored generator power she had on hand to keep the lighthouse beacon shining. She will have to go down to the village later to get some petrol to replace what she used during the night. She looks down at herself as she remembers that all she has on still is the flimsy muslin dress with nothing underneath it, which causes her to think that maybe she should run to her second floor bedroom and put on some underwear before somebody shows up at her door unexpectedly. And then, suddenly she knows that the idea of doing so is too late when Elizabeth hears somebody she doesn't recognize enter her home and say something, causing her to instinctively freeze in even more immediate fear with a hand over her mouth so she can avoid crying out, but when she hears English spoken she is in fact relieved just a little that it at least isn't as likely to be some sort of terrorist group or pirates who've arrived in the night. There's not a sound coming from the village which makes her wonder if she should take hope from that or be even more worried because of it. Still not sure yet who might be in her lighthouse home since a neighbor would have simply walked right in and yelled out her name, Elizabeth says nothing in response to the hail, and stays huddled out of view against the far counter in the kitchen with wide open eyes glued on the entry to the rest of the house. She does wonder if she should

215

try to reach into a drawer for her butcher knife, but decides doing so is too risky at the moment.

Jon hears nothing in response to his first hail, but stays on full alert because he still worries about potential enemies who could be still loose on the island, although they've found no sign of it or any sign of left behind booby traps or IEDs (Improvised Explosive Device). Frankly, Jon's tours in Afghanistan have taught him never to assume friends and never lose his alertness until sure all is secure no matter how safe things might appear. The thought reminds him that he can't assume yet that it's entirely safe for he or his men here, and he still can't be entirely sure he's even alone in the building. And, where's the woman who's supposed to live here he wonders? Frankly, he's still concerned that things have gone far easier than expected or could have hoped, too easy maybe, and he worries that his men are being set up for an ambush by the Russians, either by forces still hidden on the island or by those who could be ready to counter attack from nearby. He checks one door by gently twisting the door knob and easing it open ever so carefully with the barrel of his gun to look inside. It's a small storage room full of supplies on floor to ceiling shelves with nobody in it. Lots of food though, so this place has surely been occupied recently as the clothes on the clothes line would also seem to indicate, possibly by a Russian guard post who skedaddled when he and his guys arrived. The food not the women's clothing, those certainly wouldn't be for any guard force. Or, maybe the resident or residents of this place were down in the village when he and his squad arrived a few hours ago. He has no reason to believe he was lied to about who lived here, but he's still wary and focused just the same (again the experience of Afghanistan). He checks the other downstairs door with the same gentle twist and nudge to look inside, and it turns out to be a small bathroom with also nobody in it.

He can see that it looks like the tiny shower stall is still dripping wet from recent use (almost surely this very morning he thinks) and a damp towel is hanging on a rod on the wall. He can smell the sweet and fragrant soapy scent of a shower that appears to have just been taken not all that long ago in the air of the room. He also can see a single well used toothbrush and tube of paste on the small counter and sink along with a partially used box of tampons and a hairbrush, yet more indications that it's a woman who lives here. No signs at all of a man he notes. Jon slowly turns away from the tiny bathroom and takes notice again of the stairs to what obviously must be the floors above and the lighthouse lantern, so with quiet step after step on the rubber treaded wood steps, while stopping to pause and listen in between each of them, he starts to ease himself slowly up to take a look, taking care to stay alert and watch his 6 behind him while he does so. He realizes of course that if there are "bandits" waiting up above, they have the clear advantage as he approaches.

He softly hails again when he reaches a landing on the top step of the second level where there are windows through which he can see a wide view of the near empty ground below. Jon does note what must be a small vegetable garden. Looking back into the room he moves across the landing to the closed door beyond while he continues to check behind him and down the stairs. He eases it open with a hand twist of the knob and push. It creeks just a little when he does so, causing him to flinch and listen for a moment. Nothing, it's an empty bedroom. He does see women's clothing hanging over a chair and a bra like the ones on the clothes line outside hanging from the post like banister on the end of the bed. He notes too yet again that the owner of the undergarment is clearly a healthy girl. He also sees what looks like a pair of pink panties wadded up on the seat of the chair. But, not a soul in sight. So he turns and leaves the room, and after a quick look up the short stair way to where the high beam lantern of the lighthouse sits in its enormous enclosed globe at the ceiling of the landing above, where he makes sure nobody hides in wait, the Lieutenant heads back down the narrow stairway while he stays keenly alert as he slowly makes his way step by step just like on his way up, to check out what or who would have to be in what must surely be the kitchen down below if there is to be anybody present in the building. He realizes too late frankly that he has exposed himself to anybody who has entered the lighthouse since he's gone upstairs and could be lying in ambush down below as he carefully eases himself back down the narrow stairs. But again nobody, so Jon makes his way slowly across the first floor room to what must be the only remaining room in the building to check it out, by now reasonably sure that nobody is here.

However it's in what turns out as expected to be the kitchen beyond, in the dim light next to where the early morning sun is shining through a small window where he suddenly sees her cowering in absolute trembling fear next to a counter with a huge 14" butcher knife in her hands as she stares with undisguised dread at the weapon Jon's carrying. There's an open kitchen utensil drawer next to where she's crouching where she obviously got her weapon. He quickly aims his gun in her direction in what amounts to an instinctive reaction before thinking not to. She gasps in even more raw fear, seems to raise the knife as if to defend herself for a moment before simply putting it back in the drawer as he continues to point the gun at her while he insists that she put the weapon down, then lowers her head with closed eyes after doing so as if to receive an expected death sentence. She whimpers quietly as he continues to look around the room to make sure nobody else is present, then simply raises her head and nods in fearful wide eyed silence when asked by him if she's in fact alone in the house, which of course he knows now she must be. Jon continues to point his gun in her general direction, still not entirely sure that she's not a danger, but can even see then in the dim light that she's a strikingly beautiful woman, and most likely the owner of the underwear he's seen if he guesses right. With a flood of tears streaming down her cheeks, her eyes seem to be silently pleading for her life as she continues to stare at him without daring to say a word. Jon asks her again if she's alone, and she nods again in a rush to indicate that she is. And then, for the first time there appears a slight glimmer of hope in her eyes as he finally lowers his assault weapon to "safe it" by releasing the trigger, even though there's still a cloud of unavoidable heavy tension in the room.

Knowing not what else to say to the woman who's so obviously scared to death, Jon quietly murmurs that she's safe now and he promises not to hurt her as he allows himself to relax just a little, as his own built up tension bleeds off through his body. God, she's beautiful, he thinks to himself as he really looks her over for the first time. Knowing finally that it's surely safe to do so, he lets himself fully relax for the first time since he first entered the small house some 10 minutes ago, as he slowly undoes the chin strap of his netted Kevlar helmet with its attached night vision goggles, takes it off his head, and sets it carefully on the small table next to where he's standing. The woman's eyes flicker just a little with interest when he does so. Frankly, Jon's close cut kinky hair is matted with sweat from a night of constant vigil and alertness. The woman still hasn't moved a smidgen or said a thing except her fearful whimpers since he first entered the kitchen a moment ago.

The Marine Captain murmurs again that she's safe because he's not here to harm her and that it's frankly been a long night as he unhooks the thick nylon equipment belt around his waist that holds his canteen, sidearm, radio, ammo clips, flashlight, and other things; and then sets it all on the table with the helmet after pulling it off. While he still keeps a close eye on the woman standing before him, Jon once again checks his assault rifle to make sure it's safe but ready, then carefully stands and leans it against the table in a manner that will allow him to quickly grab it if necessary. Realizing that he should check in with his unit, Jon reaches for the radio secured on its velcro shoulder strap, toggles it, then simply says lighthouse secure, before putting it back in its proper place. Next comes the shoulder chest harness that holds more 7.62mm bullet clips and the 3 stun grenades he still has left. She continues to watch in total silence as he unbuckles and slips off the thick upper torso body armor he'd been wearing so he can put it on the table along with his other stuff while casually saying that he hopes she doesn't mind if he lightens his load a bit. As light as the armor is, Jon's still glad to finally be able to take it off because it's hot like his helmet and makes him all sweaty underneath if he has to wear it for too long. Camouflaged like the rest of his outer clothing, the armor is a high quality light weight custom model purchased for him by his parents, rather than the clunky military issue model he would normally have to wear. By now Jon can see that the woman who can't be more than his own age is clearly no threat and is unquestionably beautiful not so much in a traditional centerfold way but in a truly natural one, still he's never let his eyes wander from her or his attention from the surrounding area both inside and outside the building as he continues to watch her carefully.

He asks her kindly what her name is. She whispers almost too quiet to hear that it's Elizabeth. He tells her in a soft voice that his name is Jon, he's from Michigan, and that he's a Captain in the United States Marine Corps who are here on the island to free them from their Russian invaders, causing a quick nod of recognition and just a bare hint of a nervous smile. She murmurs back timidly that the Russians hadn't treated them poorly as a matter of fact, and Jon responds by saying that he's glad to hear it. He for some reason tells the woman that the Russians or her people won't be treated poorly by his people either. The heightened tension caused by the not violent but still frightening night time assault on the village and surrounding area continues to be bleeding off by the moment. It's getting noisier outside as the village begins to wake up to a new day, while inside the lighthouse kitchen there's another form of tension already starting to take the place of the earlier fear and is fast growing between them as the young man and young woman continue to stare at each other. She's breathing hard, maybe from what's left of the dread filled fear of before, and not for the first time Jon notices the heavy mounds of her chest moving up and down under the thin fabric of the simple but what he can now see is a surprisingly appealing looking dress she has on. For sure he thinks this woman is the owner of the large cup bras he saw both on the clothesline and in the

220

bedroom. He sees that the dress frankly outlines everything, and she appears to have little else on underneath it if anything at all, and it becomes clear that it must have been her in the shower that he saw had been used earlier since he can also see that her mid length dark hair is still wet and her feet are bare. Jon can't help but smile when he notices her rosy pink toenails, much like his little sister likes to wear on her own toes.

Jon thinks to himself that this woman would be absolutely gorgeous in the face if she would just allow herself to smile a little, but of course why would she given the current situation from her perspective with some strange uninvited guy standing before her with a gun and grenades? And, she certainly has a nice to look at body he can't help thinking to himself, but he tries to put that out of his mind for the moment as he continues to survey the situation and her. Struggling for something to say that will ease the tension some, he softly tells her she's pretty in a voice meant to be as soothing and gentle as possible, which does cause her to lift the corners of her lips just a bit and her eyes even begin to twinkle some with the knowledge of the effect that she can see that she's now having on him, something that in fact Elizabeth is not entirely unaccustomed to with the men she meets. What is surprising is her own response to that same impact which so often in her past she's resented and resisted. There's a momentary fear that flashes in her eyes that this man could decide to hurt her, but that passes quickly as she can see the man standing before her simply isn't nor could he be that sort of animal. And just as suddenly, there's that unmistakable magnetic tension of two people who inexplicably discover each other in a moment of need as another moment passes between them in a continued and uncomfortable silence. Both frankly are stunned for yet another moment or so with the sudden and undeniable realization of what they know without question is so while they continue to look without daring to blink into each other's eyes, as if he can somehow read her thoughts, and she his.

For Elizabeth's part she too has gotten over the initial shock of the upsetting and even now unexplained chaos outside and the unexpected arrival of this admittedly attractive American Marine and his associates who claim to be here to rescue her and the village from the Russians. And like the man named Jon who's staring at her so obviously now, Elizabeth is absolutely and completely dizzy with the sudden and totally unexpected realization just how much she apparently now wants something she's never in her adult life enjoyed or ever wanted. When that single moment of confusion finally passes, there arrives in its place the touch of a knowing but still somewhat shy smile along with an undeniably coy look that comes into Elizabeth's now blinking eyes as she ever so slowly and ever so casually reaches a hand and begins to unbutton each of the buttons of the dress she has on while she continues to stare deep into Jon's eyes without saying a single word.

Jon's eyes are now riveted on this beautiful creature as he stares without daring to blink at the widening gap in her dress caused by the removal of the buttons she's taken from their holes. Mesmorized by the lovely woman standing before him and now aware of what he too knows he wants, Jon's still a bit confused in a swirl of thoughts as the woman starts to undress with a look in her eyes that clearly indicates to him what she has in mind. And in that widening gap above her working hand, Jon can see a simple gold chain around her neck with the double cross of Russian Orthodoxy. Seeing it causes a flash of sudden worry that this woman could in fact be a Russian sympathizer or worse. But, she's so amazingly beautiful and the smile she now has on her face is riveting if nothing else, so the thought quickly passes and the sudden feeling that wells up in him is so filled with a desire he hasn't felt in years that his mind is closed to anything but her even if Jon is a bit confused at the moment. Jon would later realize upon reflection of the incident how careless and stupid he had been to lose his focus so. And, just as suddenly there's a new even higher but still silent tension in the room between them that's filled by the awareness of what neither of the two young people can or even want to deny as

222

she continues to stand in total silence with her dress almost completely undone and with her shining eyes now on the unmistakably growing bulge between his legs. Jon, in turn, can see her startlingly smooth olive colored flat supple stomach and her button of a belly button that causes him to smile as he remembers how his little sister would call it an "outie" while he continues to stare through the now wide open gap caused by her unbuttoned dress in his own continued silence, still not knowing quite what to say.

He can also see, as he must now admit he's eager to do, that her enormous and full melon shaped and unencumbered breasts are barely disguised by the light grey almost white and very plain but unquestionably appealing muslin cloth dress she has on. And, there's no sign of a bra underneath to hold them with their noticeably plump and dark colored nipples that show through and actually stretch the thin fabric with their own damp spots as they press against it while she stands before him with the still wet ringlets of her dark hair hanging from her head. A quick thought crosses Jon's mind as he looks at Elizabeth's wet hair and dress how much he'd like to join her in that tiny stall. The huge cleavage formed by the abundant mounds of her breasts is undeniably tantalizing as Jon brazenly continues look at it through the opening of her dress. He's quite definitely mesmorized at the view before him and their continued silence is deafening with unspoken words louder than any shouting could be as Elizabeth uses a hand to move the dress further apart just enough to let him see a little more of her impressive bosom as well as one of her nipples, and when she does so Elizabeth still says nothing but arches an eyebrow in a way that says exactly what she means and even expects. There's nothing Jon can say except to allow what amounts to a low moan of imprisoned desire escape his lips while he continues to just stand and stare without so much as a bat of his eye at Elizabeth's now succulent and incredible beauty. All of the atmosphere of fear from before is completely gone now from the room, and all thoughts of the threatening confusion that proceeded are a distant memory as both of the young people

223

are fully aware now that they have a mutual want that won't or can't allow itself to be denied. Gone too is any thought in Jon's mind that this woman could be other than somebody he desperately now wants to be his own.

Elizabeth barely manages to whisper a soft gasp when Jon moves closer and brazenly puts his hands on her for the first time through the fabric of the dress still without saying a thing. She groans more at his touch as Jon's careful not to reach underneath the damp fabric quite yet, but says nothing more as she looks down at him while she reaches and begins to tentatively unlatch and unzip the buckle and zipper of the Marine issued pants he has on while she continues to stare deep and wantingly into his eyes. So, with unblinking silence Elizabeth watches with what can now be described as a shining gleam of need in her eyes while Jon uses his own hands to push the khaki colored camoflaged pants all the way down to his ankles when she finishes unbuckling them, and then reaches for the dark green boxer shorts that are trying with little success to hide his growing desire, to jerk them off down his legs also. At the same time Elizabeth is still surprised and even still a little confused at her sudden want of a man when she's never felt so in her entire life, even when her deceased husband was alive, especially when he was alive she admits to herself.

And, only when his throbbing penis appears after Jon takes his pants and underwear off does Elizabeth respond immediately with a grunt of what has to be described as an obvious and eager anticipation while she continues to stare wide eyed at his erect post like member at the same time she licks her open and spread apart lips with her tongue with what is clearly a doubtless and undeniable carnal hunger. And, with all of its 5 buttons above the waist now undone, Elizabeth without a single word said simply uses a hand to first undo 2 more buttons at her hips then moves her other hand to lift each shoulder strap away so that the dress simply falls sliding off her body to the floor, leaving her entirely naked from head to toe where she stands with the dress crumpled at her feet.

Jon Anderson grunts loudly at the sudden nude sight of her. God she's beautiful, and she didn't even have any panties on he thinks to himself, but then murmurs an immediate mumbled appreciation for her supple blemish free shower fresh and perfectly smooth olive brown body as he continues to stare with his own unblinking eyes. Even the droplets of water still on her breasts from the earlier shower do nothing but add to her beauty. Again, Jon puts his hands on her, this time without the muslin fabric in his way. Elizabeth grunts and moans audibly in response as he tries in vain to wrap his hands around and not so gently squeeze and caress her enormous breasts. There's no denying the woman's pleasure at what he's doing which gives him more confidence as he starts to fondle her. So, with growing eagerness Jon gently pinches each of her delicious looking olive sized nipples that are now getting hard between his fingers from her own increasing excitement, causing the woman to groan even more in the sudden but appreciated erotic pain of his not so subtle touch. Elizabeth then groans some more in the undeniable obvious growing power of her increasing lust as Jon continues to silently twist, pull on, and roll her nipples with those same fingers. He wants to kiss and even bite them, but doesn't think he dares quite yet. And, while this is all taking place their eyes are literally glued to each other without so much as a blink of an eyelash to interrupt the lust filled tension that now exists between the two soon to be lovers.

Jon, still totally silent, gently lifts each heavy breast with a hand to feel the impressive weight of them, causing Elizabeth to purr almost like a kitten who's experiencing great pleasure while she watches him do so in what amounts now to her own continuing shy silence. She, even though now suddenly shy and still silent at Jon's brazen touch, does continue to stare with undisguised tongue licking approval at his hard shaft of a member and the two curly hair encased more than golf ball size testicles hanging below in their dark and fleshy sack as he continues to fondle Elizabeth's bosom with his own continued silence. By now both are breathing deep and hard from their mutual built up desire. Jon almost says something, but doesn't.

But, Jon does continue to stare into the depths of Elizabeth's lovely gray brown eyes as he slowly moves his hands from where he's been fondling her full breasts to her not too thick waist so that he can lift her up onto the counter behind. She helps him do so by lifting herself up as if Elizabeth now knows what he has in mind, which of course she does and fully approves of without any doubt or confusion. And, when Elizabeth does manage to perch herself on the edge of the counter, she immediately spreads her legs wide apart for him, which allows Jon to see and look at the dark colored curly hair of her muff and the succulently rich pink lips of her vagina for the first time. It's time for him to lick his lips now. He can also see that she's already wet from excitement. And, by now there's no question that the two of them are totally and absolutely oblivious to any of the goings on around them, they are so focused now on their mutual pent up need and lust filled desire.

Elizabeth again moans with anticipation and now has a dreamy look in her eyes, but still says nothing when Jon puts his hands on the smooth skin of the top of her spread apart thighs to gently rub up and down on her as he moves to stand even closer between her legs. And, Jon can feel the strength of this island woman's legs under the supple olive brown skin when he does so. He also notes that Elizabeth's lower legs are unshaved, which somehow excites him even more. Elizabeth then gasps loudly in immediate response when Jon moves closer and first touches her silky wetness with the hunger swollen head of his erect penis, and then she gasps even louder, crying out even, when Jon suddenly presses hard against her and pushes himself deep inside the tightness of her. It has in fact been a long time since Elizabeth has experienced a man in such a way, so the immediate pain of it overwhelms her at first, but that feeling is quickly put aside by the stretched fullness she suddenly feels. And, for a reason as yet unidentified in her mind, she welcomes the feeling in a manner she never allowed herself to do with her husband. Jon continues to hold Elizabeth's legs with his hands as he then begins to move in and out of her with increasing six inch thrusts while Elizabeth also begins to grunt in a perfect

226

rhythm to it as she tries to lean back on her hands for support against the top of the counter that she's sitting on while Jon stands before her and pounds against her harder and harder by using his pumping naked backside as the pendulum of his piston like thrusts.

Finally, Jon moves his hands from the top of Elizabeth's thighs to put them squarely on the cheeks of her naked bottom so he can hold her for better leverage, making it so that he can jam his penis even deeper inside her and make love to her even harder, as if making love is in fact what the two lust filled young people are doing can be called just then. In the fog of his carnal need, Jon does take note of the round firmness of her not entirely narrow butt in his hands. In reality what they are doing now on and against the kitchen counter isn't lovemaking at all, it's unabashedly raw and hungry sex, and both Elizabeth and Jon know it without having to ask the other. Elizabeth gasps again louder when Jon eagerly jams harder and deeper inside her when he becomes increasingly excited, and she wraps her own strong legs around his slim waist as if to grip and hold him tight against her and not let him go, and then Elizabeth literally throws her head back so that her naked melon sized breasts begin to bounce heavily, as does her gold necklace, to the even more hurried rhythm of their lust filled sex. Elizabeth's grunts are more like cries now as Jon holds her naked butt in his hands while he continues to bang against her with an almost machine gun like rhythm at the same time Elizabeth holds him against herself with her legs and thighs while she pushes back against him with her own eager loins.

And then, when it's clear that his climax is fast approaching, Jon throws his own head back in the blinding lust of his growing ecstasy while he pounds this gorgeous native American Indian woman even harder, causing Elizabeth to cry out her own lust filled gasping cry that's even louder than the one before. And finally, Jon literally jams the shaft of his penis as deep inside Elizabeth as he can get it while he holds her tight at the same time he throws his head back even further to announce the arrival of a spewing orgasmic climax. Elizabeth cries out just as loudly in response to it and even manages to gasp in her own head thrown back ecstasy as she quivers the lips of her continuing need around Jon's penis as if she doesn't want to let him go, which of course she doesn't. Jon's not sure, but he thinks the woman might have had her own orgasm. She will later admit to her unexpected lover that she did in fact do so.

Still not a word passes between them still as Jon and Elizabeth's climactic eruptions finally stop and Jon continues to stand silent before her for a long moment before he slowly pulls his still hard penis out of Elizabeth's vagina. Elizabeth watches him do so without a single word with the length of it still wet and slick from both her juices and his cum. Still breathing hard from the just finished effort and excitement Elizabeth licks her lips again as she continues to stare at Jon's member which has so recently been inside her with what is now a shy but undeniably satisfied smile of appreciation. And then suddenly Elizabeth whispers almost too quiet to hear, "thank you."

"No maim, I must thank you," Jon murmurs with a look in his eye that says so much more than he's a man who's just been sexually satiated by a woman he doesn't even know as he pulls his pants and shorts back up to cover himself.

"Stay with me," Elizabeth shyly murmurs as she steps off the counter and puts her own dress back in place before she uses a hand to straighten her still damp hair a little while she continues to stand before Jon as she slowly buttons each of the buttons back where they belong. Even while saying it, Elizabeth is shocked to hear herself do so.

And suddenly, Jon moves close and takes her breasts into his hands through the dress again with an ungentle eagerness as he kisses Elizabeth wildly on her full lips for the very first time. Elizabeth quickly moves against him in response as they continue to kiss and willingly share their tongues with a mutual hunger to experience the other, which seems to force Jon to take his hands away from Elizabeth's chest and wrap them around her body to hug her tight as they do. Quickly but not unexpectedly as one might recall later, there are immediate and mutual moans of the repeat of their mutual desire amongst the hungry mouth filled kisses as Elizabeth eagerly presses herself against Jon and he her. Jon's getting hard with renewed want again, and it's obvious that Elizabeth knows and wants it.

"Stay with me," Elizabeth murmurs again, louder this time, between even more eager kisses filled with the wanting and not to be denied desire.

With his mind slowly coming to some bit of calm following is recent lust filled excitement, Jon knows without any doubt that he's being remiss in his duties and without question should leave this woman immediately and return to his unit. Only a glimmer of his sense of duty has returned to his consciousness as he continues to stare at the gorgeous creature he's just made love to so passionately, but it's still enough to make him realize he should go. There would be consequences of course and a most likely reprimand if not more if he reported his transgression to his superiors he knows. At the same time there's also the momentary concern that his unit might become worried about his status and actually come looking for him. But, her murmured requested urging immediately stops those thoughts from going further than they do.

For her part, as stunned as Elizabeth is about what has just happened and what she's done with this admittedly attractive man she doesn't even know, she knows one thing for sure, which is that she wants him to stay with her, maybe even forever as astonishing as the completely untoward thought might be. Never in her entire life has Elizabeth remotely felt like this towards any man, but whether or not what she feels can be called love as yet or not, what she does know for sure is that she wants him again in that same way more than anything she's ever wanted in her life.

Still, Jon says nothing in response and neither does Elizabeth say more, but instead he, with a strength he would later find surprising when he thinks back about the experience, quickly buckles his pants back in place before he simply picks her up in his arms so he can carry her out of the kitchen and up the narrow stairs to her bedroom, where he lays her down on the overstuffed bed before falling on top of her with even more wild almost crazed kisses and caresses to her face and lips. Underneath the weight of the big strong man Elizabeth does nothing more than moan loudly amongst her own hungry kisses in a voice that's no longer shy at all that she needs him again. And, Jon murmurs with his lips still on hers how he so dearly wants her again.

Now lying under the man that she still doesn't even know but so wants a second time, Elizabeth struggles in a rush to unbutton the military issued khaki colored long sleeved shirt Jon has on. For the first time she notices the captains emblem and wonders to herself what rank it represents. She wants him naked this time, and to make him so she literally jerks the shirt off his shoulders and throws it to the floor along with his undershirt before turning her attention to Jon's britches where his zipper is still undone. But before she does Elizabeth eagerly caresses and kisses at Jon's naked chest with her lips and hands in what seems like an insatiate hunger as she licks at both his smooth skin and curly chest hair. When Elizabeth finishes doing so Jon helps her get off his pants, his boots and military issue dark khaki socks, and his boxer style underwear, before he returns to quickly remove Elizabeth's dress once again. And, it too is soon lying on the floor next to the bed with all of the other discarded clothing, as the lust filled eager young couple are kissing and groping each other with mindlessly wild passion amongst their intermingled naked bodies. All Jon has on now are his stainless steel plated dog tags while Elizabeth is adorned only in her precious gold necklace.

Jon's rock hard once again, but this time Elizabeth purrs with open pleasure without a hint of shyness as she holds him in her hand. There's no longer the confusion of before about her desire to have him inside her. Jon eagerly tells the beautiful woman now lying next to him on the bed that he wants to make love to her awesome breasts at the same time he makes love to her again, and Elizabeth giggles in her undenied desire and pleasure to let Jon do so as she hurries to climb on top of his body. While giggling at the same time Elizabeth then puts the fullness of her enormous ample breasts on Jon's face as if to tease him, and their huge melon like size almost feel like they might smother him as they literally wrap around his face while Elizabeth also wiggles herself onto him with an eagerness she doesn't bother to hide. Elizabeth groans in the renewed pleasure of it as Jon fills her up again with his shaft at the same time he's ravaging the deep walls of Elizabeth's cleavage with his lips and tongue, and his hands also. Elizabeth throws her head back and literally gasps out loud that she's never in her life had or enjoyed it like this as she begins to move up and down on Jon's shaft while she also takes luxury in the way he's now fondling at her breasts with his hands as he once again makes desire filled love to her.

Like only moments before in the kitchen, Jon and Elizabeth's lovemaking is hard and hungry as Elizabeth is determined to possess this lovely man in her bed at the same time that Jon eagerly gropes at her luscious and wanting body as the necklace around Elizabeth's neck is now bouncing up and down along with her heavy breasts in perfect rhythm to their urgent lovemaking. Neither worry in the least that the aging bed cries out loudly in the squeaking complaint of its inner springs while the 2 lovers do so in a mindless lust filled abandon. And, determined to finish what they've so wantingly started, Jon gently pushes Elizabeth aside off his body and rolls over on top of her so that he can then use his pumping naked cheeks as the thrusting pendulum of his boundless desire at the same time Elizabeth wraps both her legs and her arms around him while she humps him back with a matching eagerness. Too is the combined lust of Jon's orgasm as he fills Elizabeth again with his spewing eruption at the same time Elizabeth pushes herself against him as if determined to squeeze out all she can receive. This time there's no mistaking her climax since Jon can not only feel it, but Elizabeth also thanks him for it amongst more wild and eager kisses of pleasure.

Finally after it's all over once again, Jon Anderson, Marine Captain and American liberator, literally slumps on top of Elizabeth Quviariatukuluk, St. Lawrence island maiden, in apparent hard breathing exhaustion as they lay naked together on the bed in the aftermath of their twice realized mutual lust filled hunger. Their bodies are sweaty from all of the recent physical effort even though it's not at all hot in the room, and the sweet musky smell of their sex waffles in the air of the small bedroom where they lay. "You've more than likely made me pregnant Captain Jon Anderson," Elizabeth murmurs in Jon's ear as she continues to hold him in her arms. Not knowing quite what to say in response to the suggestion, Jon simply nuzzles the woman he's just made love to before admitting that duty calls and he must get dressed and return to his unit before they get too worried and come looking for him.

Without doubt, Jon's mind is in an admittedly confused swirl as he hurries to dress and leave the lighthouse so he can report back to his unit. Never could he have expected to have done anything remotely as such as what he's done. "Jesus, did I rape this woman?" he wonders to himself, but has to admit that she surely doesn't act like a girl who's been violated the way she kisses him before he leaves and begs him to return to her. "God, she's beautiful and so full of want," he can't help but think as he walks from the stone house, and knows for a fact that he's never been with a woman before who's anything like her. And, as he walks away from the 3 story stone lighthouse, he turns to see her still standing in the doorway, so waves back at her when she waves at him. And then, he remembers what she said to him after they made love that second time, that she might be pregnant. "Holly shit, wonder if she really is?" he asks himself. For Christ's sake Anderson, you have the 2 regulation condoms in your damned field kit, he muses to himself. Not once with any of the nurses or the couple of locals he's been intimate with through the years has he been so irresponsible as to not wear

232

protection, so why he asks himself did he not even think of doing so today with this girl, he wonders?

Back with his unit, Jon reports that things are "four square" with the lighthouse without of course mentioning the incident, and when asked about the gal who supposedly lives there, tells his Sergeant adjutant that she is definitely pretty, but when the man points out that one of the men in the unit who could see the large cup size of the bras hanging on the clothesline through a long distance spotting scope, Jon suggests he hadn't noticed how big the woman's bosom might have been. Not quite sure he entirely believes his Captain's claim, the man asks a bit pointedly what took him so long at the lighthouse, only to be told by Jon that all of the time he had taken after reconnoitering the place had been spent talking because the native woman had insisted she make tea for him before he left. It's pretty obvious to a Sergeant who both knows his Captain friend well and whose job it is to be aware of and understand what his unit leader is thinking and expects that Jon is leaving something out and not telling him the entire story. And besides, it's not really hard to notice a couple of odd things about his friend's attire at the moment, first that for some "unexplained reason" the buttons on the Captain's uniform shirt are in the wrong holes all of a sudden, something he's quite sure he would have noticed and pointed out had they been so earlier. The other thing he notices because elite Marines are trained to notice such fine details are that the tie strings on the Captain's combat boots have obviously been untied and retied since he can see that the mud from before has been clearly displaced on them. Also trained to piece together loose information it doesn't take the unit Sergeant a whole lot of consideration to wonder about the significance of a long time taken, buttons inexplicably out of place on a uniform shirt, and boots that have most likely been removed and put back on, and come up with the proper conclusion that the man standing before him has more than likely taken or had his clothing removed. "Holy fucking shit, the man thinks to himself when the obvious flashes across his mind,

233

certainly this straight laced by the book officer hasn't been out cavorting with the natives?

At the same time Captain Jon Anderson is still in what can only be described as a personal state of an almost fog like confusion based on the shocking but admittedly pleasing events of the last hour and twenty five minutes. Jesus, he can't help but think to himself, there's a beautifully gorgeous woman up in that lighthouse right now who might be carrying his child and he barely even knows her name for God's sakes. Likewise, Jon knows or at least suspects since he also has been well trained to observe such things, that Master Sergeant Dennis McKee, not only isn't buying his wane explanation about why he took so long to check out the lighthouse but clearly suspects the nature of what really happened back there. Dennis and he have served together now for 3 years and not only have shared more than a few local beers during their off duty hours, but have become really good friends, so it's not hard for Jon to see what's on the Master Sergeant's mind at the moment.

"Alright Dennis, tell me what you're thinking," demands Jon as he goes to the coffee pot to pour him a cup of stale but still hot coffee.

"It's not my place to say or question the Captain's actions sir," responds a man who doesn't really want to counter what his superior has told him.

"Oh come on man, we're alone. So, give it to me," demands Jon in an even more determined voice.

"Well sir, Jon (when Anderson gives him the look that indicates this is a damned personal conversation and not about rank), let me just say that it's first of all not at all like the Captain to linger so long while reconnoitering such a small building, and well given how I've noticed how the Captain's shirt buttons are out of place now that he's returned from his mission when they weren't before he left this morning, and how the strings on his boots have obviously been untied and retied since the mud has been clearly displaced all the way up and down the loops that

234

would seem to indicate that said boots have been taken off, and since I know for a fact that the person who apparently occupies that lighthouse is the most beautiful girl in town according to everybody I've spoken to, I have concluded sir that you were doing more than just taking a look around that place and talking, sir," says Sergeant Dennis McKee in one long breathless sentence.

"Is that all Sergeant," Jon says with a not quite angry look on his face.

"That would be all sir. Far be it for this measly Master Sergeant to question or judge the activities of the Captain, sir!" nearly shouts his friend.

And, the truth is that this entire conversation and it's on the surface serious and by command nature is more act than reality between two men who have shared more than life should share over the past few years. Jon and Dennis McKee have not only shared some beers and frankly shared a couple of women here and there, they have also shared the heartache of seeing men they know and care about die right before their eyes. Their respect and friendship because of that very fact runs deeper than almost any in comparison, so in a moment of honest sincerity it's not difficult at all for the two men to be openly frank with each other.

"Christ Dennis that woman back there is gorgeous, and I can't tell you exactly how it happened, but it happened so fast. Jesus man, one minute I was checking out the damned place for Russians, and the next I had my pants down to my ankles banging this gal who's sitting on the counter eagerly banging me back," gasps Jon in open admission to his friend.

"For God's sake Jon, you aren't saying that you raped that poor gal are you?" gasps a stunned man who while he might have suspected in general what his superior might have been engaged in, could have never thought this upright young man from Michigan could do such a thing.

"Oh hell no! Well, at least I don't think so Dennis. It all happened so fast. Shit, really one minute I was trying to calm her down and the next we were screwing each other. But no, I'm sure it wasn't rape. She asked me to stay with her not once but twice, and when we made love a second time up in her bedroom she held me like she didn't want to let me go," claims a man who is now focusing on and trying to analyze for the first time what really happened between him and the woman he still barely knows.

"Well, that's good at least Jon. The men say she's a hottie," observes the friend who now excepts his friend and superior's explanation.

"Oh she's a hottie alright. That I can tell you for sure," says Captain Jon Anderson. He then adds, "but you know, there's something really different about her Dennis?" It's more of a question to himself than a statement to the Sergeant.

"Should I be reading something into this sir," says the man with a suddenly official tone in his voice.

"Not at all Master Sergeant, that will be all," says Jon in mock seriousness at the same time he salutes his command inferior.

Jon says nothing to his friend about a potential pregnancy, nor does he say anything outright how truly smitten he is by this admittedly beautiful and absolutely exotic woman he just made love with not 10 minutes after he met her and before he even barely knew her name. Hell, it's not like he's not had sex before with gals he's only just met, but hell they have all been women in bars for the most part out looking for the same bit of consensual fun as he. This gal just didn't seem like that at all. It was almost as if she had been doing it for the first time as he thinks back on it, but that couldn't be since he clearly didn't break her hymen as far as he could tell that first time on the counter and there was no blood. God she was eager, and so full of love and emotion, especially that second time on her bed. "God damn, if the poor thing is really pregnant, what the hell can he do?" Jon Anderson thinks as he pours himself another

236

cup of stale coffee.   And, "What would his sister, Evelyn, do?"
he wonders as he takes a sip of the hot liquid.

22

Interlude

That very same day, after he finishes his regular duty shift and takes a mind clearing shower and puts on a freshly pressed set of khaki camouflage pattern greens, Jon makes to return trek back down to the lighthouse to visit the woman he made love to not even 12 hours before. While he's quite confident now that he in fact didn't rape or force himself on her at all, he's not so sure that he isn't guilty of taking advantage of the woman in her moment of vulnerability in a manner that's both unprofessional and unacceptable as a United States Marine. And for that reason Captain Jon Anderson has decided that he owes Elizabeth an honest and heartfelt apology, and also for that reason he has in his hand an admittedly fake bouquet of carnation like flowers to give her as a peace offering (there are no fresh flowers available on the island). And, he has to admit that on his way down the path to the lighthouse and especially up the narrow walkway to her door, there's more than a little angst about what he might run into and face when she sees him. Hell, she would have every reason to be furious with a man who so obviously and even brutally took advantage of her, and he surely wouldn't blame her at all if she either slapped his face or slammed her door in it the moment she sees him. At the same time part of him hopes beyond a reasonable hope that the woman will literally jump into his arms with excitement when he greets her, something that Jon decides sadly is more than unlikely.

Elizabeth, on the other hand, has spent the entire day since this morning with some of the same confusion as her new and unexpected lover, but not quite the same worried and swirling confusion as he. Of course, she too had been shocked and even confused by what had so unexpectedly happened between them, more so in her case since from the very beginning she'd taken no joy in being asked to have sex with her former husband so has no history of intimate bliss from the experience. Shocked too because of the erotic memory of being taken right on the counter of her kitchen in such a irreverent and brazen manner. But, like many women who are in so close touch with and have an inner confidence about their feelings, Elizabeth knows almost without thinking about it that she's already in love with the admittedly very attractive man she barely even knows, and she's pretty sure that Jon has feelings for her too that go beyond the mere physical aspects of their just begun relationship. There's no knowing of course whether or not she's really pregnant with his child as she had suggested to him, and it wouldn't matter at all in any case if she is in fact, but Elizabeth can't help but think that day how much she hopes her Captain will come back to be with her, and hopes she didn't scare him away by telling him her suspicion. She's so excited about the prospect that he might come back in fact, that Elizabeth does think about and is tempted to go speak to her mother about her experience and feelings, but she ultimately decides not to. Things have settled down to about normal by late afternoon when Elizabeth decides to make herself a simple dinner of pickled fish and vegetables after she finishes her daily duties in the lighthouse, but has to admit that she's disappointed that she never saw a glimpse of her lover the many times she peered outside hoping to do so. And then, she sees him walking up the path to her house with what are obviously newly cleaned and pressed clothes with a bundle of flowers in his hand, and she can do no more than cry with pleasure inside as she watches him approach.

"Sorry to interrupt you maim," says an obviously uncomfortable man when greeted after knocking on Elizabeth's door.

"No need Jon - or Captain - you aren't interrupting at all. Please do come in," Elizabeth murmurs shyly before inviting the man she's so glad to see into her home.

"Thank you maim, I brought you some flowers since I feel that I need to apologize for my actions this morning. I was completely out of line and I don't know what came over me maim. I've never done anything remotely like that," murmurs a clearly embarrassed Marine who is searching for how the woman before him thinks as he hands her the flowers.

"Jon - may I call you Jon Captain (nod) - you don't owe me any apology. It's I who should feel embarrassed since I too have never done anything of the sort, but I don't Jon because I took true pleasure in the experience to be honest," murmurs Elizabeth with the same searching look in her eyes.

"So, you don't feel like I forced myself on you or took advantage of you maim?" says an almost relieved Marine Captain.

"First of all as lovers I think you can feel free to call me by my first name instead of "maim" and second please feel free to take advantage of me in that same most enjoyable manner any time you like kind sir," says a woman with a twinkling look in her eyes who is now confident enough to speak her mind even though she can readily see the surprise on the face of the Marine standing before her. She then, as the man continues to stand in a moment of total silence as he processes what he's just been told, asks Jon if he might stay and have a bit of dinner with her as they continue to talk.

"I really shouldn't maim, I would be intruding," says a clearly uneasy Jon Anderson.

"First of all Captain Jon Anderson, if you call me maim one more time I do promise that I will never invite you to my bed again. Now, sit down and have some dinner with me before I decide how crazy it is that I've clearly fallen in love with you," demands a woman who now has the glow of a woman who knows what she wants and sees it before her eyes.

"Yes ma... or yes Elizabeth," stutters a man who has been entirely stunned by what he's heard the woman just say.

Elizabeth takes only a few minutes to rustle up more pickled fish, bread, and vegetables for her guest, and over an unhurried dinner the two of them begin the process of getting to know each other. Elizabeth pesters Jon about his background in Michigan and his experience as a Marine officer with true interest and excitement. She then tells him her story as a native American woman growing up in her village, including her tragic marriage experience with her dead husband and all of the physical and emotional heartache that went along with it. She admits openly to not taking any pleasure at all in her intimate obligations with her husband and that she's been sexually abstinent since his death, not because of any social mores or obligations, but because she's had no interest, that is until this morning. At the mention of this morning, Jon immediately makes an effort to once again apologize for his untoward actions, but is told in no uncertain terms by the woman sitting across the table from him that she might resent his desire to apologize if it meant he didn't take pleasure in what they'd experienced together.

"Hell no Elizabeth! Don't get me wrong! God I loved what we did this morning! Maybe more than I ever have! But, I just need to know that you are fine with it so we can move on is all," says a man who's still caught up in the emotions of his concern about the impropriety of what he's done.

"You want to know how fine I feel about what we shared this morning Captain? Well, let me tell you how I feel, which is that I liked and enjoyed it so much that I'm hoping that you might agree to go upstairs and do it with me some more right now. That's how I feel," murmurs a woman who now has what amounts to a challenging glare in her eyes.

"Are you sure," whispers a still hesitant man in a husky voice so low it can hardly be heard as he reaches across the table to take her hand in his.

"Do you love me Jon Anderson?" Elizabeth asks pointedly.

"Yes, I'm pretty sure I do," murmurs back the Marine Captain.

"Then take me upstairs and show me that you do. And after that I want you to show me again, and again, and again, murmurs Elizabeth as she squeezes the hand of the man she knows she loves so unexpectedly.

"Lights out are at 10pm," Jon observes in a quiet voice.

"You aren't going to have to worry about that Captain Jon Anderson because you will be sleeping with me," proclaims an openly defiant woman who is now determined to get what she wants.

The next morning, when Jon does finally return to his unit's temporary quarters in the village following a night of sleep robbing intimacy and some more even earlier this morning, Master Sergeant Dennis McKee greets him with a knowing look in his eyes as he says, "long night Captain?"

"You could say that Sergeant," offers a blurry eyed Jon Anderson.

"A hell of a lot of woman you have there from what I hear Jon," observes a sympathetic friend.

"You can't begin to imagine my friend. I'll be crazy if I don't grab her and hold on while I've got the chance. But, ya know I just don't know," whispers a man who is still trying to come to grips with his unexpected feelings.

"What the hell man! Do you care about her?" asks the Sergeant.

"Absolutely without question! But, Jeeze Dennis, it's all been so quick and all. It just doesn't seem really right," moans Jon Anderson to his friend.

"You know what Captain, if you think you care about and even love the woman you'd better ask what's holding you back, because my friend in the 3 years I've known you I've never seen

242

you so tied up in knots over any other gal you've just slept with," observes a very frank Dennis McKee.

So, with that well delivered knowledge and advice in mind, when Jon sees Elizabeth on the street in the village later that afternoon, he grabs her gently by the arm and quickly guides her to the privacy of a narrow alleyway to tell her in a rushed but quiet voice how much he loves and wants to be with her, maybe even for the rest of their lives. Elizabeth responds by literally gushing almost like a teenage girl with her first love, which in most ways Jon really is, as she hugs and presses herself against him. They stand and kiss wildly for a couple of moments before realizing that if they continue to do so they could be discovered doing what young lovers often do as unproblematic as being so would be.

Jon and Elizabeth would spend nineteen blissful sex and love filled days and eighteen nights together in the lighthouse before it's finally time for him to officially turn the village over once again to the civilian authorities and leave with his men to return to their base in Nome, Alaska as he must do. And every bit as much as the sex and lovemaking, it would be their mutual curiosity about the world and wondrous conversations concerning their ideals and beliefs that would continue to meld their feelings for each other during that time together. And, it hadn't at all taken Jon's men very long to realize and understand what was happening to their leader at the lighthouse between he and the undeniably beautiful young lady, but all in the unit quickly approved of the goings on as well, especially since their Master Sergeant outright ordered them to do so. To them all except for Dennis of course, their leader and commander has always been kind of the stoic by the books sort, so all of the men in the unit were glad to see him find a form of happiness that allowed him to let his hair down just a little.

In the village itself things were starting to get fully back to normal as the Marine special forces unit, along with the recovery advisors sent from Washington who followed on their heels, assessed and determined what the situation was and what would be needed to get things back to where they were before the arrival of the Russian invaders almost 61/2 months before. And, something that was appreciated by all at the time and something that in fact would serve to help normalize things with the Russians far down the line, was that the Russian soldiers had in fact acted with complete and total professionalism and compassionate understanding in all their relations with the island population, both during their occupation and after the arrival of the elite Marine force. This was stressed often and repeatedly to their liberators by the village elders and the entire population of Gambell, and they insisted to their Marine "rescuers" that the Russian soldiers be treated with the same respect.

That said, once the village and island as a whole had been quickly secured by Jon Anderson's Marine unit following a very short and not very violent firefight dominated by rubber bullets and high tech visual and hearing disruptors which resulted in only a single accidental death, the near 500 Russian soldiers on the island had been rounded up and held under loose guard (if in fact it can even be called a real security guard operation) in the large hanger type building on the military installation they had been constructing just outside of Gambell. It didn't take long for the Marines to realize that things would not be difficult as their Russian prisoners made it absolutely clear that they intended to cooperate and make things as easy as possible for the Americans. The two groups would actually become pretty friendly with each other before it would eventually be time for the Russians to leave the island in the near future. Relations between the American and Russian soldiers on the island are so good in fact in a matter of days that general Arkady Islonovich Kamanisky is even allowed to return to and live openly with his native mistress once again until it's time for him to leave the island and return to Russia. More amazing, off duty Marines could at times be seen hanging out with their Russian counterparts both in town and at the bar once the sequester of the Speznet soldiers was discontinued.

244

Over a filtered cigarette and oversized shot of decent Russian Vodka taken from his personal stash the crusty Russian Speznet general would in fact tell his young American counterpart one day how ironic it is that "we soldiers have to go out and risk our lives to implement ridiculous policies made by out of touch leaders with limp penis's that no longer work who sit in comfort far away from the dire results of their inexplicable decisions." The American Lt. Colonel can't but agree with his Russian counterpart's assessment of the situation, not at all able to ignore the sexual reference as it so obviously applies to this amorous man who is openly sleeping with one of Gambell's native citizens, then wonders along with him how the hell they ever got to this point. Lust for power, greed, and stupidity offers the Russian as he makes a jolly toast and takes another drink of Vodka. And then adds more seriously than might be thought, "we're both led by impotent men who spend far too much time lusting for power than lusting for their women."

Elizabeth is in fact already pregnant as she so accurately predicted that very first day in her lighthouse bedroom, but even though she can already feel the remarkable changes taking place in her body she fears telling her American Marine lover that she actually is for fear that he will totally freak out before he has to leave. She not only worries how he might react to the idea of being a father but really has concern that if she tells him he might do something entirely stupid like go AWOL from his unit and insist on staying with her. At least the being a father part of Elizabeth's fear for how Jon Anderson might react to the idea of being a father is entirely unwarranted as it would turn out much later, but her fear of the latter is all too true which keeps her silent with her secret knowledge.

It's only days after his arrival before Jon and Elizabeth are clearly and quite openly in love with each other, and all in the village can tell it, and most if not all are happy with the fact, especially Elizabeth's mother. When not at work with his duties as a Marine or simply being together immersed in talking about their thoughts about the world around them Jon spends virtually all of his time with Elizabeth making love, wanting to make love, or living in the bliss of having made love with the woman he's so entirely smitten by and becoming committed to. The lust filled sex in the beginning has quickly transitioned itself to intimate and unabashedly passionate lovemaking which both find so incredibly fulfilling and blissful that they can hardly get enough of it, and as things have settled down on the island there's much free time for the Marine Captain to partake in he and his lover's favorite activity. They learn quickly, in fact, that they must lock the entry door of the lighthouse while making love during the day if they expect not to be walked in on and interrupted. Never has the door been locked before, so most are fully aware of the reason why it now is. Soon, those who do approach the building at certain times will note a new sign on the door that announces that the resident is "currently indisposed." Before Elizabeth, Jon Anderson has only had a couple of what he has to admit were pretty unsatisfactory long term experiences with women besides the regular one night stands any man his age and situation might choose to partake in, and as we know Elizabeth's experience before Jon was only with her deceased husband which by her own admission had been pretty traumatic (not really his fault). And, that mutual dissatisfaction of their previous experiences only serve to make their current enjoyment only more pleasant and enjoyable.

The happy couple are laying together after yet again making passionate love to each other in their love nest one day as Elizabeth takes luxury in the finely chiseled body of her naked Marine lover. She gently rubs a hand over the tightly muscled chest of what can only be described as an excellent example of the black Afro-American male, and a perfect example of United States Marine training. She moves her hand to one of his charcoal colored almost black nipples where she uses her playful fingers to make it hard again. Elizabeth leans over and kisses it before she licks at him with her tongue as she murmurs her savory pleasure at the salty taste of his skin. And, as she moves her hand across his sculptured body, there literally isn't a hint of blubber to be found anywhere, and in fact Jonathan has only a mere 4% of body fat in comparison to his near perfect 6'2" tall and 180 pound frame. He's handsome by all measure with classic black American features, and best of all Jon is all hers, Elizabeth thinks to herself. It's Jon who will take Elizabeth out of her happy reverie by saying:

"We both know that I'm going to have to leave soon with the rest of my unit," he literally moans softly as he continues to hold Elizabeth in his arms while they lay naked together on her bed.

"I know you will my love and I hate the fact that you do," Elizabeth whispers with an unquestionably sad timber to her voice as she once again brushes his uncovered chest with her lips.

It's a warm sunny day outside, but Jon and Elizabeth have spent most of the afternoon in her second story bedroom making love over and over again as if they simply can't get enough of each other, which of course they can't. Jon has used condoms ever since that first day, as they've agreed that a pregnancy at this point would be best avoided for everybody, even though Elizabeth is more than pretty sure without admitting the fact to her lover that the decision is more than likely already too late.

"I love you my darling," whispers Elizabeth.

"Oh baby, I love you so much," murmurs Jon Anderson as he nuzzles against Elizabeth's naked breast. "Why don't we get married before I leave?" he suddenly whispers.

"Oh my darling, I could want nothing more, but we both know it would be the wrong thing to do right now," Elizabeth responds as she raises herself up to lean on her elbow while speaking to her lover of nearly three weeks now. "You have to go back with your unit, and you have another full year and a half before your current tour is up, so getting married right now would be frankly irresponsible and we both know it," the woman Jon now lovingly calls "Lizzy" murmurs with tears streaming down her eyes. "Besides, we both know that my father especially will want to make a big deal out of his only daughter's wedding," she adds.

247

Jon reaches for and again lovingly fondles the heavy naked breast that he's come to know so well over the past few weeks, as he painfully agrees with what Elizabeth is saying, but then says that he has every intention of resigning from the Marines and returning at the end of his current tour of duty to be with her. She uses a hand to rub and stroke at the thick black hair of Jon's Marine crew cut as she kisses and speaks to him.

"You would give up your Marine career just like that," Elizabeth wonders as she strokes the chest of the man she now loves more than anything?

"I would in an instant because I love you so very much," Jon murmurs back before kissing Elizabeth. "And, I do promise you that I will be back one day very soon to marry you and make a hoard of children with you my love," whispers Jon Anderson before yet another long kiss.

"Make love to me again Jon Anderson," is all Elizabeth Quviariatukuluk says as she moves to climb on top of him.

"You are one insatiably horny Indian woman Elizabeth Quviariatukuluk," whispers the Captain of the Marine Corps as he lays back on the bed to eagerly give the woman he loves what she so clearly wants yet again before it's time for them to finally quit, get dressed, and make them some dinner.

During the month that Jon Anderson stayed with Elizabeth in her lighthouse residence, when not making love or sleeping naked together in her cozy bed, they set up housekeeping when Jon didn't have duties and responsibilities to get done with his unit as if already a married man and wife, as Jon helped Lizzy do the lighthouse chores, clean and straighten up around the house, helped her cook meals (he was unexpectedly accomplished in doing so she discovers), and even goes fishing with some of the men of the village a few times. It's clear to everybody that they are in love and are seen and accepted as a couple by all in the village. They hug and kiss openly when Jon's not on duty, and do so even a few times when he is when both are sure nobody is looking.

Over that same time Elizabeth and Jon spend literally hours and hours in conversation as they sit watching the rising or setting sun while they talk about their respective heritage. Lizzy is without question interested and curious about Jon's background as a Black American and the fact that he actually hails from former African slaves who were treated brutally much of the time by their masters. She does in fact know enough about American history surrounding the Civil War to be able to appreciate what she's told. But, it's Elizabeth's native Indian and ancient Siberian heritage and traditions that they talk about most. Jon is literally spellbound by her stories about an ancient culture that's literally thousands upon thousands of years old and often voices that for the first time in his life he sees a "quieter" and gentler lifestyle with purpose that he actually thinks he can get his arms around and appreciate as something in his own future. But, in spite of their mutual desire that it be put off or never really happen, the day of Jon's departure does finally arrive.

There was one surprising and unexpected event during the almost 30 days the Marine EC5 Special Operations Unit was on St. Lawrence island when President Jeb Bush himself made an unannounced visit to Gambell village one morning. The first indication that there was something odd or out of the ordinary happening was the sudden appearance of a Navy MH53E Sea Dragon helicopter with 2 fully armed AH-64 Apache Longbow gunships in the low skies on the edge of the village. Even in the Sea Dragon as it approached were two soldiers armed with menacing looking machine guns standing in the open side doors. As if the 3 choppers weren't enough to spur interest and curiosity, there were also the 2 hovering F-35B vertical take-off and landing capable stealth fighters in the not far off attendance with the helicopters. Those who saw the helicopters land in the flat scrub next to the village with the fighters hovering in the near distance simply assumed that it must be some very important general come to see the progress being made by the Marines. That thought continued with the growing crowd of curious onlookers as first the two armed machine gun toting guards then a gentleman leaped out of the side door of the Sea Dragon helicopter that was about to land who was dressed in a classic helmeted khaki uniform with no rank patches on his chest or sleeves. He also didn't carry a gun they all noticed as the guards at his side took in all that surrounded them. And, it wasn't until he approached the villagers with a huge smile and his hand held out in greeting with several more well armed soldier types nervously fanning out behind him after themselves jumping out of the copter, that someone in the crowd finally recognized the President and shouted to his friends. Quickly, as President Jeb Bush continued to shake hands with those standing all around, the rest of the villagers were alerted to their esteemed guest with a ton of shouted excitement. And, it took only several more minutes before a microphone and speakers could be set up so that the President can address the villagers and welcome them back to the bosom of their country. And, just about before any realized it, the President was back in his helicopter and gone following some more hand shaking and back slapping to repeat his greeting and welcome back in Savoonga on the other side of the island.

Also before the Marine Special Forces unit leaves St. Lawrence island to go home, the time comes for the departure of the Russian Speznet troops, a time when to the surprise of some became a great and even sad in some cases celebration for all involved. The onetime Russian invading occupiers had in fact become friends in more than a few cases and their departure was looked upon with a sense of real sadness for many, including some of their counterparts in Marine Special Forces unit EC5. And, literally to the surprise of nobody, 21 Russian troops decide to stay on the island and ask for political asylum, since they have in fact fallen in love with some of the native girls of St. Lawrence island. Some, in fact, are already fathers of soon to be born children from the unavoidable and frankly undiscouraged relationships. And, of course, all who want to stay are gladly accepted by the islanders and immediately granted asylum from Washington.

One of the 21 who stay would not however be general Arkady Islonovich Kamanisky, to the surprise of some, but not to the surprise of Emma Vonderlinden, his native lover and mistress. Emma has never had any illusions about her Russian lover and Arkady has never been anything but honest about his intentions to return to his longtime wife in Vladivostok. Their's has for them both been a joyful and fulfilling physical and emotional relationship of convenience that has brought them both a sense of happiness in and out of the bedroom, and nothing more.

23

A Crushing Departure

For a week now the Marine Special Forces troops have been making ready to depart the island for Nome, and the same 5 Marine V-22J Osprey tilt rotor transport aircraft who brought them here a month ago are waiting with their enormous props slowly turning to transport them to the small Marine Escort Assault ship that's now anchored just off shore not a 1000 yards from the village. It's been almost two weeks now since the Russian "captives" were officially released to their Russian Naval comrades who had sent a transport ship from Vladivostok to pick them up. And quite honestly, the American Marines, the villagers, and the soon to be released Russian soldiers had held a huge celebratory party the night before where much Russian Vodka and American beer and whiskey had been shared and imbibed in.

Today, there's enough crying and wild kisses and hugs to go around as the hundreds of appreciative village citizens say their goodbyes to the men they've grown to like and even love. Honestly, Jon and Lizzy's love affair is frankly not the only one that has sprouted up over the past month. There have been a half dozen in fact. One couple is already quietly married as Jon had suggested they do, and there will be more than one additional baby born to the village as a result of the past month. There are openly stated and repeated promises of love and even more promises to return from the men dressed now in their full khakis, 100 pound packs, and full battle gear who will soon be leaving to go home.

More cries, hugs, and kisses are shared as neither side want to let the emotional moment come to an end. And, even more promises are made about the future to come, but soon what can only be described as an air of despair fills the air when the inevitable can no longer be delayed, and Jon Anderson finally and most regretfully gives the order for the Marine troops to make their way to the waiting aircraft. So after warning her that he simply hates writing letters and probably won't do so as often as she would like for him to, with one final hug and long kiss to the lips of the woman he's spent an incredible month with and knows in his heart that he both loves and wants to be with, the Marine Captain turns on his heel and strides to the tilt rotor aircraft without looking back even once for fear that he will lose his nerve. Elizabeth, in spite of her intentions not to do so, is openly sobbing as she watches the love of her life walk away and very likely disappear from her life forever.

Even though tempted and in fact strongly encouraged by her mother to do so when told, Elizabeth never does tell Jon that she is pregnant with his child before it's time for him to leave the island with his Marine unit, and 8 months and one week later she gives birth to a very healthy strapping 8 pound 14 ounce baby boy with a dark complexion, wide open eyes, and very loud voice. Many who see him for the first time take special note how much the little tyke looks like his father.

We should point out a number of unique aspects to the arrival of Joshua Kendall Anderson, the beautiful son of Marine Captain Jonathan Anderson and Elizabeth Quviariatukuluk. First of all and most importantly, there is not a bit of stigma attached to an unmarried pregnancy in the Inuit culture of the villagers of Gambell and St. Lawrence island. Such a thing as an unwanted pregnancy is unheard of in their community. Abhorrent things as rape just don't seem hardly to happen in this world to change that essential fact. And of course, as we know when it has happened like so recently at the hands of the executed Russian soldier, the child will become in fact a treasured member of the community. The father of children born on the island are mostly known but not always, but nobody concerns themselves with such "non-essentials" as the new baby is always accepted without a bit of question or hesitation into the bosom of their world with love and appreciation. In fact the entire Gambell community who all of course know well without embarrassment or judgment who the child's father is will be Joshua's extended family, always ready and willing to give him the loving support he needs, and the village elders will all willingly serve as his surrogate fathers, who will always be prepared to step up and teach their new pupil what he will need to know to take his place as a man in Inuit St. Lawrence island society. More so, Elizabeth knows without asking that her new son will be accepted and loved with open arms by her understanding parents who are now very proud grandparents for the first time.

Babies who arrive on St. Lawrence island are named in a curious and random nature, given the fact that the certain identity of their fathers might at times be in question. We should point out that still in 2018 there is not a single hospital on the island as we know them in the continental United States and only 3 doctors located in 2 urgent care centers, so babies for the most part are still born at home with the aid of a midwife. But the random nature of the naming is even more by Inuit or Siberian tradition than the fact that a father may not be known. Sometimes it's the mother's name that gets used, other times it's a treasured Inuit name, and still others it's simply a name somebody likes and wants to use. In Elizabeth's case there isn't a moment's hesitation that she will use the name of her son's biological father and her former and hopefully future lover and mate. She's always loved the name Joshua and the middle name Kendall just sounds good to her, so Joshua Kendall Anderson it is as the village Russian Orthodox priest baptizes the new child in the ocean surf just off the shore of the island on his baptizing day. Little Joshua is a strapping healthy young boy who is without question the spitting image of the combination of both his mother and his father with his rich dark olive skin, thick black curly hair, and already stocky but lean body, and by the time almost a year goes by on the island he can be seen stumbling around on his bowed legs that are getting stronger and more confident by the day. He's curious about everything and everybody in Gambell village who now call him Josh simply adore him.

While wanting to believe in her heart that the man she loves without fail and the father of her child will in fact one day return to her as he's promised her that he will do, Elizabeth is a practical person who is ready to settle down into a life as a single mother and provider for her child if in fact his return never happens as hoped. She knows without a single doubt that she has all of the support she will need for her family throughout the Gambell community to do so. And, she has her continued duties as manager of the lighthouse that she lives in with little Joshua. And, just as she'd been warned by Jon in advance would more than likely be the case, not one time over the next almost two full years would Elizabeth receive more than a short note from Jon, and only two cards at Christmas time and a single birthday card. She, on the other hand, would write several. Even though no letters came telling her what she wanted to hear, the cards Jon sent at Christmas time along with the single birthday card did express his continuing love and his desire to be with her at some point in time in the future. And, because she was so determined not to influence or put pressure on his decision Elizabeth never told Jon in any of her letters about his son. And, out of respect for her wishes do also any in the village who might be in contact with the Marine Captain.

Not unexpectedly of course, the entire incident with the Russian invasion and occupation, the following arrival of the American Marines and the Russian departure, and all of the chaos involved over a six month period has had a distinct impact on the social scene on St. Lawrence island and in Gambell village. 21 Russians did stay behind to make new lives with newfound loved ones in the island, and likewise so have several American Marines who also returned to do the same. At the same time these recent events have brought about a change in dynamics of the relationships among the men and women of the island, and

255

some of the old traditions are no longer relevant. For example Emma Vonderlinden, who before the Russian arrival was seen as nothing more than a poor two time widow to feel sorry for, is now seen as a very desirable middle aged woman with a host of men groping at the hem of her dress to share her bed and future life. And she does in fact try out a few here and there over the years, more to experience some exquisite favors than stay with for the most part. She will always for the rest of her life have a mysterious image as the one time mistress of the Russian General. Likewise after the Russian takeover incident and her so public love affair with the American soldier, Elizabeth is seen once again as a suitable potential partner or mate by the unattached adult men of the village who are in search of life partners, as well as some who are frankly already attached following an appropriate period goes by after the Marine Captain's departure.

Soon, Elizabeth is once again surrounded by more than a few eager suitors to her increasing dismay, but not so much to the dismay of either her father or mother who feel she should let go of the memory of her former lover (and father of her child) and settle down with a man who will provide for her and give her protection. And, against her mother's insistent but wizened advice Elizabeth ultimately rejects them all even though after more than a year of mostly silence she's starting to give up hope that Jon will ever really return. She knows he's promised to do so, and she knows that his tour of duty in the Marines is only soon to come to an end, but the lack of letters or communications, even though expected by Jon's own admission, are having their effect and taking a toll on her confidence.

There is in fact one incident in particular where Elizabeth comes precariously close to giving up all hope and relenting to the desires of one of her pursuing suitors. Jon has been gone from the island now for just over 22 months (just about 2 full years) and her mother is pressing her to give one fellow in the village at least a chance, and to be honest the man is a wonderful and very attractive guy with a great job who could easily provide a good and stable life for her and Joshua she knows. He's a guy with a growing fishing tour business who recently moved to the village from Savoonga on the other side of the island. So, against her better judgment, Elizabeth finally accepts an invitation to have dinner with him where a most surprising but undeniable connection is made. He makes no attempt to hide his desire and that very night following a few drinks and some dancing invites her to join him in his bed. She refuses of course, but has to admit to herself against her own wishes that there's a slight tinkling in her loins about the possibility she can't entirely dismiss. She also has to admit that she truly enjoyed the kisses good night with the feel of a man's lips on hers again. Elizabeth does turn the man's intimate suggestion down and continues to put him (and her mother who has become the man's biggest advocate) off for two full weeks afterwards in her confusion about what to do, but then at the behest and pestering of her stubborn mother, among other well meaning folks, she accepts another invitation to dinner where again she feels the strong connection and another not unexpected suggestion is made between drinks and dancing. This time she accepts the offer following a few kisses in the moonlight and soon Elizabeth and her suitor are in his bedroom smothering each other with eager kisses and groping caresses at the same time their clothing is quickly falling to the floor next to the bed they are laying together on. When her bra comes off the woman who hasn't felt the touch of a man's hand on her uncovered breast for nearly two years can't deny the pleasure of it, and when both she and he are naked she can't hide the fact that she likes the feel of a man's unclothed body against hers. But, when he climbs on top of her to mount and take her to become her lover, Elizabeth simply can't allow herself to go through with it as the only image in her mind is her former love, Captain Jon Anderson. Almost shockingly, the man understands her sudden dismay and confusion rather than get angry or upset as one might expect him to do when he's rejected right at the point when he thinks he will receive the reward he so much wants, and instead simply murmurs his continued support and willingness to wait until she's ready as he watches her hurry to dress and leave. For two long weeks afterwards Elizabeth secludes herself in her own self inflicted and conflicted confusion about what to do with her swirling emotions. There's no doubt that she still loves Jon and dearly wishes he would return to the island to be with her, but it's becoming more and more clear to her that there is the real possibility that he will never in fact return to her as promised, and there is also no doubt now that she wants the feel of a man in her bed again and that she has undeniable feelings and desires for this new man in her life. Even her mother's mostly understanding sympathy doesn't help. But finally, at the end of two stressful and thought provoking weeks of uninterrupted reflection about her life circumstance and after making all of the necessary arrangements with her parents, Elizabeth calls the man and suggests that they take a 3 day trip together to Savoonga during the coming weekend.

24

The War Ends, and a Decision is Made

In the many months that follow their departure back to the States, no less than 6 of the members of the Marine Special Forces unit do in fact return to the island to make a life with the women they had met when on the island earlier. But, to the dismay of not only Elizabeth, but to the dismay of her family and the just about the entire Gambell village, none on the island have seen any sign of or heard from their former friend and her lover since his return home and probable departure from the Marine Corps. Only those men eager to chase Elizabeth for her favors seem at all ambivalent about Jon's potential return.

Jon Anderson had in fact returned to the states as ordered and to Camp Pendleton in California with the rest of his Marine Force Recon unit to be awarded much deserved medals of battle participation and for personal valor in the face of danger for his actions during and after the assault on St. Lawrence island. And, there is no question among those who truly know Jon as a friend that he's absolutely despondent and heartbroken about being away from the woman who has literally captured his heart back on St. Lawrence island. But the fact is, that Captain of the Marine Corps Jonathan Anderson is completely conflicted about what to do. He knows without doubt that he loves Elizabeth Quviariatukuluk deeply and wants to spend the rest of his life in her arms, but he also knows how much he cherishes the opportunity to be a member of the United States Marine Corps exclusive fraternity, something that he frankly has years of investment in so needs to give much thought before making a hasty decision based solely on his emotions. And, it will in fact be more than another year before his current tour of duty is up before Jon is actually in a position where he will be allowed to make a decision what to actually do with his future life.

Even though Jon has told his lover not to expect letters or even very many cards from him while gone from her, he does repeatedly receive letters from Elizabeth that proclaim her continued love and devotion, along with her stated desire in so many words to share what they've already shared in her bed. Her letters talk openly of her sorrow at his lack of presence, especially when she talks with some obvious envy about some of the other "wartime couples" who are now moving on with their lives with marriage and children on the island. She talks frankly about how much she misses Jon and how much she would love to hear from him, but falls just short of begging him to do so. But, when she does receive a simple birthday card with a short note professing his continued love from him on her birthday, Elizabeth literally bubbles with excitement, then collapses in tears of sorrow.

Even when Jon does finally decide to resign his commission in the Marine Corps almost 13 months after leaving St. Lawrence island, his decision what to do next isn't as simple as Elizabeth might hope it would be, since he's immediately offered a couple of lucrative positions in the business world that would keep him in the continental United States. And frankly, it's his father most of all who is strongly encouraging his son to accept one of the promising jobs rather than chase off to a remote island for some "Indian girl" he barely knows. And just as frankly, Jon is powerless to know what to say or how to express his conflicted feelings to Elizabeth which further freezes his ability to communicate with her over the several months of consideration. However, from Elizabeth's point of view, she is fully aware of exactly when on the calendar her former lover would have left the Marine Corps if he indeed had, and the fact that she's not heard a word in almost 8 months since that date has her not surprisingly greatly worried and increasingly concerned about his intentions.

260

Jon, like his island lover and the mother of the child he doesn't know he has, has his own near departure from his commitment to her with another woman from his own past. She's a former high school classmate who has matured during his long absence into a beautiful young woman who's both a nurse and been recently divorced from an abusive husband and is clearly interested in forming more than a casual relationship with him. Further, her mother is a long time friend of Jon's mother, which of course means that the two women are in cahoots to get their children together in a not so subtle manner. They try all sorts of things intended to do so that Jon resists for a time, but finally he does agree to take her for a picnic to a lake in the area on a beautiful warm and sunny summer day just to get the two women off his back. She, of course, is delighted and intends to take every advantage of the opportunity the invitation to a picnic presents, so comes dressed in what can only be described as an alluring outfit of extremely short and tight cut off shorts, flip flops, and a sheer almost see through top that highlights her not overly large bosom with no hint of a bra underneath. There's no question that she's attractive and there's no doubt that Jon finds her so as they head to the lake while laughing at the obvious nature of their mother's scheming. She assures him that she's not looking for a commitment yet but just hopes they can have a little fun. Her look across the front seat of the car makes it clear what she means by some fun. It's a beautiful day and she purposely talks Jon into a location away from others on the beach that's very secluded where he puts down a blanket for their lunch and wine. They sit together on the blanket, sipping on the wine after finishing their lunch and even sharing a kiss or two (at her behest of course) while talking when she suddenly asks if Jon has ever gone skinny dipping. He says no and she admits that neither has she but has always wanted to try it with an unmistakable coy look in her eye. She dares him to do it with her, but Jon initially refuses with a hesitant chuckle. But, instead of giving up she simply unbuttons and removes her blouse as he stares in stunned surprise at her. While giggling at his obvious interest in her naked chest, she casually undoes and slips out of her cut off jeans, and then as if it's the most normal thing in the world, pulls off her panties, causing Jon to gasp at the sight of her now naked lithe body. And with that, she simply turns to walk into the lake as she looks back and challenges him to join her, which Jon finally agrees to do. The two of them make love on the blanket after frolicking together in the water, and have a torrid love affair for several weeks before Jon finally admits that he simply can't make himself get over his feelings about Elizabeth. So, to his lover's and their mother's stunned disbelief, Jon breaks off the relationship with no more explanation than that his love belongs to another.

Finally 9 full months after leaving the Marine Corps the once Captain Jon Anderson stuns his father and entire family by announcing his intentions to turn his back on the lucrative opportunities in the business world and a lovely woman who's saying she loves him to travel all the way back to St. Lawrence island so he can be with the woman he knows without question that he still loves whole heartedly and can't get out of his mind. And, he knows for a fact that Elizabeth will still be waiting for him because she continues to say so in her frequent letters and cards. There is one family member who in fact is in total agreement with and fully supports Jon's decision to return to the island and marry his native Indian girlfriend, and that is his younger sister, Evelyn.

So after literally months of indecision, confusion, and a little dallying along the way without looking back for a single moment, Jon Anderson once again packs his oversized Marine duffle bag with what few clothes and possessions he cares about, says an emotional goodbye to his family in Kalamazoo, makes a last apology to the woman he's rejected, and begins his long trek back to the Bering Strait.

(25)

Surprising but Not Surprising Return

Finally, after much confusion Elizabeth is now at complete peace with the decision she's made and isn't a bit bothered to think that 2 days from now she will be in the arms of a man she knows wants to be with her and will care for her and her child. And, after so much thought, worry, and anxiety, she's totally prepared to put her past behind her and let go of her dream of a very special love that's now surely gone forever. Having not heard a single word from Jon for nearly 4 months now Elizabeth simply can't wait any longer for something that there's not a single indication will ever happen, while in its place is this kind, compassionate, and admittedly attractive man who desperately wants her for his own. And in an honest admission to the fact, as she takes down the photograph picture of she and her Marine Captain to store carefully away for the time being, she begins to think more than just some happy anticipation about what the rest of her life might look like. The very next day Elizabeth will find out to her great surprise.

It's a late Thursday afternoon, the day before the couple are set to leave for what promises to be a much looked forward to steamy weekend in Savoonga, and the northern Pacific sun is starting to sink low in the western sky when Elizabeth Quviariatukuluk literally can't believe her eyes as she watches the yard stick strait backed man stride up the gravel path towards her house. Even in the distance she had immediately known who it must without question be, but had still held her breath not wanting to be unduly disappointed, until he got close enough so she could know for sure that it was in fact Jon. And

263

then with all that she had been thinking and planning only a moment before totally forgotten and not wanting or able to contain herself any longer, Elizabeth simply lets the wet basket of clothes she has in her arms fall to the ground before letting out a scream of excited happiness as she begins to run down the path to meet Jonathan Anderson, the true love of her life she hasn't seen for nearly two full years, nor heard from in over 4 months.

Jon is carrying only a single fully packed oversized military issue Marine khaki duffel bag slung over his shoulder, and is wearing a plaid flannel shirt with sleeves rolled loosely up his forearms and a pair of well worn blue jeans as he strides quickly up the path with a big wide smile on his face. When he sees Elizabeth begin to run towards him, Jon immediately drops the bag to the ground and starts to run to meet her.

It's a wild and eager greeting to say the least as Elizabeth literally jumps into the waiting arms of the man she's loved and waited so long for, for almost two full years in fact, and Jon lifts her up into his arms at the same time he begins to kiss the woman he knows he loves without question repeatedly while hugging her tight against his body. Minutes go by as they continue to kiss and slobber each other with the giggled delight of their unexpected reunion. Jon kisses Elizabeth all over her lips, her face, her neck, and her arms as he gushes how much he loves and has missed her. Elizabeth responds just as passionately as she returns the kisses while pressing herself against his strong body. Their need is clear and both know it as they turn to hurry together towards the lighthouse not 25 feet away, and they can't stop talking as they do. Jon also can't keep his hands off the woman he's missed being with for so long. Elizabeth literally giggles softly with admittedly anxious anticipation about what waits for them inside her home, but Jon would be highly surprised at some of the reason for her doing so.

When the eager and happy couple walk arm and arm into the front room of the lighthouse, Jon Anderson, former decorated

Marine Special Forces Captain, simply stands in stunned and silent surprise to see the 15 month old black haired and dark skinned toddler who can be no other than his son waddle up to his feet on 2 stubby legs to hold up a toy boat as he jabbers his undecipherable comments. It's obvious that Elizabeth is waiting to see Jon's reaction to the discovery that he's a father with a child he knew nothing about when he turns to look at her with a look of undisguised shock on his face. She whispers that this is Joshua, and his name is Joshua Kendall Anderson, after his father. Jon is still open mouth stunned as he turns to look at the boy again before taking him up in his arms and returning to look at Elizabeth with a huge smile on his face at the same time that he murmurs with just the tiniest bit of accusing edge to his voice that she should have told him and he would have come much sooner.

Jon and Elizabeth make long awaited love to each other soon after his arrival with their son playing on the floor in the bedroom on the very same second story bed where they did so, so often when he was on the island before. And, they make love to each other with all of the pent up desire and passion that one would expect from a couple who are completely in love and have been kept apart for so long. They also make love without a condom again, and again Elizabeth promises her lover that she's likely pregnant. This time the man who has just made passionate love to her and who will soon be her husband responds by kissing her lovingly and says he certainly hopes so. Completely forgotten of course is the trip to Savoonga that Elizabeth had been planning to take the very next day. Even more surprisingly, her clearly disappointed suitor who had been so looking forward to a much anticipated intimate weekend and the beginning of a lifelong relationship, not only expressed how he understood Elizabeth's sudden change of heart, but actually welcomed the former Marine Captain back to the island.

Life has in fact completely returned to normal on the island in the almost 2 years since Jon's departure to return home. Not that there was that much damage or death for any on the island to actually recover from, but there did take some adjustment to what had so inexplicably happened around them and all of the confusion that surrounded it. There were new members of their tiny community as represented by some of Jon's Marine unit associates left behind and the almost 2 dozen Russian soldiers who decided to stay and not go home with their comrades. There were also the 20 children who arrived as a result of the men who stayed to be with the native women they loved. There was talk of a radio station on the island and talk even of possible trade agreements with the very Russians who had invaded and occupied their island so recently. One of the former Marine soldiers and his new wife have opened a general store of sorts in Gambell where they not only sell groceries and clothing, but sell all sorts of hardware and outdoor sporting goods. Best of all, the store is booming. The buildings built by the Russians for their military installation have all been converted since their departure into a walrus, whale, and reindeer processing plant and distribution center. And, there's even some talk of converting a cove just down the shore a bit near Gambell into a small harbor for shore boats and kayaks to support a potential growing tourist trade sometime in the future. And, in addition to all of it, to the contrary of some and delight of others St. Lawrence island is experiencing a population boom due to the sudden awareness of a place never known before. Gone though are all of the signs of what had happened just a few short years ago, with the charred remains of the destroyed Russian defense weapons broken down and nicely deposited in the ocean to create much needed artificial reefs not far from shore. Gone also are the over flights of spy planes, fighters, bombers, and drones that over several months had become a common sight in the skies over the island. And gone especially is all of the tension and worry about what the island's future might be or to what country the islanders will owe their allegiance to.

Things also settle down pretty quickly between Jon and Elizabeth when he moves immediately into the lighthouse with she and their son, Joshua, who instantaneously becomes the light of Jon Anderson's life. He literally can't believe he's a father, and simply blushes with excitement when talking about teaching his son to swim, fish, hunt, play baseball, and to just love the outdoors like he does. And, as soon as he can pictures are sent to Kalamazoo to introduce his parents to the new grandson they never knew they had. Already, Jon takes the tyke on short walks along the seashore or over the small hills of the island. He figures that in a year or so the boy will even be ready to head towards the summit of Mt. Akula. But after giving her growing sense of guilt much inner thought, Elizabeth, who is in fact pregnant once again, has something she knows she has to tell the man she loves, so one day she asks her mother to watch Joshua so she can have a frank discussion with her fiancé that she has reason to fear might cause him to change his mind all together about their future.

"Jon honey, I have to be honest with you about something," whispers Elizabeth Quviariatukuluk in a voice that can only be described as trepid and a look in her eyes that can only be described as fearful.

Immediately sensing that he's about to be told something important and even distressing, Jon responds with a flash of worry across his face, "what is it dear? Are you okay? You aren't sick are you? Surely you haven't decided not to marry me?" he muses with a worried smile on his face.

"No Jon, I'm okay and not sick, and I do so much still want to marry you, but you may not want to marry me after you hear what I have to tell you," groans Elizabeth in a near sob.

"Oh baby, what is it? Surely it can't be as bad as that? What is it my love?" Jon asks as he takes the woman he loves into his arms.

"No, there's nothing at all physically wrong with me Jon. But I do have something horrible that I must tell you," and with that Elizabeth goes on to tell Jon every essential detail of the entire story of her traitorous and disloyal relationship with the fisherman tour guide and how she had gone so far as to be naked with him in his bed about to make love and only barely resisted doing so, and was even in the midst of preparing to spend a weekend filled with sex and lust with him in Savoonga and maybe the rest of her life only two days after he (Jon) had unexpectedly arrived on the island. She sobs about how guilty she feels about what she did do and very nearly did, and wouldn't blame him at all if he canceled their engagement because of it.

Jon is obviously surprised at her admission, but his only question, asked softly with the sincerest of looks in his eyes, is whether Elizabeth truly believes that she wants to be with him rather than the fisherman. She assures him that she does and that she has already told the man so, but will understand if Jon is angry about what she's done and wants to break off their impending marriage. This is when Jonathan Anderson knows that he has to make his own confession if he and this woman are to have an honest relationship, so he responds with his own admission.

"Darling, I fully understand what you went through and any transgression you feel that you might have committed is entirely my fault for not communicating better than I did. More to the point you shouldn't feel a bit guilty about wanting to be with a man who was here and ready to give you a life as compared to one who had never written and rarely sent a card for 2 years. But honey, I have to make my own admission," and this is when Jon admits to all of the graphic details of the love affair with the former high school classmate back home. And, as hard as it is he doesn't leave anything out, including the truth that he virtually lived in and out of bed with the woman for several weeks before finally breaking up with her. He tells her that he was living a life of total confusion about his future in response to what everybody around him thought he should do. Jon finishes by saying that his transgression is far more disloyal than what Elizabeth did because he actually acted upon it and was intimate with another where she hadn't allowed herself to totally be so.

Elizabeth's response is nearly identical to the one she heard from her fiancé, which is to ask about his honest feelings about

268

their future together. She assures him that she will let him go if he's only here on the island promising to marry her out of some form of obligation to either she or their child. And then, after being satisfied about Jon's claims, Elizabeth asks for more details about the woman who nearly won him away from her and their intimate activities, wonders with a glint of devious pleasure in her eyes about whose body he prefers, giggles with undisguised pleasure of course when he assures her that it's hers, then demands with pretended mock admonishment that he take her and make immediate love to her as his punishment for being so disloyal with another woman.

It also doesn't take Jon long after his arrival on the island to ask Elizabeth's dad's permission for her hand in marriage. Her dad likes Jon and looks forward to having the young man as a son in law, but a long held Inuit tradition demands that he make the young man work to prove his worth and earn the permission he must give, so even though he liked and even loved the boy he immediately put a stern look on his face, crossed his arms just so, and simply stared down the former Marine Captain before asking him what made him think he deserved to marry his only daughter. And by tradition, Jon was required to defend himself to his prospective father in law, and offer what value he would bring to a marriage partnership with Elizabeth. Some called the male suitor's required defense to a prospective father in law his marriage dowry, which of course in a way it was. Knowing the tradition and having been carefully prepared for doing so by his fiancé, Jon is in fact well prepared to play the game as dictated by her father and a thousand year old native tradition. He points out that he's a strong man who will protect the man's daughter day and night as proven by his experience in the Marine Corps. Elizabeth's dad simply grunts in response to the claim as he pretends to look Jon up and down from head to toe in appraisal. Jon then explains that he's a man of the outdoors who will hunt and fish to provide not only for his family but will bring fish and game home for the community larder as well. This Elizabeth's dad already knows about the young man's capabilities in the field and on the water since he's often been fishing or hunting with Jon, but still he challenges the claim by wondering if a man "sprouted by the softness of the continental lower 48" truly has the toughness to hunt the reindeer, the walrus, or the whale successfully when the weather is bad and food is still needed. This is done with a sly smile of course, and he only relents when Jon defends himself by promising to learn better skills from those in the community who can teach him what he will need to know, which of course is exactly what Elizabeth's dad is waiting to hear as a respectful recognition of the values and skill of the native American community and culture. But still the older man simply nods and muses that it should only be just so for one so young in years and so inexperienced in the true ways of the ancient world. Jon then assures his future father in law that he intends to raise his son in the traditions of their native culture, causing the man to nod his head in obvious approval. And then, Jon Anderson tells the elder Inuit father that he will promise to bring new life to the island and more healthy grandchildren to he and his elderly wife as a member of their family, something that he can say truthfully that he's already working on doing, knowing how both Elizabeth's mom and dad love and dote on Joshua. This finally brings a large smile to the Indian man's face as he says that it's his greatest hope that his only daughter and Jon have many healthy children born out of their love for each other, and then with great solemnity the man reaches for a traditional Inuit pipe and suggests that the two of them share a smoke as they reflect on what true love is between a man and a woman, and the great responsibility that a marriage partnership represents. He never outright says that Jon has his permission to marry his daughter, but the smoking of the pipe is the signal that the permission is implicit. And besides, Jon has known from the beginning that he has both Elizabeth's dad's and her mother's happy blessing to be their daughter's husband. While smoking the traditional pipe, Jon does share with his soon to be father in law his thoughts concerning the possibility of Jon encouraging his son at some future time to become a Marine like he, adding quickly the value he thinks doing so provides, but not entirely sure what the

270

man's response might be since military service has no strong tradition in his culture or on this island. Several puffs go by as the native man seems to be taking in and reflecting what he's just been asked, then just as if much thought has gone into what he's about to say, which in fact it has, Elizabeth's father says quietly that he would be honored and proud to be the grandfather of a member of the United States Marine Corps, as he is now honored to have a son in law who is such.

It will be a traditional Inuit outdoor wedding ceremony on the beach in June, and not only will Jon's younger sisters be attending, but so will both of his parents to his great joy. Nothing will make him happier than when he introduces his new wife and family to his mom and dad who have both come to accept their son's decision about the rest of his life and are here on the island to support him. Admittedly, they are also here to see their grandchild for the first time. Elizabeth, of course, is a little worried at first from all she's heard about Jon's father, but the fact is that the beautiful young native Indian maiden quickly has the elder man who is totally mesmorized and infatuated by his soon to be daughter in law wrapped around her finger. And, as if that weren't enough in itself, both Jon's dad and his mom are totally taken by their first grandson, Joshua, who by almost a year and a half in age looks like the perfect example of a union between their son and his native Indian Inuit wife to be. Just as nicely, Elizabeth's parents welcome Jon's to their home with all of the humility and ceremony that their native Indian culture mandates, and the two couples strike up an immediate friendship, even though in so many ways their backgrounds couldn't be more diverse. And of course, as dictated by their cultural background, any talk of staying in a hotel is squashed immediately as Elizabeth's parents insist that Jon's will be staying with them while here on the island.

Jon's younger sisters will be two of Elizabeth's three attendants (maids of honor) at her wedding, and Jon surprises many by asking a former Russian Speznet officer who has stayed and started his own life on the island to be his attendant (best man).

And what a wonderful gala event it is on a bright and sunny day with the ocean waves rolling against the shore and virtually every person who lives in Gambell attending. It is a traditional Inuit ceremony of course with a village elder statesman officiating with much prose and smoke to honor the occasion. And, even though all in the village are quite aware that the couple have for a fact already consummated their marriage many times, a mud and stick wedding night "honeymoon" hut has still been built for the purpose with all of the required traditional ceremony where they will be required to spend their first night as man and wife in all of the expected bliss, which of course both Jon and Elizabeth are completely happy to do.

The after wedding party is also the result of the long held traditions of the native people and a more recent tradition brought about by the Russian influence, making that the party will be a rousing celebration that will go well into the night, replete with massive amounts of succulent food and wondrous drink as the people dance and laugh in sacred honor of the event. Jon and Lizzy are expected by tradition to eat, drink, and dance with all of the people who are honoring them, and both are excited to do so as exhausting as the demand to do so will be. Jon is dancing so much, and in fact enjoying doing so, so much, that he fails to notice how his youngest sister is paying particularly close attention to one of his village male friends.

Another long held tradition of native Inuit culture are the wedding gifts offered to the newly married couple by family and the community. Jon's new father in law gives him a fine bolt action Winchester 30-06 rifle with a Kevlar stock and adjustable open peep sights to hunt reindeer with. His best man offers him a personal spear and finely crafted kayak to hunt the walrus that he made with his own hands. Both are modern renditions of an ageless technique for hunting the beast. Yet another friend gives him an exquisite bamboo 9' ocean fly rod and open action reel, complete with 100' of casting line and leader. Jon's mother in law gives him a hunting knife with a shiny 12" blade, a whale bone handle, and reindeer hide scabbard that she's lovingly made herself in the traditional Inuit way. Best of all, Elizabeth is presented with a traditional Inuit quilt made by the women of the village whose multitude of squares represent the thousands of year history of the people, including some of the more recent events. Two squares in particular represent the Russians who unexpectedly came to their island a couple of years back and the Marines who came to repatriate them. And, of course, the women make clear with all of the knowing giggles just how they expect the warm and cuddly quilt to be used by the couple.

Finally, near midnight, it's announced by the same village elder who married them earlier that it's time to lead the couple to their marriage hut, where they will spend the night in hopes that the seed of a new life will spark in the love of a man and a woman. And Jon and Liz will make love more than once that night before finally going to sleep in each other's arms in the warm bosom of the reindeer skins they've been so kindly provided, and again in the morning they will make love one more time before emerging from their honeymoon hut to the celebration of those outside. The truth is that the seed of a new life will not be ignited that night or morning since it already has, and so 7 1/2 months later Elizabeth and Jon will introduce a new granddaughter to their parents and to the Gambell community.

After their steamy night in the honeymoon hut, it's time for Jon and Elizabeth to set up housekeeping together in the lighthouse, where they will continue to stay and manage its operation for the island. By 2020, the St. Lawrence island lighthouse built by the Russians all the way back in 1796 is frankly in great need of some much needed repairs and upgrades, and for a couple of years doing so will occupy much of Jon's time as a new husband and member of the community. Over that time he will replace most of the wood flooring and all of the woodwork that shows much of the wear and tear of 200 plus years of existence next to the sea. A new modern furnace is put in that uses natural gas instead of coal. The recent discovery of large deposits of natural gas under the island is a modern boon to the local economy and one that will frankly revolutionize many aspects of life for all who live here. He will install a modern shower and bathroom, and fully upgrade the kitchen with a new stove, dishwasher, and microwave oven. Both Jon and Elizabeth would laugh how she had insisted that the new walk in shower only just large enough for two be christened even though her 6 month pregnant belly made things pretty tight. The new gas stove represented a major upgrade over the previous wood and charcoal model, and the dishwasher became a true convenience. Part of the storage room, Jon will wall off to create a second children's bedroom for their daughter when she arrives, and many of the things kept there previously were moved to a new basement storage area that Jon and his friends dug under the existing building for the purpose. He will also buy he and Elizabeth a very nice overstuffed queen size bed for their bedroom and a nice mirrored dressing table for his wife.

Jon and Elizabeth create a simple life for themselves as they manage the lighthouse (which in fact takes very little of their time outside of simply making residence in the building and doing what little maintenance the searchlight requires) and raise their small family. Their needs are small as they grow, hunt, or fish for most of the food they need, and what else they need is provided by the odd jobs Jon does in the community. He's always available to help with construction when needed, and is always on hand with his 4 wheeler driven snow plow when the snow needs shoveled. Jon's a dedicated participant in the walrus hunts that bring meat and blubber to the community and his own larder (his share), and he simply loves to hunt the reindeer while in season with his new Winchester. In the water Jon has become an expert at harvesting red king crab with the traps he made himself when in season along the shores of St. Lawrence island. He fishes for Pacific salmon with his fly rod and reel when they make their annual run up the one stream on the island in the late summer every year. Smoked salmon is a staple in the Anderson household, especially after Jon builds a very impressive smokehouse on the grounds of the lighthouse. He also fishes for ocean perch and even halibut from his kayak when they are in season in the plentiful waters off the Gambell shore. On many days Elizabeth can be seen hunting or fishing with her husband on or just off the shores of the island. Life in the third decade of the 21st century is pleasantly simple for Jon, Elizabeth, and their children, but life is also really good with plenty of food to eat and a great community of friends and family they can both rely on. They just love their quiet evenings together. On another corner of the lighthouse property Jon builds a very traditional Inuit sweathouse that over the coming years he enjoys sitting in with his father in law and a few close friends as they sip their drinks and smoke their cigars.

One of the results of the short war (war was never actually declared) with the Russians was a grant from the United States government to provide modern computers and digital equipment with a full time satellite internet feed that can provide the most up to date direct instruction and course material for the young people in the local schools in the St. Lawrence island villages. This for the first time brings access to a truly modern world based education opportunity for the children on the island. The systems will provide access also for the first time to internet based college courses from the Universities of Alaska, Anchorage, and Washington State who are all now beaming course networks to the island. The same computer based resources will also provide a major upgrade to the local libraries in both Gambell and Savoonga.

But, the biggest and most surprising change in Jon's life (aside from his own recent marriage and children) will be provided by his younger sister, Evelyn. Before coming to St. Lawrence island for her brother's wedding, the almost 18 year old Evelyn has been making the expected preparations to attend college at Michigan State on an academic scholarship in the coming fall semester. There's talk that she will eventually become either a surgeon or gynecologist at some future time. Evelyn, however, is without question a carefree full of life young woman who the very moment she arrives on St. Lawrence island immerses herself into the society of young people in Gambell. She attends parties and activities where she begins to meet others, one of

275

which is Randy Roskovsky, the 26 year old friend of her older brother. Also over the couple of months that Jon's sister has been in Gambell, his new wife Elizabeth has gotten surprisingly close to Evelyn to Jon's happy delight, with whom she's shared much of her experiences and feelings, as has her new husband's sister. And, it's only a few short weeks after her arrival on the island that Evelyn shares a very important secret with her soon to be sister in law, a secret that causes Elizabeth to worry with some reason.

It would only be a few weeks later when Jon and Elizabeth are out for a late evening stroll one moonlit night along the beach after the sun has gone down and disappeared over the ocean waves to the west when they unexpectedly come upon what can only be some couple obviously making love not far from the path behind some low bushes in the twilight. They had come on them so fast and so unexpectedly that doing so was unfortunately unavoidable, given the immediate result since the lovers turned out to be one of Jon's closest fishing buddies and his youngest sister, Evelyn. And, like any older and very protective brother could only expected to be, Jon is stunned to see his own little sister completely naked on the sandy beach with a man who's eagerly groping at her body, and is immediately angry even though Elizabeth makes every attempt to calm him down at the same time that Evelyn and her lover (and his friend) hurry to put their clothes back on.

"For God's sakes Evelyn what would dad and mom say if they knew you were out screwing some guy on the beach you barely even know," cries out Jon! "Hell, I'm supposed to be watching over you!"

"Oh Jon, come on, don't be such a fuddy duddy," sobs his embarrassed but contrite sister. "Besides I don't need watching over."

"Evelyn, for Christ's sake, you are still only 17, and frankly you shouldn't be having sex with guys yet," Jon cries again.

"Jesus Jon, it's 2020 for God's sakes, and just so you know, I've been having sex with guys quite nicely now for almost two years now," cries back Evelyn.

"I really didn't need to know that Ev. But, out here right in the open where anybody can see you," cries Evelyn's older brother in further complaint?

"Well Jon, at least Randy didn't take me on a kitchen counter the very first time he met me like some guys obviously like to do," cries back Jon's little sister in total frustration.

Jon's speechless now at what he's just heard her say and with the realization that his youngest sister knows his secret about that day in the kitchen of the lighthouse, and all he can do is stand watching in stunned silence as his 17 year old sister collects her things and stomps away in a huff down the beach with her boyfriend in tow. Jon simply turns to his wife and quietly says, "you had to tell her" and also begins his own walk away from the beach towards home.

Finally, once leaving the beach that night and after he's had two days to cool down while his wife has continued to counsel him, Jon asks Evelyn and Randy to sit down with them for a talk, more than sure that he's going to have to send his sister home before things get out of hand. He's in fact found out from Elizabeth that his sister has been intimate with his Inuit friend virtually from the beginning of her stay in Gambell almost two months ago, which had shocked but not entirely surprised him when he admitted it to himself. He should have seen it coming he knows, but still blames his friend for letting it happen. He should have known better. Jon's also a little frustrated with Elizabeth for not stopping his sister or telling him.

"Evelyn, I think it's time for you to go back home to Kalamazoo," says Jon to start the conversation.

"Well big brother, I knew that is exactly what you would say, but here's what I have to say. I'm not going. I love Randy and he loves me, and we plan to get married next summer right here on the island. And, Jon, don't try to stop me, I'm old enough to make my own decisions and this is what I want and intend to do. Besides, I'm pretty sure that I'm pregnant," says Evelyn Anderson to her completely stunned brother.

"Oh my God," is all Jon manages to say as he looks down in total dejected frustration. He then murmurs, "what about Michigan State in the fall? What about being a doctor? Are you ready to just throw all that away?"

"Jon, I don't give a damn about Michigan State! That's you and dad's idea not mine. And, with the new internet classes that will soon become available I can still become a doctor someday" cries out Evelyn!

"I see, so you've decided on your own to become an islander instead of going to school," offers Jon Anderson in quiet frustration.

"Well, it seems to have worked pretty well for you, so why shouldn't it for me?" points out his sister Evelyn.

"Look Ev, I didn't exactly just jump right out of high school to come out here as you know," responds Jon.

"Jon you have to listen, I love your sister more than you could know. I didn't plan for it to happen my friend, but it did, and I'm not going to apologize for being in love with and wanting to spend the rest of my life with Evelyn dude," offers Randy Roskovsky. And before Jon can say anything, his friend adds that he knows that he knows that he's a good person who would never hurt his best friend's sister, then adds that he plans to expand his fishing business to help support them and that he and Evelyn also plan to start a radio station on the island when they collect enough money to do so. He then says that he wants his soon to be wife to someday become a doctor since the need is increasing with all of the people now moving to the island.

"Jon, it will be okay," offers Elizabeth as she puts a hand on his upper arm as is to emphasize the fact.

"You're really pregnant," Jon whispers?

"Yes brother, I'm pretty sure that I am," returns Jon's little sister.

For the first time Jon and Evelyn's sister, Kate, speaks up by telling her older brother that he and their father can't always have things their way and that Evelyn has to find her own path in life. She adds that she thinks Jon knows that Randy is a good guy who will love and cherish their sister, and that he also should realize from his own experience that when you find true love you have to follow the path to see where it goes, even if it's an unexpected and surprising one.

"I'm just concerned about what mom and dad will say Ev," murmurs Jon Anderson.

"Well don't be Jon, first of all it really isn't their say or business, well it kind of is I guess, but I've already written mother to tell her my intentions," says Evelyn.

"Really, have you heard back from her," wonders Evelyn's older brother?

"I have in fact, and while I admit that she's not entirely thrilled with my choice mom does respect it as I think you know she would. She even says that she's going to try and talk dad into coming back for the wedding next summer, and I think they will," responds Evelyn Anderson.

"Did you tell her you're pregnant," whispers Jon again?

"I did," responds Evelyn.

"What did she say," wonders her older brother with a look on his face that shows his shock?

"She said that while it wouldn't have been her choice for me to be so at such a young age, she loves and supports me," murmurs Evelyn with a smug look on her own face.

"Does dad know," asks Jon with a look that's now worried?

"No I don't think mom has told him yet, but look Jon both mom and dad met Randy when they were here last month and really liked him," offers Evelyn.

279

"I think they did dude and will approve when they have a chance to get used to the idea," throws in Randy Roskovsky.

"For God's sake, am I the only person around here who hasn't known what's going on," bleats Jon Anderson to all around him.

"Oh Jon, I just wish you could accept this and know that I'm a woman now and not just your little sister. Randy and I are going to be okay I promise," says an almost pleading Evelyn.

"Is this where I'm supposed to surrender and give my approval," smiles Jon Anderson.

"Jon, my dearest elder brother, I think you know that I don't need nor will I ever ask for your approval," giggles Evelyn knowing her brother has finally relented.

"Oh, how I know that is true little sister," laughs Jon Anderson who is now comfortable knowing that his little sister is interested in more than a "who cares what it may be dalliance," appears to have found meaningful love with his friend, and even seems to have a sort of plan for the future. He then asks one last final question, which is: "so, are you really and truly pregnant or was that just a fib intended to shock me into agreeing."

"I'm more than pretty sure I am Jon," answers Evelyn as she pats her still flat belly with her hand.

"Well, as we all know, you Anderson's do appear to be pretty fertile," offers Elizabeth with a big smile on her face and her own tiny beginnings of a baby bump on her belly.

"Well damn, Randy you had better take good care of my little sister or I will literally hunt you down and drown you in the surf with my own two bare hands. You got it," Jon says with an almost teasing smile on his face? Jon then adds that he plans to hold his friend to his promise that he wants his little sister to eventually study to become a doctor.

"Got it dude," is all that his friend says in response as he puts his arm around Jon's sister, Evelyn.

With that everybody laughs and hug with a sense of relief before they decide to fix and eat some dinner together in celebration of Evelyn and Randy's announced plans.

In the spring of 2021 the KVCD radio station opens for business in Gambell with moneys provided by another United States government grant along with the savings the owners have contributed, and Randy Roskovsky is the station program manager and his soon to be wife, Evelyn Anderson, is the operations manager for the 2 person business. Their plan for the station is for it to have a multiple format that will include current event information both about the local community, the island, the north Pacific region, as well as a full schedule of reported national and international news on a daily basis. They also hope to schedule how to shows on activities such as hunting, fishing, food preservation, gardening, quilting, and canning by reaching out to subject experts. They also intend to have modern, classical, country western, and even Russian music hours as part of their weekly itinerary. And, of course, of key importance will be the weather and fishing reports that will be so important to many in the community.

It's another gorgeous June day on the beach just outside of Gambell St. Lawrence island where the crowd has gathered once again for Randy Roskovsky and Evelyn Anderson's wedding ceremony. Like Jon and Elizabeth's before, the ceremony is to be a traditional Inuit affair with the bride and groom standing before all of their friends and family with their 2 month old daughter in their arms. Almost the entire town is here to celebrate the occasion, while Jon, Kate, and Evelyn's mother has in fact gotten their father to bring her to the island to participate. Unfortunately, due to their never ending business responsibilities, Evelyn's to eldest brothers couldn't attend as they had hoped to do. Jonathan Anderson Sr. would proudly present his youngest daughter to the man she plans to marry, while Mary Anderson looks on in her lovely blue chiffon dress with huge tears streaming down her cheeks while holding her tiny granddaughter in her one arm with her 3 year old grandson's hand held tightly in hers. And, when all of the partying is finally finished at the end of the evening the newly married couple are led to their own traditional Inuit wedding night hut to consummate their marriage.

The spring snow is still falling as the village men mount their kayaks and prepare to paddle far out into the surf to intercept the massive blue whale that has been sighted by the islanders. Each of the 48 hunters is armed with his own traditional looking spear with its modern 4"wide stainless steel and very, very sharp pronged point. Each of their individual spears have been custom made personally out of a well honed and varnished 6 foot length of 11/2 inch thick perfectly straight cured ash wood and has attached to it a deceptively frail looking but exceptionally strong 50' ribbon looking synthetic cord followed by a 100 foot length of 3/8" polyester nylon rope that's anchored tightly to the kayak. 12 selected hunters will be the first to surround the surfacing whale before throwing their spears to injure and slow it down with deep thrusts, after which those sitting behind waiting in their own kayaks move in for the kill. Jon is one of the 12 given the honor to make the first throws, but even with 48 hunters and their spears it will take more than an hour for the whale to finally surrender to its wounds, and almost half a day before it finally succumbs to its injuries. And then, it will take the party of 4 dozen hunters a full 4 hours to drag the whale with their spear attached ropes to shore where it can finally be beached where their fellow villagers wait in preparation for the celebration and butchering party.

After a solemn dedication given by the local Russian Orthodox vicar and village elders, a great celebration is held on the shore of St. Lawrence island for the bounty provided by the mammoth beast of the sea where, like all 11 of his first rank spear throwers, Jon Anderson is honored with one of the first bites of uncooked fresh whale heart which he chokes down with great pride. In the thousands of year traditions of the Inuit people, the Gambell villagers will celebrate for 3 full days with food, drink, and dance as they prepare the smoking and rendering fires that will allow the women folk of the village to butcher and smoke the meat and render the blubber for much needed fat and oil for the coming winter. This has been a long held native tradition conducted for over 2000 years, ever since the day the first blue whale was sighted and harvested by the people on the very day of Christ's birth. It's a tradition that is now being proudly passed on to the newest St. Lawrence island generation as represented by the children of Jon Anderson and his wife, and Evelyn Anderson Roskovsky and her husband.

The Aftermath

No less than 21 out of nearly 500 Russian soldiers do in fact decide to stay to make their lives and become Americans on St. Lawrence island, adding their own special flavor to the now fast changing culture on the island. Moscow did complain for a short while about the unacceptable and unquestionably brazen "kidnapping and brainwashing" of their soldiers, but didn't actually dare complain too loudly and the issue dropped almost immediately between the two recent antagonists as the men hurried to marry their American girlfriends so they could begin their lives as respected members of the Gambell and Savoonga communities. And, also without question, the newest members of the island community were accepted with open arms by the natives on the island in the best traditions of the Inuit culture.

A direct and measurable consequence of the entire St. Lawrence island incident would be the 2020 census, whose increase in numbers represented a dramatic growth in population in comparison to the 2016 numbers only 4 short years before. In the 2016 census report there were listed a grand total of 1296 souls on the entire island, while in 2020 there would be an amazing 1569 officially people counted, or a full 22% increase in only 4 years. The great irony of the number increase of course is that before 2016 not a person in a thousand had ever heard of St. Lawrence island, but by 2020 it had become one of the fastest growing places in America (albeit still very small in comparison to many, many other places). Almost more astonishingly still, it had taken 10,000 years for the island's population to grow from the original 35 immigrants to the 1296 folks on the island in 2016, and a mere 4 years to increase that number substantially. So, just how exactly did it happen. This is how...

Between the census years of 2016 and 2020 there were no fewer than 12 sad deaths on the island, which included 10 elderly members of the community who all died of natural causes, one adult who died of cancer, and an infant who died tragically from SIDS.

And, as we know a total of 7 American soldier Marines, including Jonathan Anderson, decided to stay on the island when their units returned home in 2019, and we know as stated before that 21 Russian soldiers also decided to stay behind and join the St. Lawrence island community when their units left to go home to Russia in 2019. We also know that one Evelyn Anderson, younger sister to Jon Anderson, has come to Gambell, fallen in love, and made a home on the island as well.

But, here's the most astonishing news of all. Between 2016 and the 2020 census there were an earth shattering total of 259 births, which all by themselves represent a 5% rate annually in the short 4 year period, but when you look further into the numbers you discover even further that over 200 of those births actually took place in 2018 and 2019 alone. What this tells you is that during those 2 latter years of supposed upheaval and chaos as a result of the invasion there was a whole lot of intimacy and lovemaking taking place all across the island.

Of real interest is that starting in 2019, many dozens of the Russian Speznet troops who had served for a short time on the island during the occupation and their families, including the commanding general himself, attend an annual reunion held on the island where they celebrate their short residence with the local population. And, surprising as it may sound, a few of them actually decide to stay behind when they do, adding even further to the population numbers and diversity on the island.

But, it would be in 2021 when things really start to change. St. Lawrence island has now captured the heart of not only folks all across America, but has become of great interest to people all across the world in fact. So, to the dismay of more than a few islanders, by that year the quiet solitude of their former lives was being trampled on by increasing numbers of tourists who just wanted to see the place for themselves as well as more and more folks looking for an escape from the hectic nature of modern life throughout the world. And the truth is that it would be the 2030 census that would show the true ultimate consequential impact of what had happened between 2016 and 2020 on the island, with the counted population having more than doubled from 1296 souls in the 2010 census to an amazing 2813 full time residents in 2030. Factually, in a place only 100 miles long and 20 some miles wide, population growth and overcrowding are actually becoming an issue on the island for the first time since its formation 10,000 years ago.

In 2020, to the absolute dismay of Jon Anderson and even to a point to some concern of his wife Elizabeth, Jon is nominated by his peers in the village then elected by near acclamation to be the official mayor and "city manager" of Gambell, where he would serve in his post "unwillingly but voluntarily" for a period of just under 35 years. For the first time the mayoral position will have a salary of $25,000.00 per annum which isn't a whole lot of money actually, but the additional salary adds nicely to a household budget that always seems to fall a little short at the lighthouse. The lighthouse management position also now includes a stipend of $6,000.00 per year plus expenses, by that year Jon and Lizzie are in much better financial shape than they could have expected. In fact, with his pretty steady income from his odd jobs and light construction business and the traditional native dresses and infant outfits that Elizabeth makes to sell in the community, to go with Jon's not overly large Marine pension, they have a nice income that will allow them to make plans for their children's college education when the time comes in the not all that distant future. Frankly, Jon Anderson would discover that he actually has a flare for politics and an even better flare for effective and efficient administration of policies. And unexpectedly, it will turn out that he will have a future in politics, not only in the Gambell and on St. Lawrence island, but a future that will eventually expand on a national basis.

One of the biggest consequences of the entire St. Lawrence island incident is the reelection of Edward Jeb Bush to a second term as President of the United States in what amounts to an electoral landslide (a staggering 56% of the popular vote, and almost 300 electoral votes in comparison to 39% and 139 for his closest Democratic rival), mostly because most Americans have become super patriotic with the overthrown Russian occupation of American territory and the vast majority of those people give Jeb Bush the lion's share of credit for getting it back. And, following the election Jeb Bush is sitting in the Oval Office of the White House with his closest advisors, and they are talking frankly about where they stand now and what has been accomplished in reality since the beginning of the entire St. Lawrence island incident in 2016 or so.

"Well, Mr. President I think you can take great pleasure and pride in what's been accomplished with the ouster of the Russkies from the Bering Strait and its aftermath," says Roger Noriega.

"Oh, I'm not so sure about that Roger," offers a thoughtful and honest thinking but highly popular President.

"Just what do you mean Mr. President," wonders John Negroponte.

"What I think the President means is that while the island has in fact been taken back and returned to its previous peaceful status, and that yes he's immensely popular for making that happen, that in reality nothing much has really changed for the most part, except we and the Russians brought the world precariously close to another world wide war. Would that be right Mr. President," offers Vice President Mia Love.

"Now Mia, I don't think.... " says Robert Natter the Secretary of Defense before he's uncharacteristically interrupted by the President.

287

"Mia's right Bob. When you consider all that happened during the incident in reality and how many lives were impacted in a most negative manner (how about all those poor Russian oil workers who lost their jobs because we undermined their industry) as well as what we know we came so very close to letting happen between our armed forces, it does seem that not much substantial was actually accomplished," muses the President.

"Mr. President, I do take exception to that outlook. Geopolitically, we trumped the Russians and forced them to back down from their aggression in the Bering Strait, we put a major hurt on their economy, we made the Castros come back to the negotiating table in Cuba, we embarrassed the Russian military at every turn, and we made the Saudi's very happy by handing them a major new customer in the Euro Zone, urges Roger Noriega yet again.

"Oh sure, we did all of that I know Roger. But, so what? Here's the reality folks, it all started if you remember with our standing up to Putin in the Ukraine and the Crimea am I right? Our goal at the time if I remember correctly was to force he and his government to back off and return freedom of choice to that area of the world. With that said, where do we actually stand geopolitically Roger? Well, let me answer it for you. All of the area once referred to as the Crimea, including the economically important city of Odessa and the strategically critical warm water port of Sevastopol is now officially part of the Russian Federation instead of a Ukrainian province, and even worse than that there's now a government in power in Kiev who walks in lockstep with Vladimir Putin and his Russian super nationalists. Worse yet, every eastern European government (Estonia, Finland, Latvia, Lithuania, Romania, Georgia, and even Poland have all rushed to make accommodations with Moscow, which has done much to unravel the fabric of the expanded NATO alliance and Euro Zone. Oh yes, we won a small victory over the Russian military in the Bering Strait and that victory supplied us with a second term in office, but here's what I really think

288

happened folks. I think a cagy Vladimir Putin got exactly what he wanted at a very cheap cost. Sure his armed forces were momentarily humiliated on St. Lawrence island, but were they really? To be honest, we've even quietly paid the families of those 2 Russian Mig pilots several million apiece and even paid millions to the Russian soldier's wife and kids who died during our reoccupation. I don't particularly think those are bad things, but just the same everybody we talk to mentions how the Russians acted as occupiers and how readily they stood down then we arrived. I think the truth is that the Russian President caught us with our pants down by invading and occupying an island we barely knew was there but would have to do all we could to recapture it, and it's become my opinion that from the very beginning Putin intended to give us that island back without a fight because he knew that by the very taking of it he'd accomplished his ultimate goal of taking our attention away from the Crimea. And guess what else has happened everybody, interest and support for the sanctions put in place against Russia has disappeared and most of them have been dismantled as we know. We also know that Brazil, China, and India have all made agreements with them for low cost oil so that the loss of production and sales due to our Saudi / Euro Zone strategy has been replaced and as so the Russian economy has rebounded. That's our reality everybody," says a President who knows what the truth is.

"Well Mr. President, I'm thinking that we should just keep all of that to ourselves," says John Negroponte.

"Oh I agree whole heartedly with that John. But, how long will the smart guys decide to play along when they begin to write the history of the whole thing?" says President Jeb Bush.

"Oh, I'm pretty sure Mr. President that those "smart guys" you mention already have it all figured out," offers Mia Love.

Unintended consequences are without question a constant axiom of human relations, and the entire Crimea / Bering Strait incident will surely be seen as such when the history does actually get written for future generations. And, one of the more important "unintended consequences" will be a strong relationship that gets forged surprisingly between one Vladimir Putin, President and sometimes called dictator of the Russian Federation, and Edward Jeb Bush, the 45th President of the United States. It's a surprising relationship that's built on an understanding of what really did happen in the confrontation between their two countries and its significance for the future of their mutual understanding for each other.

(27)

The World Changes, but Not All That Much

While it's frankly improbable or maybe even pretty unlikely that war would or could break out between Russia and the United States in the near future and even more unlikely that the Russians would actually dare to invade and occupy any part of our territory if it did in fact happen, the possibility isn't entirely impossible. Many people aren't aware at all that the world (the U.S. and Russia in particular) came precariously close to a nuclear conflagration during 1983 due to a series of misunderstandings, skewed perceptions, and a number of actions that would be seen later as not just confrontational but damned inappropriate. It's often been stated that war mostly represents nothing more than the result of failed policies, missed opportunities, miscommunications, or leaders who should know better simply sliding unknowingly into an ibis that leads to unspeakable misery for the people they work for, for the simple reason that they don't know what else to do. That's exactly what happened in 1983 when the Soviets, not knowing what else to do when they feared that the U.S. was finally gaining a military hegemony over them under President Reagan, darned near pushed to button for a nuclear preemptive strike.

A Sudden War in the Bering Strait is such a story about two countries with a history of being antagonists who suddenly find themselves in a direct confrontation blows up into quite something else. We take a real life situation as now does in fact exist in 2015 throughout the war torn regions of the Eastern Ukraine (Crimea) where rebellious ethnic Russian "freedom fighters" or "terrorists" depending on which side you agree with in the dispute are battling for independence from the Ukraine and are receiving direct support from the Russian Federation who themselves would like to see a return of the region to their direct control and use it as fuse for our story. To us here in the United States the situation in Eastern Europe appears both deplorable and unacceptable as it seems like the Russians are once again meddling in what should be on the surface an internal Ukrainian issue or problem. And, of course, it is truthfully both deplorable and unacceptable what's currently happening where a region and all of its people are being literally torn apart by civil war and all that makes a civilized life possible.

But, the situation in the Eastern Ukraine frankly isn't quite as simple as we Americans would like it to be or think it is. Our problem is that we tend to be so driven by our long stated ideals of democracy and freedom that we want to or insist on viewing the world only through a narrow prism of our closely held beliefs, which unfortunately causes us to misunderstand the true dynamics of what is really going on in other places where those traditions aren't as strong. Worse yet, those very assumptions which all seek our version of freedom and democracy are off. Frankly, there is no strong tradition of either in that part of the world in the western liberal democratic sense, so to call anybody involved in the fight in the Crimea "freedom fighters" or to assume they are fighting for a "democratic right" is far from the point and not even relevant much at all. What we American television viewers don't know or refuse to understand is that the situation in the Ukraine and Russia is grounded in hundreds of years of history and more recently due to a seemingly unimportant administrative decision by a country that no longer exists. The region is frankly ethnic Russian historically with close ties to the Russian motherland, and not until 1984 was it ever a part of the Ukraine. And, in the classic modern nation state way of handling border lines and locations, the Soviet government of the old USSR then in power in Moscow made a completely administrative decision to change the borders on the map and put the Crimean region with its strategically important Black Sea warm water naval port in

Sevastopol under the control of their underlings in the Ukrainian Soviet Socialist Republic. It seemed like a credible thing to do in a country so vast and hard to manage as the old Soviet Union, right up until the sudden break-up of the trans European Asian empire in 1988 and 1989 where the Soviet Socialist Republics overnight discovered their newfound independence from their Moscow masters.

And here's the 2 additional key points we need to know if we are to truly understand what's going on over there. First, Russia and the Ukraine have never in the last thousand years gotten along that well with each other. Historically, the Ukraine has been the "most western oriented" of all of the former east European or southern Soviet satellites (including even the Baltic states, Belo Russia, Georgia, etc.) and has always remained highly suspicious of and nervous about her much larger eastern neighbor. So much so in fact, that in 1941 when the German Nazi armies arrived during their invasion of the Soviet Union they were immediately welcomed with open arms, not as invaders but as liberators from a repressive regime. The Russians my friends have never forgotten this nor forgiven the Ukrainians for doing so. The second issue of importance that drives the situation is the 500 year old prioritized policy of every Russian monarch or leader to have access to the warm water port at Sevastopol on the Black Sea. Without it Russia is limited to being nothing more than a seasonal sea power since all of her northern ports are iced over during the winter months. The bulk of the Russian (and Soviet before) Navy is based at the Naval Station outside of Sevastopol. Up to now, under the agreements signed between the new Russian Federation (government in Moscow that replaced the fallen Soviet government) and the independent country of Ukraine in 1992 the Russians were given "managerial control" over the Naval Base at Sevastopol and rights to supply it across what was now Ukrainian territory in the Crimea. The problem is simple, neither does Mother Russia enjoy having their most important Naval installation under the control of another nation regardless what promises have been made, nor do the ethnic Russians in the

293

area either enjoy being Ukrainians or told what to do by a Ukrainian government in Kiev that they both dislike and distrust.

So ergo, "Houston we have a problem" as the old saying goes. And, here's the problem that I foresee could be a remote possibility if we don't take great care to avoid it, which is that if our leaders and decision makers fail or refuse to understand the historical or emotional realities involved in the Ukrainian dispute and it continues to fester or get worse as I fear it most likely will (these sorts of things never seem to go away quietly all by themselves), we will ultimately begin to move down the road to that ibis of a shooting war that appears so unimaginable to us today. Would we actually shoot at each other? Of course we would. When we start encroaching on each other's territories in a tit for tat manner with armed military aircraft and ships as both we and the Russians are even now currently doing in 2015, an incident or incidents are bound to happen at some point. And, if great care is not taken on both sides, those incidents can lead to more claims and counter claims to a point where there is no backing off by either side. We must remember that this is exactly the situation that started World War I, a war that frankly neither side or any country wanted and actually professed must be avoided. But, a devastating war happened anyway since nobody could make themselves see the other point of view or back off before the shooting really started.

And likewise, the entire region of the northern Pacific, the Bering Strait in particular, serves as a potential flash point in the situation if things continue to spin out of control. Not unlike the Ukrainian situation in the Crimea, the Russians greatly regret selling "Alaska" to the Americans with all of the valuable geographic resources they represent. The Russians frankly see the area as a natural sphere of influence while we more often see the islands in the Bering Strait region as outlying and remote. So, to suggest that the Russians would never dare consider a surprise move in the area if things got difficult between the U.S. and them is frankly unrealistic, since all through the decades of the cold war and even today to some

294

degree the entire region is a "contested area" where our respective military forces often come into contact as we continue to push and probe each other. And then, there's Vladimir Putin, a man who is without fail a true unapologetic Russian nationalist who not only knows his history but is more than willing to roll the dice in a manner that is far less risky with a much larger upside than one might in the beginning. His on the surface unconventional moves in Syria and elsewhere point to the fact. So, the very idea that he might shuffle the deck with a lightning invasion of a place nobody knows or cares about, be determined to be good citizens as occupiers and managers, and then simply back away when the rescuers arrive in a manner that makes the world turn its back on things that are a higher priority, such as the Crimea, seems fairly credible to me.

Sadly, it's these kinds of circumstances where we seem to never learn from history, and become doomed to repeat ourselves to the misery of many. And quite honestly, for the most part, not all that much ever really changes when all of the killing and destruction is said and done, although I did choose for personal reasons to limit the death and violence in my story. A Sudden War in the Bering Strait is a message to that very point where, yes the inexplicable and seemingly impossible can in fact happen, and yes when it's all said and done nothing really much changes after all of the damage and chaos has been inflicted. Admittedly and unrealistically in fact, I did chose to keep the actual violence and resulting death to a minimum in my story, but my honest opinion is that if ever a shooting war at any level ever took place between the United States and the Russian Federation, the consequences in loss of life and property would be staggering almost without question before we could ever manage to stop ourselves.

Part of the A Sudden War in the Bering Strait story is about the military equipment and techniques that would most likely be used, and I hope I did so without making too many stupid or blatant mistakes in the process. I admit openly that I played fast and loose with the realities, or lack of for the most part, in the intelligence capabilities of both sides in a way that did nothing more than served the purposes of my story, since in today's world it would be extremely difficult to move naval task forces or an elite attack force without the other side seeing it from above.   I also took advantage of a number of current international circumstances to build my story, including the aforementioned Crimean situation, a potential return to the bad old days in Cuba, discussions about anti-missile systems in Poland, an arbitrating role played by both Angela Merkel (Germany) and David Cameron (England), cheap Saudi Oil, Islamic terrorism, as well as a silent non-participating role by China in a manner that fits their tradition of doing so.

In the end I wanted A Sudden War in the Bering Strait to be a story about relationships, newfound love, and a reminder of who we are as Americans and what our hopes are, a conglomerate of peoples and ethnic groups that have come from many places and backgrounds throughout our history to live in mutual freedom and happiness. And honestly, I also wanted to describe those relationship circumstances (some of them intimate) in their rawest detail. I hope I haven't upset anybody by doing so.